International Financial Management

International Financial Management

Angelina Gleason

STATES
ACADEMIC PRESS
www.statesacademicpress.com

States Academic Press,
109 South 5th Street,
Brooklyn, NY 11249, USA

ISBN: 978-1-63989-296-9

Cataloging-in-Publication Data

International financial management / Angelina Gleason.
p. cm.
Includes bibliographical references and index.
ISBN 978-1-63989-296-9
1. International finance. 2. International finance--Management.
3. International business enterprises--Finance.
4. Financial institutions, International. I. Gleason, Angelina.
HG3881 .I58 2022
332.042--dc23

For information on all States Academic Press publications visit our website at www.statesacademicpress.com

STATES
ACADEMIC PRESS

TABLE OF CONTENTS

PREFACE

The purpose of this book is to help students understand the fundamental concepts of this discipline. It is designed to motivate students to learn and prosper. I am grateful for the support of my colleagues. I would also like to acknowledge the encouragement of my family.

The management of finance in an international business atmosphere is known as international financial management. It refers to the exchange of foreign currency for trade and make money. It helps organizations to contact overseas business partners like suppliers, lenders and customers for international deals. The goal of this area of study is the maximization of stakeholders and shareholders. Enhanced opportunity sets, foreign currency, political risks and market imperfections are the four primary areas of this discipline. Foreign investment, earning higher returns, gaining essential raw materials for production, wider and larger markets and efficient production are some of the advantages associated with it. This book is a valuable compilation of topics, ranging from the basic to the most complex theories and principles related to international financial management. While understanding the long-term perspectives of the topics, the book makes an effort in highlighting their impact as a modern tool for the growth of the discipline. This book, with its detailed analyzes and data, will prove immensely beneficial to professionals and students involved in this area at various levels.

A foreword for all the chapters is provided below:

Chapter - Introduction

The management of finance in an international business environment is termed as international financial management. It helps the organizations to connect their international dealings with overseas business partners- customers, suppliers and lenders. This is an introductory chapter which will briefly introduce about international financial management.

Chapter - Foreign Direct Investment

Foreign direct investment refers to the investment of funds by an organization or a firm from one country into another. A few of its concepts are foreign ownership, global capital markets, foreign exchange controls, etc. This chapter has been carefully written to provide an easy understanding of foreign direct investment.

Chapter - Foreign Exchange Market

A global decentralized market for trading of currencies is called foreign exchange market. Forex includes all aspects of buying, selling and exchanging currencies at current or determined prices. This chapter closely examines foreign exchange market to provide an extensive understanding of the subject.

Chapter - Financial Globalization

The global linkages through cross-border financial flows fall under the domain of financial globalization. It further includes domestic and global financial system, trade finance, etc. The topics elaborated in this chapter will help in gaining a better perspective of financial globalization.

Chapter - International Trade

The exchange of goods, capital and services across international borders and territories is known as international trade. Some of the aspects studied under it are export and import trade, international trade theory, mercantilism, etc. All the aspects related to international trade have been carefully analyzed in this chapter.

Angelina Gleason

Introduction

CHAPTER 1

The management of finance in an international business environment is termed as international financial management. It helps the organizations to connect their international dealings with overseas business partners- customers, suppliers and lenders. This is an introductory chapter which will briefly introduce about international financial management.

International finance sometimes is also known as international macroeconomics and it is a section of financial economics that deals with the monetary interactions that occur between two or more countries.

International finance research deals with macroeconomics; that is, it is concerned with economies as a whole instead of individual markets. Financial institutions and companies that conduct international finance research include the World Bank, the International Finance Corp. (IFC), the International Monetary Fund (IMF) and the National Bureau of Economic Research (NBER). There is an international finance division at the U.S. Federal Reserve that analyzes policies relevant to U.S. capital flow, external trade and development of markets in countries around the world.

Concepts and theories that are key parts of international finance and its research include the Mundell-fleming model, the International Fisher Effect, the optimum currency area theory, purchasing power parity, and interest rate parity.

Example of International Institutions of International Finance.

The Bretton Woods System

The Bretton Woods system, which was introduced in the late 1940s, after World War II, established a fixed exchange rate system, having been agreed upon at the Bretton Woods conference by the more than 40 countries that participated. The system was developed to give structure to international monetary exchanges and policies and to maintain stability in all international financial transactions and interactions.

The Bretton Woods conference acted as a catalyst for the formation of essential international institutions that play a foundational role in the global economy. These institutions the IMF and the International Bank for Reconstruction and Development (which became known as the World Bank) continue to play pivotal roles in the area of international finance.

Special Considerations

International or foreign trading is arguably the most important factor in the prosperity and growth of economies that participate in the exchange. The growing popularity and rate of globalization have magnified the importance of international finance.

Another aspect to consider, in terms of international finance, is that the United States has shifted from being the largest international creditor (lending money to foreign nations) and has since become the world's largest international debtor; the United States is taking money and funding from organizations and countries around the world. These aspects are key elements of international finance.

COMPONENTS OF INTERNATIONAL FINANCE

Foreign Exchange Market

Foreign exchange market is the market in which money denominated in one currency is bought and sold with money denominated in another currency. It is an overthe counter market, because there is no single physical or electronic market place or an organized exchange with a central trade clearing mechanism where traders meet and exchange currencies. It spans the globe, with prices moving and currencies trading somewhere every hour of every business day. World's major trading starts each morning in Sydney and Tokyo, and ends up in the San Francisco and Los-Angeles.

The foreign exchange market consists of two tiers: the inter bank market or wholesale market, and retail market or client market. The participants in the wholesale market are commercial banks, investment banks, corporations and central banks, and brokers who trade on their own account. On the other hand, the retail market comprises of travelers, and tourists who exchange one currency for another in the form of currency notes or traveler cheques.

Currency Convertibility

Foreign exchange market assumes that currencies of various countries are freely convertible into other currencies. But this assumption is not true, because many countries restrict the residents and non-residents to convert the local currency into foreign currency, which makes international business more difficult. Many international business firms use "counter trade" practices to overcome the problem that arises due to currency convertibility restrictions.

International Monetary System

Any country needs to have its own monetary system and an authority to maintain order in the system, and facilitate trade and investment. Some countries have their own monetary policies The same is the case with world, its needs a monetary system to promote trade and investment across the countries. International monetary system exists since 1944. The International Monetary Fund (IMF) and the World Bank have been maintaining order in the international monetary system and general economic development respectively.

International Financial Markets

International financial market born in mid-fifties and gradually grown in size and scope. International financial markets comprises of international banks, Eurocurrency market, Eurobond market, and international stock market. International banks play a crucial role in financing international business by acting as both commercial banks and investment banks. Most international banking is undertaken through reciprocal correspondent relationships between banks located in different countries. But now a days large bank have internationalized their operations they have their own overseas operations so as to improve their ability to compete internationally. Eurocurrency market originally called as Eurodollar market, which helps to deposit surplus cash efficiently and conveniently, and it helps to raise short-term bank loans to finance corporate working capital needs, including imports and exports. Eurobond market helps to MNCs to raise long-term debt by issuing bonds. International bonds are typically classified as either foreign bonds or eurobonds. A foreign bond is issued by a borrower foreign to the country where the bond is placed. On the other hand Eurobonds are sold in countries other than the country represented by the currency denominating them.

Balance of Payments

International trade and other international transactions result in a flow of funds between countries. All transactions relating to the flow of goods, services and funds across national boundaries are recorded in the balance of payments of the countries concerned.

Balance of payments (BoPs) is systematic statement that systematically summarizes, for a specified period of time, the monetary transactions of an economy with the rest of the world. Put in simple words, the balance of payments of a country is a systematic record of all transactions between the 'resident's of a country and the rest of the world. The balance of payments includes both visible and invisible transactions. It presents a classified record of:

- All receipts on account of goods exported, services rendered and capital received by 'resident's.

- Payments made by then on account of goods imported and services received from the capital transferred to 'non-resident's or 'foreigner's.

Thus the transactions include the exports and imports (by individuals, firms and government agencies) of goods and services, income flows, capital flows and gifts and similar one-sided transfer of payments. A rule of thumb that aids in understanding the BOP is to "follow the cash flow". Balance of payments for a country is the sum of the Current Account, the Capital Account, and the change in Official Reserves.

FOREIGN PORTFOLIO INVESTMENT

Foreign portfolio investment (FPI) refers to investing in the financial assets of a foreign country, such as stocks or bonds available on an exchange. This type of investment is at times viewed less favorably than direct investment because portfolio investments can be sold off quickly and are at times seen as short-term attempts to make money, rather than a long-term investment in the economy.

Portfolio investment typically has a shorter time frame for investment return than direct investment. As with any equity investment, foreign portfolio investors usually expect to quickly realize a profit on their investments.

As securities are easily traded, the liquidity of portfolio investments makes them much easier to sell than direct investments. Portfolio investments are more accessible for the average investor than direct investments because they require much less investment capital and research.

BALANCE OF PAYMENTS

Balance Of Payment (BOP) is a statement which records all the monetary transactions made between residents of a country and the rest of the world during any given period. This statement includes all the transactions made by/to individuals, corporates and the government and helps in monitoring the flow of funds to develop the economy. When all the elements are correctly included in the BOP, it should sum up to zero in a perfect scenario. This means the inflows and outflows of funds should balance out. However, this does not ideally happen in most cases.

BOP statement of a country indicates whether the country has a surplus or a deficit of funds i.e when a country's export is more than its import, its BOP is said to be in surplus. On the other hand, BOP deficit indicates that a country's imports are more than its exports. Tracking the transactions under BOP is something similar to the double entry system of accounting. This means, all the transaction will have a debit entry and a corresponding credit entry.

Why Balance of Payment is Vital for a Country?

A country's BOP is vital for the following reasons:

- BOP of a country reveals its financial and economic status.
- BOP statement can be used as an indicator to determine whether the country's currency value is appreciating or depreciating.
- BOP statement helps the Government to decide on fiscal and trade policies.
- It provides important information to analyze and understand the economic dealings of a country with other countries.

By studying its BOP statement and its components closely, one would be able to identify trends that may be beneficial or harmful to the economy of the county and thus, then take appropriate measures.

Elements of Balance of Payment

There are three components of balance of payment viz current account, capital account, and financial account. The total of the current account must balance with the total of capital and financial accounts in ideal situations.

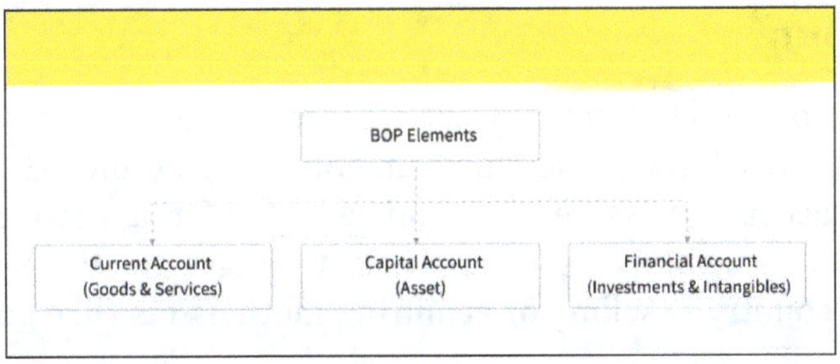

Current Account

The current account is used to monitor the inflow and outflow of goods and services between countries. This account covers all the receipts and payments made with respect to raw materials and manufactured goods. It also includes receipts from engineering, tourism, transportation, business services, stocks, and royalties from patents and copyrights. When all the goods and services are combined, together they make up to a country's Balance Of Trade (BOT).

There are various categories of trade and transfers which happen across countries. It could be visible or invisible trading, unilateral transfers or other payments/receipts.

Trading in goods between countries are referred to as visible items and import/export of services (banking, information technology etc) are referred to as invisible items. Unilateral transfers refer to money sent as gifts or donations to residents of foreign countries. This can also be personal transfers like – money sent by relatives to their family located in another country.

Capital Account

All capital transactions between the countries are monitored through the capital account. Capital transactions include the purchase and sale of assets (non-financial) like land and properties. The capital account also includes the flow of taxes, purchase and sale of fixed assets etc by migrants moving out/in to a different country. The deficit or surplus in the current account is managed through the finance from capital account and vice versa.

There are 3 major elements of capital account:

- Loans & borrowings: It includes all types of loans from both the private and public sectors located in foreign countries.
- Investments: These are funds invested in the corporate stocks by non-residents.
- Foreign exchange reserves: Foreign exchange reserves held by the central bank of a country to monitor and control the exchange rate does impact the capital account.

Financial Account

The flow of funds from and to foreign countries through various investments in real estates, business ventures, foreign direct investments etc is monitored through the financial account. This account measures the changes in the foreign ownership of domestic assets and domestic ownership of foreign assets. On analyzing these changes, it can be understood if the country is selling or acquiring more assets (like gold, stocks, equity etc).

INTERNATIONAL FINANCIAL CRISES MANAGEMENT

Managing financial crises includes measures that reduce their economic damage and costs. Numerous and creative monetary and fiscal policy or financial interventions have been deployed either in the European Union or in the US, China and Japan to mitigate the impacts of the crisis.

When confronted with emergencies never experienced before, strategic crisis managers hasten to mobilize expertise to come up with crisis decision-making. They should be able to make sense of the crisis and identify the core values that are threatened.

When we talk about crises in relation to businesses, it is the owner's responsibility to develop crisis management capacities to cope with the impacts of a disaster on stakeholders and on their companie's value. Regardless of its size, every company can follow the necessary steps in crisis management. Advanced planning is regarded as the key to survival. A written plan including specific actions is important to make when things are running smoothly. A badly managed crisis can ruin decades of hard work and company value within hours. A crisis can strike any company anytime, anywhere.

As far as natural disasters are concerned, prevention and mitigation policies against them require massive investment but help to reduce the exposure and to increase the adaptation of affected countries.

Disruptive events still continue to occur. We can say their characteristics change over time. They can stem from unprecedented, poorly understood or ignored threats and hazards. The 2008 financial and fiscal crisis, although it demonstrates features that are similar to those in the past, has been much greater in its severeness and intensity. In terms of falling output and rising unemployment, it has proved to be the most serious recession since the war. The crisis has posed new challenges to fiscal and monetary policies in all the countries, including the euro area. Without the creative monetary and fiscal policy tools applied in the European Union or in the US, China and Japan, the meltdown of the global financial system could hardly have been avoided. Global leaders have recognized that further systemic shocks could severely challenge even political stability.

The recent global financial crisis demonstrated some new factors in terms of its roots: widespread implementation of complex and nontransparent financial instruments, the high level of national and cross-border interconnectedness of financial markets, banks and institutions, the high degree of leverage of financial institutions and the role of the household sector.

Owing to the interconnected nature of the global economy, crises can spread beyond national borders. Globalization has also resulted in an increased interdependence of production and delivery systems as well as a globalized financial system. It is a key responsibility for governments to manage new crises while building resilience to shocks at all levels.

Learning from the Past and Revealing New Strategies of Managing Crises

Today's crises demonstrate a diversity and complexity that challenge crisis management in many ways. Hazards including industrial accidents, natural disasters, terrorist attacks, infection, refugee crises and financial threats have a cardinal feature in common: their socioeconomic impacts spread fast across borders, making modern societies vulnerable to a wide range of large-scale shocks. Innovative crisis management responses became vital, which was the case in coping with the consequences of the global financial crisis of 2008. European, the US, Chinese and Japanese policy makers initiated fiscal expansions to boost growth, while their central banks introduced unconventional monetary policies including quantitative easing, forward guidance and negative interest rates on bank's deposits with the central bank.

The complexity of managing today's crises calls for the efficient coordination of emergency responses to defend citizens and businesses and mitigate the harsh impacts. Similarly to emergencies that threaten businesses, response plans are fundamental tools for governments to manage "conventional" crises. To design such plans, it is necessary to study past events and draw the conclusions and the lessons, which could function well for routine events.

Banks, financial institutions and trading firms are vulnerable to hazardous "black swan" events like the global financial crisis of 2008, and are exposed to huge losses beyond the realm of normal expectations due to their flawed financial models. The term is based on an ancient saying which presumed black swans did not exist, though the observation of a single black swan was enough to disprove that belief in the seventeenth century.

Finance professor, writer, and former Wall Street trader Nassim Nicholas Taleb's "black swan theory" describes an event that comes as a big surprise and has a major impact. His book "The Black Swan: The Impact of the Highly Improbable" was published in 2007 and focuses on the extremely strong impacts of rare, unexpected and impossible-to-predict events referred to as "outliers", which is a point in a statistic that does not "fit" in the overall trend. The metaphor also sheds light on the fragility of any system. The idea in Taleb's book is not to attempt to predict "black swan" events, but to create robustness and build resilience. Humans tend to find oversimplified explanations and later convince themselves that these events are explainable in hindsight. Analyzing black swan events, however, helps us to gain a better understanding why certain events are recurring in history and what consequences they have.

The concept of resilience applied to societies, businesses, infrastructure, services and financial systems requires strong governmental or central bank commitment under fast-changing economic and social conditions which create higher probability for unexpected and uncommon crises.

When Bubbles Burst

The Great Recession was triggered by a bubble in housing and derivatives, which became entangled in the financial markets. The term "Great Recession" applies to both the US economic downturn, officially lasting from December 2007 when the US housing market went from boom to bust to June 2009, as well as the ensuing global recession in 2009.

Derivatives built on mortgages spread quickly and became the new, attractive thing that everybody wanted. Based on mortgages, there were so many of them available that when the prices were bid upward with supply lagging, a bubble was formed. When the real estate market collapsed in 2007, large amounts of mortgage-backed securities and derivatives declined sharply in value, jeopardizing the solvency of over-leveraged banks and financial institutions.

The classic example for a bursting bubble is the Great Tulip Mania of 1637 in the Netherlands. Tulip bulbs became extremely valuable as the rich bid up their prices in the belief that there would always be a market for the exotic tulips, no matter how high their prices soared.

A bubble is usually fueled by speculation or The Greater Fool Theory. A speculative bubble is usually triggered by the prospect of a greater profit and exaggerated expectations of future growth, rise in prices or other events that could result in an increase in asset values. This pushes up trading volumes, while supply remains at about the same level but demand increases. Price inevitably exceeds the asset's intrinsic value, an objective analysis would indicate that.

Value is what someone is willing to pay for. The Greater Fool Theory of investment suggests that someone is sure to seek your appreciated item, no matter how high its price is at the moment, and willing to pay an even greater price for it later on.

When the Greater Fool stops being the Greater Fool and prices are too high for the market to be sustainable, the bubble bursts. A crash is inevitable as the bubble must go down.

Burst of financial bubbles that brought underlying economic problems to the surface developed into a financial and economic crisis at global level in 2008. The financial crisis turned into a debt crisis and a euro crisis. There were three main factors existing in the precrisis period that resulted in the escalation of the economic and financial crisis in the Eurozone. The financial dimension of macroeconomic stability was largely overlooked: the deepening of the financial integration and the expansion of the financial sector at the same time undermined financial and macroeconomic stability, the banking system was highly interconnected and lightly regulated and Economic and Monetary Union (EMU) member states made imprudent fiscal policy steps.

The economic situation within the euro area in 2007–2009 stemmed from its vulnerability and fragility owing to its architecture. The phenomenon that bank portfolios from the Northern part of the euro area were diverted toward the periphery of economies in Southern-Europe strengthened risk. Low nominal interest rates and easy access to credit-fostered demand and inflation reducing real interest rates, which had destabilizing effects such as housing booms accompanied with an increase in investment of nontradable construction or high government borrowing. This process ended up in cumulating current account deficits and external liabilities.

At the union level, the crisis has highlighted that institutional reforms are necessary to implement for two main reasons. One is that the euro area should develop effective mechanisms of fiscal supervision and policy coordination to prevent a crisis as severe as the recent one from occurring in the future. The other is: should a recession occur in any EMU country, it is important to stop its escalation in the particular country and its contagion to other countries.

Theories on Business Cycles

Minsky maintained that "To understand the short-term dynamics of the business cycle and the longer term evolution of economies it is necessary to understand the financing relations that rule, and how the profit-seeking activities of businessmen, bankers and portfolio managers lead to the evolution of financial structures".

According to Schumpeter's theory on business cycles "cycles are the essence of the organism that displays them". The starting point of his analysis is stable equilibrium with the aim of identifying the economic factors arising from the economy itself that destroy the equilibrium and lead to evolution. These real economic processes are referred to as the "circular flow" and "develop", which creates the economic evolution: changes in the economy that arise from itself. Contrary to Keynes, Schumpeter presumed that in the circular flow, there is a constant tendency toward an equilibrium which, under competitive capitalism, tends to maintain the optimal allocation of available capital and labor. In the "circular flow", the role of money is to facilitate the circulation of commodities. It is basically entrepreneurial demand that determines the credit supplied by the banks; consequently, the money supply is an endogenous variable. Schumpeter argued that in a developing economy, where an innovation prompts a new business to replace the old called by him "creative destruction", booms and recessions are inevitable.

Minsky adopted Schumpeter's idea of the innovating entrepreneur. Minsky regarded, however, financial innovations produced by financial institutions as the source of financial fragility, which lead to financial crisis and instability. Schumpeter contrarily stated that innovation was the main source of stability. Minsky concluded that Schumpeterian entrepreneurship, evolution and change are the most evident in banking and finance, where the drive for profits is the clearest factor to make a change. Financial institutions were essential to Schumpeter's theory and in the development of Minsky's thought. The advanced market economie's institutional arrangements are the setting within which innovation is financed by entrepreneurs.

Financial innovations including "exotic" securitizations, nonbank financial intermediation, trading in derivatives, unconventional mortgages, hedge funds and the globalization of finance markets are behind the recent global economic crisis.

Monetary policy rules on the central bank's systematic adjustment of its interest rate to respond to developments in inflation and macroeconomic performance are referred to as Taylor rules. Taylor offered a framework for the analysis of historical policy and for the econometric evaluation of specific alternative strategies that a central bank can make. The framework links interest rate decisions directly to inflation and economic performance abstracting from a detailed analysis of the demand and supply of money. These reactive rules facilitate the discussion of systematic monetary policy.

Where does Credit Expansion Lead to?

The question arises if the recent business cycles in the US and Japan can be explained on the basis of the Austrian business cycle theory (ABCT) since they display some of its signs. ABCT suggests that an economic boom is sustainable if it is the result of an increase in investment funded by an increase in saving, while an economic boom which stems merely from credit expansion is not sustainable.

Excessive growth in bank credit is owing to the artificially low interest rates set by a central bank or through expansionary monetary policy. These interest rates are below the rate of the market for loanable funds that supply and demand clear. As a result, the information embedded in market prices or interest rates is distorted. Entrepreneurial decisions are affected, which causes a misallocation of capital across the economy and the credit-sourced boom results in a widespread malinvestment. Consequently, a sustained period of low interest rates and excessive credit creation leads to an unstable imbalance between saving and investment. The boom fed by the credit expansion turns to recession when the money supply contracts and eventually resources are reallocated back toward their former uses.

Mainstream economists have concluded that the housing boom, subsequent to the 2001 recession, was mainly due to the Fed's accommodative monetary policy, which means expanding the overall money supply to boost the economy when growth is slowing—as measured by GDP—to encourage more spending from consumers and businesses.

Between 2002 and 2005, the US monetary policy was far more accommodate than an approach based on an interpretation of inflation and output data would have called for. White and other Austrians predicted that a burst of an asset bubble, specifically, the real estate bubble would trigger a crisis while forecasts of some non-Austrian economists, such as Nouriel Roubini and Stephen Roach focused more on macroeconomic imbalances such as the current account deficit or the federal government debt.

Public Expectation from Central Banks

Monetary policy is supposed to support the objectives of general economic policy for the purpose of achieving sustainable growth and a high level of employment. Inflation-targeting framework (ITF) sets two goals. One is the central bank's commitment to keep inflation low, and the other is to keep the variance of inflation right. While the ITF can greatly promote attaining the first goal, attaining the second provides more room to debates. At the same time, a strategy for monetary management, namely inflation-targeting policies, conducted mainly in a discretionary form have been considered to be capable of keeping inflation low while supporting the central bank's flexibility to manage monetary policy with their independence being emphasized.

It is widely agreed that central bank transparency can make the policy more effective. According to inflation-targeting framework, it is possible to create a "nominal anchor" to the price level by the communication to the public. The target would result in certain "psychological" market conditions which are favorable to reaching the very same inflation goal. The only way for central banks to earn credibility is to demonstrate that they have the tools and the willingness to curb inflation and to keep it low for a period of time. In addition, the element of discretion provides the central bank with the capacity to pursue other political objectives thought necessary in a certain case without compromising the attainment of the stated goal.

Public expectation from the central bank should be met, by suggesting that the bank has the power to expand or contract the money supply, to raise or to sink interest rates, to impose exchange controls, to alter the level of obligatory reserves, to alter the classes of assets and the conditions of granting access to discount facilities and to impose new bank regulations. Both critics and supporters of the ITF, claimed, however, that the ITF does not constitute best-practice in resolving the question of other goals such as real and financial stability. Nevertheless, stabilizing inflation is the best way to achieve that goal. The view of the ITF is supported by Bernanke, Laubach, Mishkin and Posen commonly referred to as "BLMP", who conclude that should a great supply shock of some unexpected origin in particular arise, missing or changing a previously communicated inflation target may even be justified.

Why do Financial Crises Occur?

The conduct of economic and financial policies is strongly affected by the substantial implications of financial crises. A thorough analysis of the consequences of and best responses to crises has become an integral part of the policy debates. Crises manifest the linkages between the financial sector and the real economy. Theories focusing on the sources of financial crises have recognized the importance of sharp movements in asset and credit markets.

A financial crisis often occurs together with one or some of the following phenomena: a remarkable change in credit volume and asset prices, disruptive financial intermediation, immense balance sheet problems of firms, households, financial intermediaries and sovereigns or significant government support in the form of liquidity support and recapitalization.

The question may arise why neither financial market players nor policy makers anticipated the risks and tried to slow down the expansion of credit and increase in asset prices. Such phenomena have been around for centuries. Asset prices sometimes deviate from what fundamentals would suggest and move differently from the patterns of standard models. Asset prices can also be affected by investor's behavior or information asymmetries, changes in international financial and economic conditions. Information asymmetries exist among intermediaries and in financial markets. Safety deserves a premium, and perverse spirals can be created. When the demand for quality assets increases, some of the lower quality may experience a sharp decline in their prices. The crises in the past exhibit the signs of those of recent recessions when the collapse of banking systems was preceded by a sharp increase in credit in real estate investment.

The East Asian financial crisis, for instance, in the late 1990s is similar to the ones in the Northern countries. The experience of the United States in the Great Depression shows some similarity to the way leading to the recent global financial crisis in terms of an increase in household leverage or asset prices.

Credit booms can be triggered by a wide range of factors, for example, shocks such as positive productivity shocks, economic policies and capital flows. Lagged GDP growth is positively associated with the probability of a credit boom. Increases in international financial flows can strengthen the credit booms. Global conditions also affect the national financial markets resulting in asset bubbles easily spill across borders.

Capital inflows can extend the availability of funds for banks leading to relaxing credit constraints for corporations and households. Accommodative monetary policies have been connected to credit booms and excessive risk taking. Asset prices and borrower's value are affected by interest rates so are the conditions of lending. Risk-taking is usually higher when interest rates are lower and a shift to quality, when interest rates rise. The rapid increases in real estate prices and household leverage are explained by the relatively low interest rates in the US during the period 2001–2004.

Structural factors such as financial liberalization and innovation facilitate more risk-taking and can also trigger credit booms. Empirical studies found that crises were often preceded by financial liberalization. Shocks or liberalization keeps innovation in move. Regulation, supervision and market discipline are not quick enough to catch up with greater competition and innovation. Vulnerabilities in credit markets can emerge. A decline in lending standards owing to stronger competition in financial services may contribute to financial fragility in the short run in particular.

During financial crises, asset prices and credit booms and busts differ from the movements of a normal business cycle: booms are shorter and more intense than other upturns, and crunches and busts are longer, deeper and more violent than regular downturns. The violent episodes last longer.

Reinhart and Rogoff distinguished two groups of crises, both including two types. The first group is classified on the basis of quantitative definitions, and the other depends mainly on qualitative and judgmental analysis. Currency crisis and sudden stop belong to the first group since these are measurable variables and allow the use of quantitative methodologies. Other crises are connected to adverse debt dynamics or banking system turmoil. Since these variables are not easy to measure, the use of qualitative methodologies is more appropriate.

When a country cannot service its foreign debt, the financial crisis takes the form of a sovereign or private (or both) debt crisis. In a systemic banking crisis, bank runs and failures can make the banks suspend the convertibility of their liabilities or force the government to intervene to prevent that by extending liquidity and capital assistance on a large scale.

Research that has been conducted on the causes of the recent crisis revealed some factors similar to previous crises. Although these factors may differ on the exact weights in different results features concluded in common are as follows: unsustainable asset price increases, credit booms leading to excessive debt burdens, build-up of marginal loans and systemic risk, and that regulation, supervision, and market discipline is too slow to catch up with greater competition and innovation. Nonetheless, the recent global financial crisis demonstrated some new factors in terms of its roots: widespread implementation of complex and nontransparent financial instruments, the high level of national and cross-border interconnectedness of financial markets, banks and institutions, the high degree of leverage of financial institutions and the role of the household sector. These new and common factors in the framework of the "new financial architecture" led to the severest financial crisis since the Great Depression.

Restoring confidence in the financial system, if possible at all, required immense government participation, outlays and guarantees. As for real and financial implications, they are hard and show common features with other episodes. They include large output losses and declines in consumption, investment and industrial production. Financial crises have large economic costs. Crises impact economic activity and can trigger recessions worse than a "normal" business cycle recession. The average duration is longer, and output losses are larger than those of a recession not triggered by a financial crisis. So is the cumulative loss, the output loss relative to the peak before recession.

Various approaches are used for measuring the real impact of a crisis on output. The traditional business cycle's methodology implies that recessions associated with credit crunches and housing busts are costlier compared to those associated with equity price busts. Adding up differences between trend growth and actual growth for some years after the crisis can show overall losses, which vary in different countries. On this basis, according to Laeven and Valencia, emerging markets tend to suffer larger losses due to the recent crisis than advanced economies, which can also differ significantly. An indication of the significant costs that crises incur is consumption and overall welfare. In recessions associated with financial crises, a fall in consumption is 7–10 times larger than in those without such crises in emerging markets and consumption still keeps growing, though at a slower pace.

Financial variables show with large downward corrections. In advanced countries, credit falls by about 7.0%, house prices drop by about 12.0% while equity prices decline by more than 15.0% during credit crunches, house and equity price. The most remarkable hit on the real economy from a financial crisis is the lack of credit. After banking crises, sectors grow more slowly, so they naturally need more external financing owing to bank's limited lending capacity. Recoveries in aggregate output after credit crunches tend to take place before the revival of credit growth and turnaround in house prices. Sectors more dependent on external finance grow relatively less. "Creditless recoveries" are more common after banking crises and credit booms.

Financial crises are associated with reductions in investment, R&D and employment and firm's giving up on growth opportunities. The timing of crises is more difficult or even impossible to predict than identifying vulnerabilities. The phrase "Minsky moment" refers to the situation when a market fails or falls into crisis after a long period of speculation or unsustainable growth. What we have seen in the recent case of the financial crisis was a slow movement of the global financial system toward" money manager capitalism", as Minsky put it, that collapsed in 2007. Wray named it the "Minsky half-century".

Financial Innovation and the New Financial Architecture

In the late 1970s, a radical financial deregulation process began that accelerated the evolution of financial markets. Financial innovation took various forms and stimulated strong financial booms that ended up in crises. The "new financial architecture" (NFA) refers to the integration of financial markets with light government regulation of the era characterized earlier. NFA created a framework for flawed practices and institutions which can be regarded as the deep financial roots of the recent crisis.

As a result of financial innovation, complex and opaque financial products became available in financial markets. They lacked transparency, which made it impossible to be priced correctly and therefore, lost liquidity when the boom ended. The explosion of these securities flowing through banks at a high rate created large profits, while destroyed the transparency which is necessary to ensure market efficiency. Large investment banks like Lehman and Merrill Lynch were given high ratings by international rating agencies enabling them to borrow at a low price. Instead of exposing risk, the agencies systematically disguised it.

The recent economic crisis was remarkable not only because of its severity and size but of its nature. The true nature of the underlying situation seems to be difficult to reveal since trading of over-the-counter (OTC) derivatives, especially the ones which take the form of collateralized debt obligations (CDOs), accounts for confusing those who attempt to paint a clear picture. Collateralized debt obligations are structured financial products that pool together assets such as mortgages, bonds and loans which serve as collateral for the CDO. The creation of asset-backed securities enabled the banks to increase their leverage significantly. These structured financial products were particularly attractive assets for banks to keep because they could be held off-balance-sheet with no capital adequacy requirements.

Derivatives are financial contracts that derive their value from the performance of the underlying asset, the most common of which contain commodities, stocks, bonds, interest rates, currencies or other. The risk of derivatives stems from using leverage, which means that investors can earn large returns from minor changes in the underlying asset's price. On the other hand, however, they can suffer massive losses in case of opposite moves in price.

The Third Basel Accord is a global regulatory standard on bank capital reserves. According to the Basel III rule, the banks are required to hold 4.5% of common equity and 6.0% Tier I capital of risk-weighted assets (RWA) besides introducing additional capital buffers during periods of high credit. There was no need for a percentage of the value of these assets to be held as a capital reserve. CDOs, which comprised loans of different quality, and other derivatives were distributed widely between the dominant institutions in the financial system. They were regarded as relatively safe, since they were given a high rating by rating agencies, while in fact, their credit worthiness and cash flow possibilities were doubtful. This was an unsustainable situation. In late 2007, the whole financial network came under strain questioning the viability of many financial instruments leading to the withdrawal of these funds from Wall Street investment banks and associated institutes.

The collateralized debt obligation "market" was impossible to sustain. Wall Street investment banks were able to evade regulatory constraints. A "shadow banking" was constructed alongside the regulated sector. These banks do not take deposits and have no access to central bank funding or debt guarantees. They deal with short-term funding on asset-backed commercial papers and provide cash loans against collateral as security or long-term loans like mortgages. Shadow banks with less-risk aversion did not mind having clients not eligible to applying for loans. Due to high interconnectedness, they can contribute to increasing systemic risk indirectly as well. Without the support of their central bank as lender of last resort, they are unable to refinance their short-term liabilities. The shadow banking system is blamed for significantly contributing to the global financial crisis of 2007–2012.

Since OTC derivatives are not traded in an exchange, there are no central counterparties (CCPs). As a part of the financial sector reform, noncleared OTC transactions are to be shifted to central counterparties, which would result in a better risk management and resiliency in accordance with giving more transparency to the OTC market.

The conduct of economic and financial policies is strongly affected by the substantial implications of financial crises. A thorough analysis of the consequences and best responses to crises has become an integral part of the policy debates. Crises manifest the linkages between the financial sector and the real economy.

The Euro Area Crisis and its Lessons

The euro area crisis that began in 2009 stems from the financial/fiscal trilemma. Obstfeld suggested a new policy trilemma for currency unions: (1) cross border financial integration, (2) financial stability and (3) national fiscal independence cannot be simultaneously maintained within the union after a certain level of the financial integration has been reached. Conclusively, financial integration and independent national fiscal policy do not create financial stability.

Consequently, if countries sacrifice the options of financial restraint and capital controls, they cannot credibly backstop their financial systems without external fiscal support. A country reliant mainly on its own fiscal resources will likely give up on financial integration as well as stability because financial risks will be assessed nationally by the markets. As an alternative, if a country with limited fiscal space withdraws from the integrated financial market, it may control and insulate its financial sector in order to reduce fragility to the minimum level. Any diagnosis that overemphasizes the lack of enforcement of existing fiscal rules is partial.

Argument is that the turmoil in euro area in the period after the outburst of the crisis finds its roots in financial vulnerabilities of the incomplete design of Economic and Monetary Union (EMU). Initially, architects were concerned with monetary policy, fiscal policy and structural reform in nonfinancial markets, for example, labor markets, leaving the financial dimension out of scope. The process of financial integration, ruling optimism concerning risk and growth, as well as global liquidity, created credit conditions at the time when monetary union began to work resulted in excessive borrowing. Asset price bubbles occurred in housing and in the sovereign debts increasing bank's exposure to the risk of collapse creating the "too-big-to-fail" (TBTF) issue. It means that when a systemically important financial institution (SIFI) fails, losses or disruptions could be severe enough to lead to failure of third parties. The problem is rather the fact that financial institutions are too interconnected to fail. It is necessary to prevent TBTF banks from failing in order to maintain the stability of the financial system in the short run. Nonetheless, bailing out TBTFs will result in a less stable financial system and raises the issue of moral hazard.

The theoretical basis of the creation of the monetary union is optimal currency area theory that considers exogenous shocks rather than the endogenous dynamics of capitalism. Diagnostic failure prevailing in the North blames government profligacy for the euro crisis. Both allow disguising the design flaws of the euro area. Argument is that endogenous dynamics of booms and busts work also on the level of national economies, which remained so within EMU. The central bank as the lender of last resort is supposed to counterbalance the instability of capitalism, which stems from its nature. It implies two responsibilities: injecting liquidity in the banking sector and to the government bond markets. When problems in the government arise, sovereign bond prices drop, extending the problem to the banks and causing insolvency, thus developing a vicious circle. The European Central Bank (ECB) as a lender of last resort in the government bond markets has an infinite capacity of buying government bonds. The European Stability Mechanism (ESM) that became operational in October 2012 cannot commit to such an outcome due to its limited resources. It is only the infinite resources that enable the central bank to stabilize bond rates. This is the only way to gain credibility in the market.

The structure of the balance sheets of both the banks and the sovereign is unbalanced in terms of maturity. It refers to the liquidity difference of their liabilities and assets, thus a collective move of distrust can trigger a liquidity crisis that can cause sovereign default. This also underpins the necessity of the central bank's extended core responsibility. Stabilizators can be built in the government budget. The private sector's postcrash deleverage may carry the threat of a deflationary spiral. Increased savings together with reduced consumption output and national income will decline leading to the savings paradox. It can be offset by the government's saving less and borrowing more. The private sector's asset sales can trigger a downward spiral by causing insolvency for those holding these assets. The harmful effect can be stopped by the government's taking over them. These processes moved by the stabilizing elements are not organized on the level of EMU. Monetary integration does not obviously include economic integration.

According to the theory of optimum currency areas (OCA), sufficient real wage flexibility and labor mobility can compensate for real divergences. The lack of those in Europe makes it less likely for the requirements of a sound monetary union to meet. In addition, market efficiency with prices fully reflecting available information has not been constituted by the European Union, which also suggests that monetary integration does not imply economic integration. Maastricht has brought the loss of two economic policy levers, monetary and exchange rate policies, and has left two other, the national fiscal policies and the EU budget itself. It means national governments are restrained in reacting to asymmetric shocks, the outcome of which depends to a great extent on the relative phasing of business cycles between each member state and on the ability that cycles can be responded through the EU budget. Since monetary sovereignty and exchange rate tool are no longer accessible, fiscal latitude is needed for the members to treat shocks, particularly in an environment where labor migration has failed to function as a valve for dealing with asymmetric shocks.

Emphasizing the lack of enforcement of existing fiscal rules provides a partial diagnosis to the euro crisis. The euro area's inherent weaknesses revealed by the crisis have made euro area vulnerable. At the core of its vulnerability stands the impossible trinity of strict no-monetary financing, bank-sovereign interdependence and no co-responsibility for public debt. Secondly, the euro area has deprived itself of the shock absorbers most economies can lean on to reduce the negative effects of demand shocks and fully expect a central bank to respond an economic downturn.

Argument is that euro area crisis was not a sovereign debt crisis. The fact that Belgium and Italy, which entered the crisis with extraordinarily high debts did not land in serious trouble, while Ireland and Spain, which entered the crisis with low levels of sovereign debt needed bail-outs, underpins this statement. The problem was massive capital flows across borders, which encouraged high levels of private borrowing in the economies which at last got into trouble. A reversal in those flows generated by the financial crisis made private borrowers and banks get into big trouble, which turned into serious economic downturns and bank failures and led to explosive growth in sovereign debt burdens. Massive sovereign debt was the symptom rather than the cause of the crisis.

Countries without a single currency have the option of turning to the tool of money creation to support their financial systems in hard times. Financing public debt in such a way leads to destabilized price level ending up in a quadrilemma: at least one of (1) strong capital market integration, (2) financial stability, (3) national fiscal independence and (4) price level stability must be given up.

As it comes to discussing, the fragility of EMU by examining the role of the central bank as a lender of last resort and the automatic stabilizers in the government budgets, it is significant to see the existence of a "deadly embrace" between the sovereign and the banks. It refers to the case when falling government bond prices threaten the banks, or sovereigns are threatened with insolvency. As a result, when one is endangered the other follows. This creates a good starting point to analyzing the operation of the ECB.

Accumulation of private debt resulted in developing bubbles. Deleverage as a consequence of bursts got the deflation dynamics going thus, pushing the economy into a deflationary spiral.

The idea of the financial instability hypothesis (FIH) was pioneered by Hyman Minsky. He argued that financial crises are endemic in capitalism; the model does not based on exogenous shocks to arouse business cycles of various massiveness, instead, it suggests that business cycles are generated from the internal dynamics of capitalist economies, the fragility of financial markets and the system of interventions and regulations necessary to keep the operation within bounds. Capitalism is prone to move from periods of financial stability to instability, which is a type of market failure and needs government regulation.

Effective Crisis Management Measures to Avoid the Worst

The global financial crisis and associated recessions have shown the ability of macroeconomic and financial sector policies to mitigate the costs of such episodes.

The measures implemented aimed specifically at enhancing credit support. They are defined as "nonstandard, unconventional measures" and are considered as part of the central bank's toolkit, but "by definition exceptional and temporary in nature". In the wake of the Lehman collapse and exploding sovereign debt crisis in the Eurozone, the unconventional measures taken by the central banks were mainly aimed at stabilizing specific segments of financial systems. They are referred to as "credit easing".

Central banks like the ECB, the Federal Reserve System (Fed), the Bank of England (BoE), the Bank of Japan (BoJ) or the People's Bank of China (PBC) differ in terms of their tasks or legal statuses while they show more similarities in their institutional structures, monetary frameworks and in the use of instruments. Central banking practices in the world have evolved toward greater independence, transparency and the adoption of monetary policy committees. This trend has contributed to reducing the differences among these five institutions and can also be seen among other central banks. The differences include communication strategies; nevertheless, the responsiveness of the financial market seems to be high for both the Eurosystem and the Fed in terms of monetary policy inclinations and views on the economic outlook. The ECB and the BoJ quantify their definitions of price stability, while the Fed does not. All these central banks mentioned earlier had to face a series of diverse challenges, which were rather country-specific in Japan or more global in the other economies.

The Fed made clear its objective of preventing a meltdown and gained credibility in spite of the fact that it temporarily suspended its commitment to price stability. Euro area's output had fallen behind that of the US in 2009 and had not been able to catch up.

It was due to the delay in economic stimulus. In addition, the credibility of the ECB was not strengthened by its deeds. With the core inflation rate in below 1% a year, the euro area slipped into a low inflation trap, well below its stated target of 2% a year.

The epicenter of the crisis was located in the US during the period between 2007 and 2009. It moved to the euro area at the end of 2009 and at the beginning of 2010. It was the reason why monetary policy responses to the crises of Fed, BoE and ECB were done at different times. A decline in financial asset prices escalated in a financial crisis, but while in the US and in the UK, it was centered around subprime assets; in the euro area, it was centered around government debt. Subprime assets did not actually have the value they were supposed to and sovereign debt was considered risk-free, which is used by banks as collateral.

As for monetary transmission mechanism, in the US 25.0% of corporate external financing is done by banks, while 75.0% through financial markets. In comparison, in the euro area 75.0% of corporate external financing is conducted by banks and 25.0% through financial markets. This proportion in the UK is approximately 50–50%.

In addition, the US and the UK have a single sovereign Treasury bond and Treasury bill market. It is easier for the Fed and the BoE to perform monetary policy than for the ECB, which has to deal with 19 different Treasury bond and bill markets.

The ECB has one primary objective, price stability and the other goals are subordinated to the first. The Fed and the BoE have more than one objectives, monetary stability and financial stability. The financial stability goal consists of a sound and stable financial system. The BoE has explicitly stated that financial stability is regarded as a major goal. The three main objectives set by the Fed besides monetary stability are: permanent economic growth, maximum employment and low long-term interest rates. Its target for price stability is measured by the consumer price index, which is 2%. Its present estimated long run unemployment rate will increase from around 5.2 to 6.0%.

The BoE has expressed the "lender of last resort" operations as a mean to ensure financial stability. Compared to the ECB, this function is stronger for the BoE. The ESCB1 is allowed to buy debt instruments from euro area member states in the secondary markets, as the ECB has done so during the crisis, on the condition, it is necessary to meet the ESCB objectives.

In the euro area, monetary easing has been low compared to the US or the UK. Several major advanced economies got close to a liquidity trap. At that point, standard monetary policy becomes ineffective because nominal interest rates hit zero, both money and bills have a close to zero interest rate so they become close to perfect substitutes, short-term interest rates cannot drop further. Given these circumstances and the economy needs more monetary stimulus, demand is still insufficient to reach full capacity in the medium and long term, the central bank deploys unconventional or nonstandard monetary policies. Negative interest rates are employed to avoid a recession after reaching a liquidity trap. There are theoretical options that can be considered to escape.

Owing to the higher debt levels in the US and the UK compared to the euro area, the political constraints are high. The central bank can buy government debt or private debt in primary or secondary markets. In these circumstances, the Fed purchases Treasury bonds and bills and mortgage-backed securities (MBS). To buy private debt, Congress approval is needed. The BoE bought only UK Treasury bonds and did not purchase private debt. The ECB bought some government debt from peripheral member states in the secondary markets, but sterilized its purchases. Raising inflation expectations to lower real interest rates may be a radical but effective solution by allowing inflation to be above the central bank normal target at least for some time.

Having assessed the effects of unconventional or nonstandard monetary policies, without a swift deployment of innovative policy tools, the meltdown of the financial sector could not have been avoided. These measures mitigated the harsh impacts of the global financial crisis on the real economy in terms of output, unemployment and inflation.

Taking into account the effects of the asset purchases deployed as unconventional stimulus, the purchases were targeted toward long-term assets held by nonbank financial institutions, like insurance companies and pension funds, which may be encouraged to use the funds to buy other, riskier assets like corporate bonds and equities. Asset purchase announcements had an impact on long-term asset yields, interest rate futures and measures of financial market uncertainty, which supports the importance of the signaling transmission channel. In the US, asset purchase shocks had an effect on long-term yields and the real exchange rate, underlining the role of the portfolio rebalancing channel.

Unlike the Fed and the BoE, the ECB responded to the crisis in terms of asset purchasing too late and in a limited scale. The Eurosystem had to face a continuous decline of inflation to a level below its definition of price stability of close but below 2.0%. To bring inflation back to 2.0% in the medium term, the ECB announced a broad package of measures in June 2014 to deal with the deflationary risks, which was present in the Eurozone since late 2013.

The current global financial crisis has had a significant negative impact on the Chinese economy affecting exports, foreign exchange reserves and structural adjustments. Since China is over-dependent on exports to stimulate its economic growth, weakening external demand means an adverse impact on the Chinese economy. In November 2008, China's continued GDP growth was disturbed by both losses in export-led manufacturing and reduced foreign direct investments from the international capital market. When external demand collapses, overheating caused by strong investment demand and strong export demand will turn into overcapacity, and inflation into deflation, immediately. It was the case in September–October 2008 since in the second half of 2008, export demand collapsed due to the global financial crisis causing the overcapacity come to the surface.

The global economic crisis exposed the vulnerability of China's growth pattern. The overcapacity of its economy would have surfaced and called for correction without the global financial crisis as well. The investment-driven and export-led growth pattern is not sustainable as the investment rate cannot increase forever and the growth rate of China's exports cannot stay persistently higher than that of the global economy.

At the end of 2008, the Chinese central bank held foreign exchange reserves worth US$1.95 trillion, the majority of which were denominated in US dollars comprising mainly the US treasury bonds and agency bonds. The deepening of the subprime crisis meant a potential threat of devaluation and downgrade of its US bonds, thus eroding the international purchasing power of China's foreign exchange reserves. In addition, to prevent a slowdown of economic growth, the Chinese government had to consider postponing or even canceling some structural adjustment policies necessary to ensure the sustainability of the growth of the economy such as bursting the price bubble in the real estate sector and increasing the flexibility of the RMB's exchange rate mechanism. From the second half of 2009, the largest developing country managed to regain its previous GDP growth levels while most advanced economies were still struggling to recover. The global crisis affected China only for a limited period, from late 2008 until late 2009. The Chinese Government's reaction had proved effective in boosting short-term economic growth, but was insufficient to ensure sustainable long-term development and to avoid new risks from arising. The structural problems of the economy were exposed further by the crisis.

China's exposure to the global financial crisis is moderated by its lack of direct exposure to the subprime mortgage issue. The economy applies numerous restrictions on capital flows, particularly on outflows of capital. Limiting the ability of the Chinese citizens and private firms to invest abroad, the policies compel them to invest domestically. Even if these restrictions could be evaded by some who invested abroad in subprime mortgages, the extent of this investment is unclear and is probably relatively small.

Although the People's Republic of China's (PRC) government made a bulk of foreign investment overseas owing to China's massive foreign currency reserves, most of these investments went to safe, low-yielding instruments, such as the US Treasury securities. PRC officials are cautious and conservative by nature in their investment strategies; they are unlikely to invest in mortgage-backed securities and other innovative financial instruments, which they do not know or may be viewed as speculative.

While China's direct exposure to subprime mortgages seems to have been limited, the impact of the subprime mortgage problem did affect China via its harsh impact on the economies of China's two largest trading partners: the US and the EU. Economic downturn in the economies throughout the world made the Chinese economy slow down significantly due to their lower purchases of Chinese exports, which began to decline. So did the FDI inflows.

The Chinese government's economic policy reaction to mitigate the impact of the global financial crisis includes stimulating household consumption effectively, reducing the pressure of unemployment and diversifying China's foreign exchange portfolio. China was one of the first major economies to recover from the spillover effects of the crisis. Thus, its economic policy responses, particularly those of the PBC are assumed to have been effective.

Before the global financial crisis, the PBC was a central bank in a transition economy. Financial liberalization was incomplete, and the Bank applied both direct and indirect tools. During the crisis direct controls dominated as risk management solutions, and further market-oriented principles were replaced by administered interest rates and exchange policy.

Due to the crisis, direct government intervention intensified, which continued to limit the PBC and even threatened China's market-oriented reforms. Nonetheless, in the frame of the fiscal stimulus package, the Chinese property market quickly returned to its previous growth after the decline in 2007 and 2008 attracting a great volume of commercial loans. With low deposit interests and in the lack of diversified investment products, household savings were continuously invested in the property and stock markets, which made government intervention only rarely successful.

Nonetheless, the global financial crisis challenged the Chinese central bank to such a degree that explicit government intervention seemed to threaten China's continuing market-oriented reforms. While demonstrating proactive risk management, the bank remained constrained by political domination. The Chinese government has intensified direct controls over both the central bank and wider financial markets.

The global crisis called for cross border cooperation, and the internationalization progress continued toward further Asian regionalization. To offer liquidity support, different institutions were established including a Credit Guarantee and Investment Fund (CGIF), an Asian Development Bank (ADB), the Associations of Southeast Asian Nations "ASEAN+3" and Macroeconomic Research Office (AMRO). The Chiang Mai Initiative (CMI) has evolved from a bilateral US dollar-denominated exchange arrangement to a multilateral facility. The establishment of the Asian Infrastructure Investment Bank (AIIB), which has attracted economies outside Asia as well, indicates that China has reached a new stage of financial integration.

Owing to China's crisis management, the economy was able to achieve its GDP growth targets for 2008 and 2009. In January 2010, the GDP growth rate of over 10% exceeded that of previous years on average. The Shanghai Stock Exchange Composite Index rose by 45.0% and retail sales rose by 14.8% on a year-on-year basis. Industrial output increased by 7.3% and investment in real estate by 6.4%. With regard to these figures, Chinese policy responses to the global financial crisis seem to be effective.

Compared with the US and the UK, severe housing collapses or banking failures did not hit Japan during the global crisis. Japanese banks were less innovative and continuous recapitalization rather than profitability created a sound financial environment. The Japanese stock market indicated the external instability by gradual sustained decline. Fiscal stimulus and monetary expansion were employed to deal with the global crisis. Owing to its over-dependence on exports, thus being vulnerable to external shocks Japan and its underperformed peers and emerging countries in Asia in 2008 and 2009. As foreign banks largely reduced their investment in the interbank market and their holdings of Japanese stocks negative outward portfolio investments increased from 2007 while inward portfolio investment turned negative in 2008 and 2009 leading to a credit crunch on Japan. Japan's economy turned into a serious economic recession from late 2008.

As Japan still suffered huge losses, the BoJ was required to pursue unconventional measures. Regarding these points, the selected crisis management solutions were similar, including interest rate cuts, clarified commitment and asset purchase programs, but monetary easing was more aggressive during the global financial crisis.

As for the timing, the BoJ was late to deal with the bubble economy and its impacts, although it acted proactively mainly in cross border cooperation. Regarding the independence of the central bank, it can be stated that in a financial crisis, a central bank is likely to have to sacrifice at least part of its independence. This was the case with the

BoJ while it increased its direct control over financial markets. As the banker's bank, by taking over credit risks from the private sector, the BoJ directly affected resource distribution. By providing commercial loans to contracted institutions, the Bank ensured liquidity while intensified its on-site examination and off-site monitoring in order to assist to improve liquidity risk management at the firm level. The key crisis management solutions can be summarized as ample liquidity provisions, support for credit market functioning, macroeconomic stimulus and injections of public capital and elimination of balance sheet uncertainties. Under the crisis challenge, the Bank's role as a government-driven monetary authority further strengthened and so did its function to promote the government's strategy.

References

- International-finance: investopedia.com, Retrieved 13 July, 2020
- Components-of-international-financial-environment, international-finance: mbaknol.com, Retrieved 16 April, 2020
- What-difference-between-foreign-portfolio-investment-and-foreign-direct-investment-060115: investopedia.com, Retrieved 30 May, 2020
- Balance-of-payment: cleartax.in, Retrieved 11 April, 2020
- Managing-international-financial-crises-responses-lessons-and-prevention, crisis-management-theory-and-practice, books: intechopen.com, Retrieved 13 March, 2020

Foreign Direct Investment

CHAPTER 2

Foreign direct investment refers to the investment of funds by an organization or a firm from one country into another. A few of its concepts are foreign ownership, global capital markets, foreign exchange controls, etc. This chapter has been carefully written to provide an easy understanding of foreign direct investment.

According to the IMF and OECD definitions, direct investment reflects the aim of obtaining a lasting interest by a resident entity of one economy (direct investor) in an enterprise that is resident in another economy (the direct investment enterprise). The "lasting interest" implies the existence of a long-term relationship between the direct investor and the direct investment enterprise and a significant degree of influence on the management of the latter. Direct investment involves both the initial transaction establishing the relationship between the investor and the enterprise and all subsequent capital transactions between them and among affiliated enterprises, both incorporated and unincorporated. It should be noted that capital transactions which do not give rise to any settlement, e.g. an interchange of shares among affiliated companies, must also be recorded in the Balance of Payments and in the IIP.

IMF's Balance of Payment Manual defines the owner of 10% or more of a company's capital as a direct investor. This guideline is not a fast rule, as it acknowledges that smaller percentage may entail a controlling interest in the company (and, conversely, that a share of more than 10% may not signify control). But the IMF recommends using this percentage as the basic dividing line between direct investment and portfolio investment in the form of shareholdings. Thus, when a non-resident who previously had no equity in a resident enterprise purchases 10% or more of the shares of that enterprise from a resident, the price of equity holdings acquired should be recorded as direct investment. From this moment, any further capital transactions between these two companies should be recorded as a direct investment. When a non-resident holds less than 10% of the shares of an enterprise as portfolio investment, and subsequently acquires additional shares resulting in a direct investment (10% of more), only the purchase of additional shares is recorded as direct investment in the Balance of Payments. The holdings that were acquired previously should not be reclassified from portfolio to direct investment in the Balance of Payments but the total holdings should be reclassified in the IIP.

Concerning the terms direct investor and direct investment enterprise, the IMF and the OECD define them as follows. A direct investor may be an individual, an incorporated or unincorporated private or public enterprise, a government, a group of related individuals, or a group of related incorporated and unincorporated enterprises which have a direct investment enterprise, operating in a country other than the country of residence of the direct investor. A direct investment enterprise is an incorporated or unincorporated enterprise in which a foreign investor owns 10% or more of the ordinary shares or voting power of an incorporated enterprise or the equivalent of an unincorporated enterprise. Direct investment enterprises may be subsidiaries, associates or branches. A subsidiary is an incorporated enterprise in which the foreign investor controls directly or indirectly (through another subsidiary) more than 50% of the shareholder's voting power. An associate is an enterprise where the direct investor and its subsidiaries control between 10% and 50% of the voting shares. A branch is a wholly or jointly owned unincorporated enterprise.

It should be noted that the choice between setting up either a subsidiary/associate or a branch in a foreign country is dependent, among other factors, upon the existing regulations in the host country (and sometimes in its own country, too). National regulations are often more restrictive for subsidiaries than for branches but this is not always the case.

It should be mentioned that in the case of affiliated banks (depository institutions) and affiliated financial intermediaries such as securities dealers, transactions recorded under direct investment are those associated with permanent debt (loan capital representing a permanent interest) and equity (share capital) investment or, in the case of branches, fixed assets. Deposits, loans and other claims and liabilities related to usual banking transactions of depository institutions and of other financial intermediaries are classified, as appropriate, under portfolio investment or "other investment", but never as direct investment. The stock of foreign assets and liabilities of banks and other financial intermediaries should be treated in a parallel manner.

The OECD recommends in its Benchmark definition that for the existence of a direct investment relationship the "full consolidated system" should be followed. In other words, it means that when there is a cascade of participations, the percentage of the parent company in any affiliated companies should be calculate assuming the 100% of the subsidiaries and the corresponding percentage of the associates. This criterion does not correspond with the consolidation concept in the accounting statement.

From an accounting standpoint, bank branches are wholly considered as being an integral part of their parent company and, therefore, do not have separate accounts. However, the requirement for affiliated companies to be included in bank's consolidated financial statements is twofold: (i) they themselves must carry out a financial activity; and (ii) at least 20% of their capital must be owned by their parent bank, together with the latter's exerting an effective control over them. Non-compliance with any of these requisites entails that the affiliated company is not consolidated, although it should be valued according to the "equity method" in its parent bank's financial statements. In accordance with these consolidation rules, a bank will not include in its consolidated statements the assets and liabilities of all its associates, despite the fact that such associates may obviously be direct investment enterprises from a BOP/IIP viewpoint.

Direct Investment Classification, Components and Sectorial Breakdown

The classification of direct investment is based firstly on the direction of investment both for assets or liabilities; secondly, on the investment instrument used (shares, loans, etc).; and thirdly on the sector breakdown.

As for the direction, it can be looked at it from the home and the host perspectives. From the home one, financing of any type extended by the resident parent company to its nonresident affiliated would be included as direct investment abroad. By contrast, financing of any type extended by non-resident subsidiaries, associates or branches to their resident parent company are classified as a decrease in direct investment abroad, rather than as a foreign direct investment. From the host one, the financing extended by non-resident parent companies to their resident subsidiaries, associates or branches would be recorded, in the country of residence of the affiliated companies, under foreign direct investment, and the financing extended by resident subsidiaries, associates and branches to their non-resident parent company would be classified as a decrease in foreign direct investment rather than as a direct investment abroad. This directional principle does not apply if the parent company and its subsidiaries, associates or branches have cross-holdings in each other's share capital of more than 10%.

As for the instruments, direct investment capital comprises the capital provided (either directly or through other related enterprises) by a direct investor to a direct investment enterprise and the capital received by a direct investor from a direct investment enterprise. Direct investment capital transactions are made up of three basic components: (i) Equity capital: comprising equity in branches, all shares in subsidiaries and associates (except non-participating, preferred shares that are treated as debt securities and are included under other direct investment capital) and other capital contributions such as provisions of machinery, etc. (ii) Reinvested earnings: consisting of the direct investor's share (in proportion to direct equity participation) of earnings not distributed, as dividends by subsidiaries or associates and earnings of branches not remitted to the direct investor. If such earnings are not identified, all branche's earnings are considered, by convention, to be distributed. (iii) Other direct investment capital (or inter company debt transactions): covering the borrowing and lending of funds, including debt securities and trade credits, between direct investors and direct investment enterprises and between two direct investment enterprises that share the same direct investor. As it has been mentioned before, deposits and loans between affiliated deposit institutions are recorded as other investment rather than as direct investment.

Finally, there are several sector breakdowns of FDI flows and of IIP. The IMF has chosen a breakdown by four institutional sectors, defined according to the sector to which the resident party belongs. However, reporting on this sector breakdown is not compulsory in the Fifth IMF Manual. In national statistics, some countries (among which Spain) publish their FDI data providing this breakdown. Nevertheless, in practice the only relevant breakdown is Banks and Other sectors and it is blurred by the fact that national banks often invest in foreign enterprises via resident non-banking holding companies. Such transactions would be recorded as being carried out by other sectors rather than by Banks, thus distorting both categories.

By contrast to the classification according to the institutional sector, the OECD Benchmark definition favours an "industrial" breakdown, which includes nine economic sectors. The OECD specifically recommends, for the purpose of this classification, that FDI carried out via a resident holding company be classified according to the industrial sector to which the parent company belongs. Under this criterion, when the parent company is a bank, FDI transactions carried out by a non-banking holding company would be attributed to the Banks.

Institutional sector (IMF)	Economic or industry sector (OECD)
• Monetary Authority	• Agriculture, hunting, forestry and fishing
• Banks	• Mining and quarrying
• General Government	• Manufacturing
• Other resident sector	• Electricity, gas and water
	• Construction
	• Wholesale and retail trade and restaurants and hotels
	• Transport, storage and communications
	• Financing, real state and business services
	• Community, social and personal services

Valuation of FDI Flows and Stocks and Relations between both of them

The Balance of Payments and the International Investment Position are compiled under the same framework of methodological rules laid down in the Fifth edition of the IMF Balance of Payments Manual. According to this, FDI transactions should be recorded in the Balance of Payments at the accrued value, i.e. "transactions are recorded when economic value is created, transformed, exchanged, transferred, or extinguished". Thus, the flows recorded do not necessarily coincide with the liquid proceeds and payments generated. In practice, it is very difficult to apply the accrued principle to all transactions and many of them are therefore recorded at the time when the proceeds or payments are generated.

Moreover, the IMF recommends the using of market price as the basis for valuation of flows and stocks, although this means different approaches for both types of data: (i)

For flows, market price refers to the actual price agreed upon by transactors on the date of the transaction and should not reflect changes induced by fluctuations in exchange rates or in the market price of the financial assets of liabilities in question. (ii) For stocks, the market price at the time of the compilation of the stocks is recommended. Nevertheless, it is recognized that in practice, book values from the balance sheets of direct investment enterprises (or investors) often are used at a proxy of the market value of the stock of direct investments, when the company has no a market price. These balance sheets values, if recorded on the basis of current market value, would be in general accordance with the principle. If based on historical cost or on an interim but not current revaluation, such balance sheet values would not conform to the principle. But this practice reflects the fact that enterprise balance sheet values represent the only source of valuation of assets and liabilities readily available in most countries.

The difference between the stock at the beginning of the year and its value at year-end must be equal to the flow recorded in the Balance of Payments, which reflects the transactions on these assets or liabilities that actually took place; plus the change in the value of the stock induced by swings in the exchange rate; plus the change caused by alterations in the price of the related assets or liabilities; and plus other changes in the volume of financial assets and liabilities:

> Position at the end of the period = Position at the beginning of the period + FDI flows + price changes + exchange rate changes + other adjustments.

With regard to the "other adjustments" although some of them may be explained by the use of different sources to compile both statistics, main conceptual ones are re-classifications in the IIP (but not in the Balance of Payments) e.g. portfolio to direct investment.

As for the international comparison of data, despite a common international methodological framework, discrepancies between countries do occur. In fact, the worldwide discrepancy between outward and inward direct investment flows should be zero, if all flows were recorded fully and consistently by both sides. Nevertheless, according to Lipsey "the asymmetries have been no higher than 8% in any year from 1993 to 1999, as contrasted with 40 or 50% for portfolio investment".

Discrepancies are mainly due to the use of different criteria for valuation or for geographical allocation of transactions. The increasing complexity of enterprise groups poses a further challenge to the correct application of the directional principle for accurately assessing FDI. Similarly, it is rather difficult to consistently capture loans granted to or received from related enterprises and they are often incorrectly considered as "other investment", rather than as "direct investment". This problem does not arise, however, in the case of loans between banks since they are not considered as "direct investment". Additional circumstances resulting in discrepancies between countries are, among others: The lack of information on reinvested earnings, the use of a percentage-ownership threshold different from the recommended 10% level for identifying an investment as direct, and the use of different reporting systems and exemption threshold by countries for collecting and aggregating data on international transactions. Most countries use a combination of sources to compile their balance of payments and international investment position statistics. Data collection may be based on the compulsory reporting of individual transactions or on aggregates, or alternatively data may be collected by the statistical agency from an intermediary (such as a dealer that handles security transactions for clients) or directly from the transactor by means of mandatory surveys.

FDI Data

Data on FDI flows and stocks are offered by several sources, the most important of which are explained in the Annex. Within them, however, only the OECD and EUROSTAT provide a sector breakdown of FDI flows and stocks. Since both institutions do only cover a very limited number of world countries, the total direct investment received by the financial sector of any given country cannot be wholly assessed.

Due to this significant restriction, we focus on showing the trend of total FDI flows and stocks. We use both data published by the UNCTAD with those published by the IMF, to assess the extent of the discrepancies. Note that the former provides a break down into two different categories (FDI figures for developed and for developing countries) so the IMF FDI data has been harmonised with this breakdown (by adding up individual countrie's figures according to the geographical classification of the World Economic Outlook, WEO). Therefore, a preliminary reason for discrepancies may be the criterion for classifying some countries as "developed" or "developing" that differs between the UNCTAD and the WEO.

In rough terms, both sets of data reveal a similar pattern for all countries, albeit significant differences in magnitude, especially with regard to stocks and with regard to developing countries. More specifically, the following statistical issues can be observed:

- Concerning flows, the differences between both sources are more relevant in the case of developing countries, especially for the year 2000 but they are relatively limited (UNCTAD data reach a peak of USD 264 billion, while IMF data initiate a downward trend).
- Concerning stocks, differences are larger, especially for developing countries. The main reason is the lack of information for many developing countries in the IMF data. For developed countries the differences between IMF and UNCTAD data are more significant from 1994 onwards, IMF data henceforth always being higher than UNCTAD data.

As for the general trends, it is interesting to note a couple of things:

- Even if flows to emerging countries have grown, the bulk of them continue to go to industrial countries.

- The large reduction in FDI flows to emerging countries in 2001 in the UNCTAD statistics is much milder in the IMF ones and is not perceived in the stock data.
- Total stock, as well as the stock received by industrial countries, seems to have reached a plateau in IMF statistics but not in the UNCTAD ones.

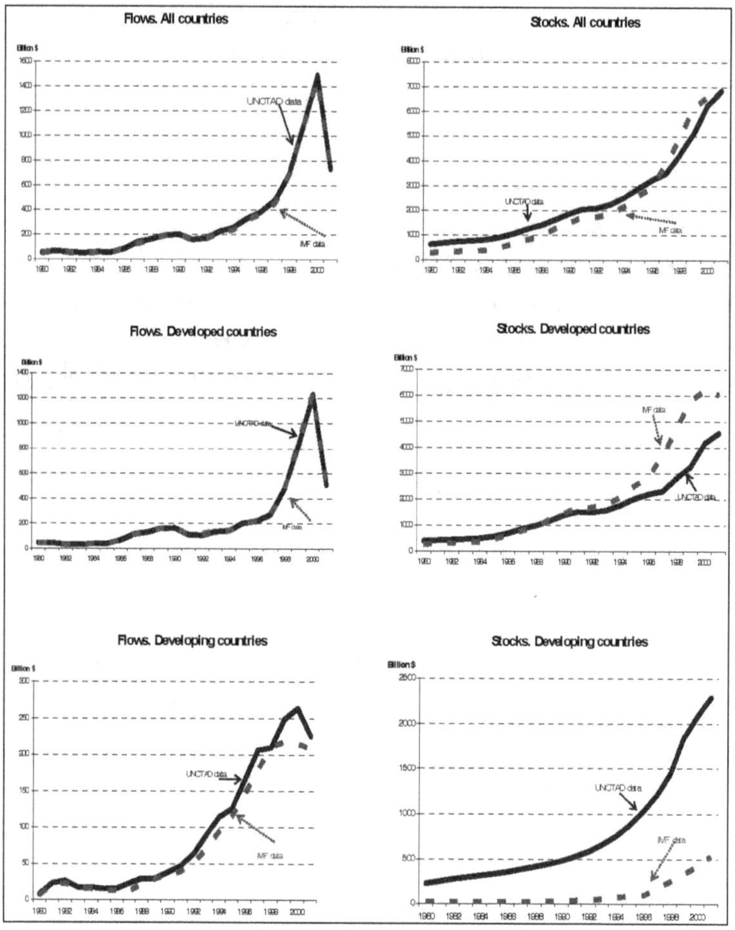

Inward Foreign Direct Investment: flows and stocks data.
Comparisson between IMF and UNCTAD data.

Example of Foreign Direct Investments

Examples of foreign direct investments include mergers, acquisitions, retail, services, logistics, and manufacturing, among others. Foreign direct investments and the laws governing them can be pivotal to a company's growth strategy.

In 2017, for example, U.S.-based Apple announced a $507.1 million investment to boost its research and development work in China, Apple's third-largest market behind the Americas and Europe. The announced investment relayed CEO Tim Cook's bullishness toward the Chinese market despite a 12% year-over-year decline in Apple's Greater China revenue in the quarter preceding the announcement.

China's economy has been fueled by an influx of FDI targeting the nation's high-tech manufacturing and services, which according to China's Ministry of Commerce, grew 11.1% and 20.4% year over year, respectively, in the first half of 2017. Meanwhile, relaxed FDI regulations in India now allows 100% foreign direct investment in single-brand retail without government approval. The regulatory decision reportedly facilitates Apple's desire to open a physical store in the Indian market. Thus far, the firm's iPhones have only been available through third-party physical and online retailers.

Types of FDI

Strategically, FDI comes in three types:

- Horizontal: In case of horizontal FDI, the company does all the same activities abroad as at home. For example, Toyota assembles motor cars in Japan and the UK.
- Vertical: In vertical assignments, different types of activities are carried out abroad. In case of forward vertical FDI, the FDI brings the company nearer to a market (for example, Toyota buying a car distributorship in America). In case of backward Vertical FDI, the international integration goes back towards raw materials (for example, Toyota getting majority stake in a tyre manufacturer or a rubber plantation).
- Conglomerate: In this type of investment, the investment is made to acquire an unrelated business abroad. It is the most surprising form of FDI, as it requires overcoming two barriers simultaneously – one, entering a foreign country and two, working in a new industry.

FDI can take the form of greenfield entry or takeover:

- Greenfield entry refers to activities or assembling all the elements right from scratch as Honda did in the UK.
- Foreign takeover means acquiring an existing foreign company: as Tata's acquisition of Jaguar Land Rover. Foreign takeover is often called mergers and acquisitions (M&A) but internationally, mergers are absolutely small, which accounts for less than 1% of all foreign acquisitions.

This choice of entry in a market and its mode interacts with the ownership strategy. The choice of wholly owned subsidiaries against joint ventures gives a 2x2 matrix of choices – the options of which are:

- Greenfield wholly owned ventures,
- Greenfield joint ventures,
- Wholly owned takeovers,
- Joint foreign acquisitions.

These choices offer foreign investors options to match their own interests, capabilities, and foreign conditions.

Factors affecting Foreign Direct Investment

Wage Rates

A major incentive for a multinational to invest abroad is to outsource labour-intensive production to countries with lower wages. If average wages in the US are $15 an hour, but $1 an hour in another country (say x), costs can be reduced by outsourcing production.

- However, wage rates alone do not determine FDI, countries with high wage rates can still attract higher tech investment. A firm may be reluctant to invest in Sub-Saharan Africa because low wages are outweighed by other drawbacks, such as lack of infrastructure and transport links.

Labour Skills

Some industries require higher skilled labour, for example pharmaceuticals and electronics. Therefore, multinationals will invest in those countries with a combination of low wages, but high labour productivity and skills. For example, A country x has attracted significant investment in call centres, because a high percentage of the population speak English, but wages are low. This makes it an attractive place for outsourcing and therefore attracts investment.

Tax Rates

Large multinationals, such as Apple, Google and Microsoft have sought to invest in countries with lower corporation tax rates. For example, Ireland has been successful in attracting investment from Google and Microsoft. In fact, it has been controversial because Google has tried to funnel all profits through Ireland, despite having operations in all European countries.

Transport and Infrastructure

A key factor in the desirability of investment are the transport costs and levels of infrastructure. A country may have low labour costs, but if there is then high transport costs to get the goods onto the world market, this is a drawback. Countries with access to the sea are at an advantage to landlocked countries, who will have higher costs to ship goods.

Size of Economy / Potential for Growth

Foreign direct investment is often targeted to selling goods directly to the country involved in attracting the investment. Therefore, the size of the population and scope for economic growth will be important for attracting investment. For example, Eastern European countries, with a large population, e.g. Poland offers scope for new markets.

This may attract foreign car firms, e.g. Volkswagen, Fiat to invest and build factories in Poland to sell to the growing consumer class. Small countries may be at a disadvantage because it is not worth investing for a small population. China will be a target for foreign investment as the newly emerging Chinese middle class could have a very strong demand for the goods and services of multinationals.

Political Stability / Property Rights

Foreign direct investment has an element of risk. Countries with an uncertain political situation, will be a major disincentive. Also, economic crisis can discourage investment. For example, the recent Russian economic crisis, combined with economic sanctions, will be a major factor to discourage foreign investment. This is one reason why former Communist countries in the East are keen to join the European Union. The EU is seen as a signal of political and economic stability, which encourages foreign investment.

Related to political stability is the level of corruption and trust in institutions, especially judiciary and the extent of law and order.

Commodities

One reason for foreign investment is the existence of commodities. This has been a major reason for the growth in FDI within Africa – often by Chinese firms looking for a secure supply of commodities.

Exchange Rate

A weak exchange rate in the host country can attract more FDI because it will be cheaper for the multinational to purchase assets. However, exchange rate volatility could discourage investment.

Clustering Effects

Foreign firms often are attracted to invest in similar areas to existing FDI. The reason is that they can benefit from external economies of scale – growth of service industries and transport links. Also, there will be greater confidence to invest in areas with a good track record. Therefore, some countries can create a virtuous cycle of attracting investment and then these initial investments attracting more. It is also sometimes known as an agglomeration effect.

Access to Free Trade Areas

A significant factor for firms investing in Europe is access to EU Single Market, which is a free trade area but also has very low non-tariff barriers because of harmonisation of rules, regulations and free movement of people. For example, UK post-Brexit is likely to be less attractive to FDI, if it is outside the Single Market.

There are many different factors that determine foreign direct investment (FDI) and it is hard to isolate individual factors, given there are many different variables. It also depends on the type of industry. For example, with manufacturing FDI, low wage costs tend to be the most important, as they are a labour-intensive industry. For the service sector, FDI, macro-economic stability and political openness tend to be more important.

Also, it depends on the source of FDI, American firms may value political openness more than Chinese firms. Or American firms may have a preference for countries where English is spoken more.

Advantages of FDI

The advantages of FDI are as follows:

Increased Employment and Economic Growth

Creation of jobs is the most obvious advantage of FDI. It is also one of the most important reasons why a nation, especially a developing one, looks to attract FDI. Increased FDI boosts the manufacturing as well as the services sector. This in turn creates jobs, and helps reduce unemployment among the educated youth - as well as skilled and unskilled labour - in the country. Increased employment translates to increased incomes, and equips the population with enhanced buying power. This boosts the economy of the country.

Human Resource Development

This is one of the less obvious advantages of FDI. Hence, it is often understated. Human Capital refers to the knowledge and competence of the workforce. Skills gained and enhanced through training and experience boost the education and human capital quotient of the country. Once developed, human capital is mobile. It can train human resources in other companies, thereby creating a ripple effect.

Development of Backward Areas

This is one of the most crucial benefits of FDI for a developing country. FDI enables the transformation of backward areas in a country into industrial centres. This in turn provides a boost to the social economy of the area. The Hyundai unit at Sriperumbudur, Tamil Nadu in India exemplifies this process.

Provision of Finance and Technology

Recipient businesses get access to latest financing tools, technologies and operational practices from across the world. Over time, the introduction of newer, enhanced technologies and processes results in their diffusion into the local economy, resulting in enhanced efficiency and effectiveness of the industry.

Increase in Exports

Not all goods produced through FDI are meant for domestic consumption. Many of these products have global markets. The creation of 100% Export Oriented Units and Economic Zones have further assisted FDI investors in boosting their exports from other countries.

Exchange Rate Stability

The constant flow of FDI into a country translates into a continuous flow of foreign exchange. This helps the country's Central Bank maintain a comfortable reserve of foreign exchange. This in turn ensures stable exchange rates.

Stimulation of Economic Development

This is another very important advantage of FDI. FDI is a source of external capital and higher revenues for a country. When factories are constructed, at least some local labour, materials and equipment are utilised. Once the construction is complete, the factory will employ some local employees and further use local materials and services. The people who are employed by such factories thus have more money to spend. This creates more jobs. These factories will also create additional tax revenue for the Government, that can be infused into creating and improving physical and financial infrastructure.

Improved Capital Flow

Inflow of capital is particularly beneficial for countries with limited domestic resources, as well as for nations with restricted opportunities to raise funds in global capital markets.

Creation of a Competitive Market

By facilitating the entry of foreign organisations into the domestic marketplace, FDI helps create a competitive environment, as well as break domestic monopolies. A healthy competitive environment pushes firms to continuously enhance their processes and product offerings, thereby fostering innovation. Consumers also gain access to a wider range of competitively priced products.

AGREEMENT ON TRADE-RELATED INVESTMENT MEASURES

The Agreement on Trade-Related Investment Measures (TRIMs) are rules that are applicable to the domestic regulations a country applies to foreign investors, often as part of an industrial policy. The agreement, concluded in 1994, was negotiated under the

WTO's predecessor, the General Agreement on Tariffs and Trade (GATT), and came into force in 1995. The agreement was agreed upon by all members of the World Trade Organization. Trade-Related Investment Measures is one of the four principal legal agreements of the WTO trade treaty.

TRIMs are rules that restrict preference of domestic firms and thereby enable international firms to operate more easily within foreign markets. Policies such as local content requirements and trade balancing rules that have traditionally been used to both promote the interests of domestic industries and combat restrictive business practices are now banned.

In the late 1980s, there was a significant increase in foreign direct investment across the world. However, some of the countries receiving foreign investment imposed numerous restrictions on that investment designed to protect and foster domestic industries, and to prevent the outflow of foreign exchange reserves.

Examples of these restrictions include local content requirements (which require that locally produced goods be purchased or used), manufacturing requirements (which require the domestic manufacturing of certain components), trade balancing requirements, domestic sales requirements, technology transfer requirements, export performance requirements (which require the export of a specified percentage of production volume), local equity restrictions, foreign exchange restrictions, remittance restrictions, licensing requirements, and employment restrictions. These measures can also be used in connection with fiscal incentives as opposed to requirement. Some of these investment measures distort trade in violation of GATT Articles III and XI, and are therefore prohibited.

Until the completion of the Uruguay Round negotiations, which produced a well-rounded Agreement on Trade-Related Investment Measures (hereinafter the "TRIMs Agreement"), the few international agreements providing disciplines for measures restricting foreign investment provided only limited guidance in terms of content and country coverage. The OECD Code on Liberalization of Capital Movements, for example, requires members to liberalize restrictions on direct investment in a range of areas. The OECD Code's efficacy, however, is limited by the numerous reservations made by each of the members.

In addition, there are other international treaties, bilateral and multilateral, under which signatories extend most-favored-nation treatment to direct investment. Only a few such treaties, however, provide national treatment for direct investment. The Asia-Pacific Economic Cooperation Investment Principles adopted in November 1994 are general rules for investment but they are non-binding.

Legal Framework

GATT 1947 prohibited investment measures that violated the principles of national treatment and the general elimination of quantitative restrictions, but the extent of the prohibitions was never clear. The TRIMs Agreement, however, contains statements prohibiting any TRIMs that are inconsistent with the provisions of Articles III or XI of GATT 1994. In addition, it provides an illustrative list that explicitly prohibits local content requirements, trade balancing requirements, foreign exchange restrictions and export restrictions (domestic sales requirements) that would violate Article III:4 or XI:1 of GATT 1994. TRIMs prohibited by the Agreement include those that are mandatory or enforceable under domestic law or administrative rulings, or those with which compliance is necessary to obtain an advantage (such as subsidies or tax breaks).

Figure contains a list of measures specifically prohibited by the TRIMs Agreement. Note that this figure is not exhaustive, but simply illustrates TRIMs that are prohibited by the TRIMs Agreement. The figure, therefore, calls particular attention to several common types of TRIMs. We would add that this figure identifies measures that were also inconsistent with Article III:4 and XI:1 of GATT 1947. Indeed, the TRIMs Agreement is not intended to impose new obligations, but to clarify the pre-existing GATT 1947 obligations. Under the WTO TRIMs Agreement, countries are required to rectify any measures inconsistent with the Agreement, within a set period of time, with a few exceptions.

Examples of TRIMs Explicitly Prohibited by the TRIMs Agreement			
Local content requirement	Trade balancing requirements	Foreign exchange restrictions	Export restrictions (Domestic sales requirements)
Measures requiring the purchase or use by an enterprise of domestic products, whether specified in terms of particular products, in terms of volume or value of products, or in terms of a proportion of volume or value of its local production.	1.Measures requiring that an enterprise's purchases or use of imported products be limited to an amount related to the volume or value of local products that it exports. (Violation of GATT Article III:4)2. Measures restricting the importation by an enterprise of products used in or related to its local production, generally or to an amount related to the volume or value of local production that it exports.	Measures restricting the importation by an enterprise of products (parts and other goods) used in or related to its local Production by restricting its access to foreign exchange to an amount related to the foreign exchange inflows attributable to the enterprise.	Measures restricting the exportation or sale for export by an enterprise of products, whether specified in terms of particular products, in terms of volume or value of products, or in terms of a proportion of volume or value of its local production.

Exceptional Provisions of the TRIMs Agreement		
Transitional period	Exceptions for developing countries	Equitable provisions
Measures specifically prohibited by the TRIMs Agreement need not be eliminated immediately, although such measures must be notified to the WTO within 90 days after	Developing countries are permitted to retain TRIMs that constitute a violation of GATT Article III or XI, provided the measures meet the conditions of GATT Article XVIII which allows specified derogation	To avoid damaging the competitiveness of companies already subject to TRIMs, governments are allowed to apply the same TRIMs to new foreign direct investment

the entry into force of the TRIMs Agreement. Developed countries will have a period of two years in which to abolish such measures; in principle, developing countries will have five years and least-developed countries will have seven years.	from the GATT provisions, by virtue of the economic development needs of developing countries.	during the transitional period described in (1) above.

FOREIGN EXCHANGE CONTROLS

Foreign exchange controls are various forms of controls imposed by a government on the purchase/sale of foreign currencies by residents, on the purchase/sale of local currency by nonresidents, or the transfers of any currency across national borders. These controls allow countries to better manage their economies by controlling the inflow and outflow of currency, which may otherwise create exchange rate volatility. Countries with weak and developing economies generally use foreign exchange controls to limit speculation against their currencies. They may also introduce capital controls, which limit foreign investment in the country.

Common foreign exchange controls include:

- Banning the use of foreign currency within the country.
- Banning locals from possessing foreign currency.
- Restricting currency exchange to government-approved exchangers.
- Fixed exchange rates.
- Restricting the amount of currency that may be imported or exported.

Today, countries with foreign exchange controls are known as "Article 14 countries", after the provision in the International Monetary Fund's Articles of Agreement, which allows exchange controls only for "transitional economies".

Foreign exchange controls used to be common in most countries. For example, many western European countries implemented exchange controls in the years immediately following World War II. The measures were gradually phased out, however, as the post-war economies on the continent steadily strengthened; the United Kingdom, for example, removed the last of its restrictions in October 1979. By the 1990s, there was a trend toward free trade and globalization and economic liberalization.

Often, foreign exchange controls can result in the creation of black markets in currencies. This leads to a situation where the actual demand for foreign currency is greater than that which is available on the official market. As such, it is unclear whether governments have the ability to enact effective exchange controls.

FOREIGN OWNERSHIP

Foreign ownership or control of a business or natural resource in a country by individuals who are not citizens of that country or by companies whose headquarters outside that country.

In general, foreign ownership occurs when multinational corporations, which do business in more than one country, inject long-term investments in a foreign country, usually in the form of foreign direct investment or acquisition.

If a multinational corporation acquires at least half of a company, the multinational corporation becomes a holding company, and the company receiving the foreign investment becomes a subsidiary. Also, foreign ownership can occur when a domestic property is acquired by a foreign individual. An example is an Indian businessman buying a house in Hong Kong.

Assessment

According to the US Department of Defense, the following factors relating to a company, the foreign interest, and the government of the foreign interest are reviewed in the aggregate in determining whether a company is under foreign ownership, control, or Influence:

- The record of economic and government espionage against US targets.
- The record of enforcement and engagement in unauthorized technology transfer.
- Type and sensitivity of the information that is accessed.
- The source, nature, and extent of the foreign ownership.
- The record of compliance with pertinent US laws, regulations and contracts.
- The nature of any bilateral and multilateral security and information exchange agreements that may be pertinent.
- The ownership or control, in whole or in part, by a foreign government.

Benefits

- The transfer of technology and organisational knowledge can lead to higher productivity, and the company in the host country can learn from multinational corporations.

- It increases employment and wages. Inward foreign direct investment has an overall positive effect in employment, as companies have more capital to expand.
- It lowers prices and improves the quality of products. That is a result of higher productivity, which is beneficial for consumers and the company's competitiveness for exports.

Drawbacks

- Foreign ownership can increase the demand of products, leading to price increases.
- The increase in productivity in the firms in foreign ownership can cause other domestic companies to become relatively less competitive, which reduces profits.
- Multinational corporations may use their power to influence government policies, especially in underdeveloped countries. That may have an adverse impact on economic development.
- A lowering of employment because of operational optimization or an increase by a planned expansion can occur. Wages can be reduced for new employees by new corporate policies, and an optimized employee benefits package can reduce benefits for all.
- The demise of local economies can be caused by siphoning money from communities to global elites.

Policies

Indonesia

The House of Representatives of Indonesia passed the plantation bill to set stricter rules on foreign ownership in the plantation sector to prioritise smaller local plantation firms. There is no specific percentage value on the limit on foreign ownership, but a 30% foreign ownership ceiling had been demanded by the House's Commission IV.

Plantation business groups as well as the Ministry of Agriculture had previously voiced criticism of the bill, expressing concern that it would negatively impact plantation firms and growers, as foreign investment might be reduced.

Even though the bill was passed to limit foreign ownership, the law encourages cooperation research and development between domestic and foreign businesses, universities and individuals.

A reduction in foreign ownership limit may reduce foreign investment, but it can help boost revenue for domestic firms and economic development.

Qatar

As part of financial reforms, Qatar's emir has issued a law, allowing foreign investors to obtain up to 49% of listed Qatari companies for expansion in the stock market and to stimulate development in the financial industry.

Prior to the law, ceilings on listed Qatari firms restricted foreign ownership to 25%.

The reform aims to help attract more foreign investment in the long run. However, according to a wealth manager in the Gulf, "It's a step in the right direction, but it will have to be backed up by good performance from companies in order to attract foreign investment. Also, there should be limited impact from the law in the short term due to liquidity issues and limited numbers of shares available".

Russia

The Russian Duma has passed a law, reducing the foreign ownership ceiling for print publications and radio and television outlets from 50% to 20%; it was passed by with a vote of 430-2. The legislation forbids foreign governments, organisations, companies and individuals from founding or holding more than a 20% stake in Russian media businesses.

According to Vadim Dengin, one of the bill's authors, " the tighter limit on foreign ownership would help protect Russia from western influence". However, publishers and editors of independent media companies in Russia argued that the new law would further reduce diversity of opinion.

FOREIGN DIRECT INVESTMENT AND THE ENVIRONMENT

Foreign direct investment and the environment involves international businesses and their interactions and impact on the natural world. These interactions can be observed through the stringency applied to foreign direct investment policy and the responsiveness of capital or labor incentive for investment inflows. The laws and regulations created by a country that focuses on environmental regimes can directly impact the levels of competition involving foreign direct investment they are exposed to. Fiscal and financial incentives stemming from ecological motivators, such as carbon taxation, are methods used based on the desired outcome within a country in order to attract foreign direct investment.

External funding sources that come from foreign direct investment, stimulates the increase of innovative ideas surrounding technological advances while it also holds the potential to decrease unemployment. When financial and fiscal motives are combined with environmental consciousness, the promotion of green and sustainable innovations increases. Such environmental consciousness can result in the decrease of industrial pollutants, which contributes to infant mortality and other health issues. Policies created that attract innovative and environmentally conscious technological advancements have been stated as a great way to encourage increase in the abundance of environmentally friendly foreign direct investments. The Organization for Economic Co-operation and Development promotes policies that can have positive social and economic impacts.

Foreign direct investment does have the potential in initiating negative effects on countries as well. Foreign direct investments allow for the chance of compromise and collaboration between policies of negotiating countries which brings the opportunity for new perspectives on green innovation. However, intensifying regulations around production costs, such as environmental effect, can decrease the attraction of foreign direct investment to that country. Businesses or governments may wish to negotiate with a country with less complicated policies therefore decreasing a country's competitive edge on the international market.

Environmental Regulation and Foreign Direct Investment Incentives

A complete list of foreign direct investment incentives that can be applied in regards to international business can be found in Foreign direct investment.

Some researchers find foreign direct investment leads to strict environmental policy. Environmental consciousness has been a pressing topic for discussion and concern in the global community as has been seen in the recent Paris Agreement. For a country to become more attractive to foreign investors, one may consider implementing incentives that simultaneously reduce cost while also enabling environmental initiatives. Incentives are policy or regulation measures that are implemented to serve both as a reason to increase foreign direct investment while also maintaining control over the impact investment may have.

Fiscal incentives alone, such as taxation laws that aim to reduce the tax burden of a firm, do not largely contribute to attracting foreign direct investment in research and development. Financial incentives direct monetary contributions from a government to a firm; this could include direct capital subsidies or subsidized loans. Incentives that combine both fiscal and financial aspects, have the capacity to increase interest in investment.

Foreign Direct Investment and Environment in Different Countries

Canada is part of the OECD, an amalgamation of countries dedicated to working in unison to increase environmental sustainability. Research shows that the total amounts of

CO_2 emissions have been increasing for Canada. One study shows that Canada is not prepared to avoid the effects of environmental issues that come with economic growth as it does not have a high level of per capita GDP to avoid these negative effects at this time. While another study shows that Quebec which is a major exporter of hydropower, decreased their green house gas emissions by 35%.

Since the 1980s, Canada has developed more lenient foreign direct investment policies in order to attract investment. For example, recent Chinese investment in Canada's oil and gas industry has raised concerns that such investments may increase global emissions. Furthermore, Canada is involved in trade agreements over water with the United States such as NAFTA. Researchers argue trade agreements concerning water is affecting the sustainability of water management. It is stated that water governance and management is changing in Canada. There are many commodities that are produced with water, which may increase the competition for water resources and this may affect water security.

Canada has been taking preliminary steps to become more environmentally conscious within their trade agreements and environmental regulation policies. In order to address air pollution and its effects on the environment such as acid rain, Canada has partnered with the United States through Canada-United States Air Quality Agreement. Canada and the United States work together to address acid rain issues. Moreover, chemicals and waste industries have economic benefits however also pollute the environment. Canada is part of multiple groups such as United Nations Commission for Sustainable Development and Stockholm Convention on Persistent Organic Pollutants, to ensure waste management is effectively managed. In addition, Canada is part of multiple trade agreements to ensure economic growth as well as protection of the environment. Canada has made trade agreements that focus on both labor and the environment with countries such as Chile, which focus on promoting environmental transparency and strengthening the effectiveness of domestic environmental laws and regulations.

For the past 30 years China has experienced rapid economic growth. Many studies have been dedicated to documenting the impact foreign direct investment has on the environment in China. However, there have been varying conclusions as to whether or not such investment is environmentally beneficial for the country. Jiajia Zheng and Pengfei Sheng discovered that provinces in the East have higher evidence of market development and lower CO_2 emissions while provinces in the West have lower evidence of market development and higher CO_2 emissions. It has been documented by the scientific community that there is a correlation between foreign direct investment and increases in China's CO_2 emissions as energy consumption in the long term impacts CO_2 emissions. Researchers found that a 1% increase in foreign direct investment stocks, increase industrial SO2 levels by 0.099%, which shows that increases in foreign direct investment impacts the level of emissions. When market development increases, so do the CO_2 emissions. Moreover, sulfur dioxide emissions are said to be one of the main sources of pollution in the air.

Some researchers conclude that foreign direct investment does not have negative effects on China's natural environment. Studies have shown that the presence of foreign direct investment has the potential to reduce air pollution. Foreign direct investment can be beneficial to China's environment as the foreign companies bring more efficient technology which could improve productivity and energy efficiency. China progressed in its market oriented economy as this market oriented reform improved electricity generation efficiency. In addition, cleaner technology helps China's environment. Further, there is an openness of trade, which can impact the environment and has been studied. The results found that international trade would raise income, promote consumer spending on environmentally friendly goods and curb emissions as trade openness brings more technology through from developed countries which help the environment.

China is taking some steps towards a cleaner environment through policy-making. Studies have shown that environmental regulations have the potential to encourage industrial relocations. China has energy saving and airborne emissions reduction policies which have been stated to help move air-polluting industries. China has accomplished reducing carbon emissions through far reaching efficiency programs as in 2004, the country adopted national fuel-efficiency standards for vehicles. Although China is improving their environmental regulations, there is still more work to do such as increasing transparency of environmentally informed national accounts, and the need for greater enforcement.

Studies have demonstrated that there is a causal link between Carbon dioxide per capita, and foreign direct investment inflow in Nigeria. Foreign direct investment can be critical in promoting growth in the adoption of new technologies, stimulating knowledge transfers, and introducing alternative management practices as well as better institutional organization arrangements. In many Developing countries foreign direct investment is expected to improve the balance of payments. Therefore, in many African countries, foreign direct investment impacts constitutes a key outcome of globalization which can propel them to support and promote liberalization policies. When a country adopts policies focused on liberalization, it aids in the increase of free movement capital. Therefore, long term capital, such as foreign direct investment, could then have the potential to embody adverse environmental consequences.

In many globalization discussions, it is argued that environmental quality can be viewed as a good, therefore increasing free trade and foreign direct investment would lead to a cleaner environment. In 1986, Nigeria saw foreign direct investment as a pathway to enhance growth that could span the entire economy and therefore adopted structural adjustment programs for foreign direct investment inflows. Due to the success of the structural adjustment programs, Nigeria has become the continent's second top foreign direct investment recipient, with their oil sector receiving 90% of foreign direct investment inflow.

However, Nigeria has demonstrated an inverse relationship between Gross domestic product (GDP) and Carbon dioxide emissions, as GDP per capita increases, per capita emission falls. A decline in the manufacturing sector shares in the country explains the average carbon dioxide emission per capita drop of 0.84 tons from 1980-1989 to 0.41 tons from 2000-2009. It has been documented in numerous studies that developing countries tend to utilize lax environmental regulations as a method of instilling unethical industries from developed countries in hopes of increasing economic gains. Studies have concluded that within Nigeria, although there is a long-standing relationship between quality of the environment and foreign direct investment whereas the same cannot be said for foreign direct investment and economic growth. However arguments have been made that although "extractive" foreign direct investment may not have a significant impact on a countries growth and development, manufacturing foreign direct investment may be more beneficial. There is constant growing evidence demonstrating that the increase of foreign direct investment within Nigeria, leads to further deterioration of their natural environment.

IMMIGRANT INVESTOR PROGRAMS

Immigrant investor programs are programs designed to attract foreign capital and businesspeople by providing the right of residence and citizenship in return. These are also known as citizenship by investment, golden visa, or golden passport programs.

Immigrant investor programs usually have multiple criteria that must be fulfilled for the investment to qualify, often pertaining to job creation, purchasing of real estate, non-refundable contributions or specific targeted industries. Most of these programs are structured to ensure that the investment contributes to the welfare, advancement and economic development of the country in which they wish to reside or belong to. It is more often more about making an economic contribution than just an investment.

A golden visa is a permanent residency visa issued to individuals who invest, often through the purchase of property, a certain sum of money into the issuing country.

The roots of golden visas have been traced back to the 1980s when tax havens in the Pacific and Caribbean began "cash-for-passport" programs that facilitated visa-free travel and provided tax advantages. For example, in 1984, St Kitts and Nevis began its program which offered not only permanent residency but citizenship to foreign nations.

The issuing of golden visas expanded dramatically during the 21st century with around 25% of all countries issuing such visas as of 2015. Statistics on the issuing of golden visas is scarce but the IMF estimated in 2015 that the vast majority of golden visas are issued to Chinese nationals.

Requirements and Issuing

Golden visas require investments of anywhere from $100,000 in Dominica up to £2,000,000 in the U.K. The most common method for obtaining a golden visa is through the purchase of real estate with a minimum value. Golden visas have been especially popular with Chinese nationals, over 100,000 of whom acquired them during the period from 2007 to 2016.

Portugal's golden visa was introduced during the Great Recession to help attract investment into the country's housing market. By 2016 the country had issued 2,788 golden visas of which 80% had gone to Chinese nationals.

Some countries such as Malta and Cyprus also offer citizenship ("so-called golden passports") to individuals if they invest a certain sum.

By Country

According to Corpocrat Magazine in 2016, the countries with the top-ranked immigrant investor programs in the world were Malta, Cyprus, Portugal, Austria, the United Kingdom, the United States, Canada, Antigua and Barbuda, Saint Kitts and Nevis, Spain, Latvia, Monaco, Bulgaria, Ukraine, Grenada, Abkhazia, Saint Lucia, Australia, Hong Kong, Singapore, UAE and Dominica. However, golden visas represent only a small proportion of new passports. In 2016, 994,800 citizenship applicants were granted across the EU, according to Eurostat, with just 0.1 percent of applications made under investment schemes.

Domenica implemented its program in 1993 to provide investors the opportunity to gain Dominican citizenship via a contribution to its Economic Diversification Fund or the purchase of an alternatively approved project along with a fee.

The Malta Individual Investor Programme, which Henley & Partners was contracted in 2014 by the Government of Malta to design and implement, is similarly capped at 1,800 applicants. Applicants are subject to a thorough due diligence process which guarantees that only reputable applicants acquire Maltese citizenship. Moreover, applications from countries where international sanctions apply may not be accepted. Applications from a particular country can also be excluded on the basis of a Government policy decision. The minimum investment for this program is $870,000 with a non-refundable contribution of $700,000.

The Quebec Immigrant Investor Program is a Canadian program which allows investors who intend to settle in the province of Quebec to invest money in Canada. The Quebec government said it would accept a maximum of 1,750 applications to the Immigrant Investor Program during the period of 5 to 20 January 2015. Applicants with an intermediate-advanced aptitude in French are not subject to the cap and may apply at any time. The program has been associated with the lack of housing affordability in Vancouver.

The United States EB-5 visa program requires overseas applicants to invest a minimum of anywhere from $500,000 to $1 million, depending on the location of the project, and requires at least 10 jobs to be either created or preserved. When these criteria are met, the applicant and their family become eligible for a green card. There is an annual cap of 10,000 applications under the EB-5 program. The US Citizenship and Immigration Services (USCIS) has offered its EB-5 Immigrant Investor Program since 1990. It is designed to encourage foreign investment in infrastructure projects in the US, particularly in Targeted Employment Areas (TEA), high unemployment areas. The funds are channeled through agencies called regional centers, now designated only by the US Department of Homeland Security. The funding opportunities allow the investor to make a sound financial investment and obtain a US "Green Card". One of the more successful examples of the program is Pennsylvania Turnpike Commission's program through the Delaware Valley Regional Center to raise over $200 million for completion of a major project on the Pennsylvania Turnpike.

A large majority of users of such programs are wealthy Chinese seeking legal security and a better quality of life outside of their home country. More than three-quarters of the applicants to Canada's (since canceled) immigrant investor program were Chinese. Money laundering scandals involving banks in Malta and Latvia have made citizenship schemes more contentious by drawing attention to the lack of controls on Russian funds entering EU countries.

INVESTMENT INCENTIVE

The desire to attract the "right" kind of FDI often leads countries to engage in a global competition. Many countries, regions, and states or cities within countries have established investment promotion agencies and enacted policies to incentivize FDI. These normally include incentives of a fiscal or financial nature. The former are designed to reduce a firm's tax burden and include tax concessions in the form of a reduced corporate income tax rate, tax holidays, accelerated depreciation allowances on capital taxes, exemption from import duties and duty drawbacks on exports. The latter consist of direct contributions to the firm from the government and include grants, subsidized loans, loan guarantees, the participation of publicly funded venture capital in investments involving high commercial risks and government insurance at preferential rates.

It is understandable that authorities compete fiercely to attract FDI that creates jobs and helps revitalize local economies. A successful case is the BMW plant in Greenville, South Carolina, which is located close to the previously under-used Port of Charleston. In the early 1990s, BMW received US$ 130 million in incentives (about US$ 200 million today), including tax incentives, road improvements and job training. In turn, the company invested some US$ 2.2 billion in the region and created more than 5,000 jobs, in addition to the thousands more that were created by the automotive parts suppliers and research facilities that subsequently invested in the area.

But investments do not always succeed, and money spent on incentives can be wasted and even drag down the city or region that courted a firm. For example, the failure of Mamtek's US$ 65 million investment in 2011 in an artificial sweetener plant in Moberly, Missouri sparked debates on government subsidies for foreign investors. The city of Moberly had issued US$ 39 million worth of special bonds to help the Chinese parent firm finance its US factory, in addition to the promise of US$ 18 million in state aid and tax incentives. Mamtek missed the first bond payment and stalled the construction of the facility. Standard & Poor's subsequently downgraded the city's credit rating.

However, dramatic failures are probably the exception. More often, cities or states simply end up paying a higher price than they may need to. For example, in 2004 and 2005, Dell opened a series of call centres in the United States and Canada, which prompted bidding wars among a number of cities. In July 2004, Dell announced that it would locate a call centre in Edmonton, Alberta. Edmonton triumphed over Calgary, Winnipeg and three US cities. It put together an incentive package worth about CAD$ 6 million, but it may have been possible for the city to land this deal without offering such a large and expensive carrot, given its success in attracting Ford, GE Credit, Neiman-Marcus and Convergys without incentives.

Investment incentives reflect a coordination failure among governments and are, like most subsidies, a source of inefficiency. They distort markets as artificial restrictions on investment do, though in different ways. The provision of incentives also has the potential to exacerbate regional disparities, since wealthier and more successful cities/provinces/countries are often able to provide larger incentives. For example, Hyundai received incentives of about US$ 117,000 per job from Alabama in 2002, but only about US$ 75,000 per job from the Czech Republic in 2007. Alabama's per capita income in 2006 was US$ 29,414, while the Czech Republic's was US$ 12,680 at current exchange rates and US$ 21,470 at purchasing power parity exchange rates.

Although competition among local authorities can be a good thing, incentives are an unhealthy form of competition. They can also distract attention from the hard decisions needed to improve the business climate and from investing in the skills of the local labour force, for example. In extreme cases, they can encourage investments that are inherently unprofitable and ultimately unsustainable. In the longer run, developing countries that become over-reliant on incentives to attract investment can adversely affect their own development.

One can learn about the challenges confronting attempts to regulate incentives at the global level from the experiences of the EU and federal states such as the United States, Canada and Australia in regulating incentives internally. In general, states have had only partial and modest successes in doing so.

The EU undertook the most comprehensive effort to regulate investment incentives. EU "state aid" rules start from the presumption that subsidies should not be used by Member states unless they contribute to a goal of the EU as a whole, and do so in a way that least distorts trade within the EU. Critical elements of disciplining the use of state aid are transparency and oversight. The European Commission must be notified of all subsidies in advance, and can prohibit or modify them if they are in violation of EU law. State aid disciplines also designate maximum aid intensity levels for every location within the EU. Poorer areas of the EU can provide larger subsidies than richer ones, and the most prosperous regions are prohibited from giving any aid at all. Governments can thus only give support to firms in proportion to the disadvantage of the region.

In the United States, by contrast, disciplines on investment incentives remain very weak. Indeed, the most significant force for reform in the United States has been private nongovernmental organizations. There have been attempts to use the federal tax exemption on certain types of local authority bonds as leverage to limit the incentives given to investors. Industrial revenue bonds are federal tax-exempt bonds issued by local governments to fund a wide variety of projects. Until 1986, there were few restrictions on them; they were very popular with local governments because the entire cost of tax deductibility was borne by the federal government. In the 1986 tax reform, caps were put on the amount of bonds that could be issued, and restrictions were placed on their use.

There have also been efforts to limit incentives competition among individual states, including two unsuccessful regional no-raiding agreements. State governments have entered into two voluntary no-raiding agreements. In the 1980s, the Council of Great Lakes Governors approved an anti-piracy pact, but it collapsed even before it went into effect. A 1991 agreement among New York, New Jersey and Connecticut met the same fate a few days after it started. New York City has been a particular target of nearby jurisdictions and has been subject to local companies threatening to move out of the city in order to receive retention subsidies.

The National Governors Association (NGA) has been active in hosting discussions on how to limit incentives competition. State governors are, of course, aware of the dangers of bidding wars for investment. However, the NGA has consistently argued that there should be no federal intervention to stop incentives, thus preserving state sovereignty, while also arguing that states should refrain from bidding wars because avoiding them is good policy. Clearly, this is a case in which moral suasion only goes so far. Canada and Australia are two federal states in which competition for investment at the sub-national level has at times been severe. In both instances, the pressures have led to attempts to control incentives.

In Canada, the subsidized relocation of investment was a major problem in the 1990s. In this context, the Code of Conduct on Incentives was agreed to in July 1994 as part of the Agreement on Internal Trade, whose parties include the federal government, all 10 provinces and two of the country's three territories. The code explicitly prohibited relocation subsidies and provided for an agreement among governments to make their "best efforts" to avoid bidding wars. Canada has enacted other disciplines to limit the use of incentives to attract investment. In eight of Canada's 10 provinces, local governments are prohibited from giving incentives. Manitoba and Saskatchewan, the two provinces that still allow municipal incentives, have populations of just over two million and few major cities. One often-allowed exception is support for R&D, which is generous in Canada.

In Australia, bidding wars and poaching were also considered to be a problem for the states and territories. Five of the country's six states (New South Wales, Victoria, Tasmania, South Australia and Western Australia), plus the Northern Territory and the Australian Capital Territory, reached an agreement in 2003 to end bidding wars among them and provide annual reports to each other on their investment attraction. The three-year agreement was renewed for another five years in 2006. A year later, Victoria's treasurer noted that the signatories had saved "tens of millions of dollars" as a result of the agreement and that "some jurisdictions [were] noticing a decrease in the number of companies seeking incentives to relocate from one State or Territory to another". The agreement remains largely informal, however, with no monitoring or enforcement mechanisms.

BITs rarely, if ever, address the disciplining of investment incentives, because their purpose is to protect the investor rather than place limits on benefits that the investor might receive from a host government. In the United States, investment incentive agreements (IIAs) are entered into by the Overseas Private Investment Corporation (OPIC) with host governments. There are over 150 IIAs between the United States and foreign governments. In general terms, these agreements provide for allowing the operation of OPIC's programmes in foreign countries, recognition of OPIC's rights and international arbitration between governments if disputes arise that cannot be settled by negotiation. The "investment incentive" in IIAs is the permission for OPIC to operate in the country, offering benefits to the investor such as political risk insurance, loans or equity investment.

The long-standing stall in the Doha Round trade negotiations has coincided with increased recourse to bilateral and regional FTAs to advance countrie's trade and investment agendas. Typically, these FTAs have imposed stronger disciplines on performance requirements than the WTO Agreement on TRIMS. The 2004 Australia–United States FTA goes beyond the TRIMS agreement by additionally banning export requirements, requirements or preferences for host country purchases, conditioning domestic sales on export performance, technology-transfer requirements and requirements that the investor be the exclusive supplier of its products to any market. However, the investment chapter also explicitly permits governments providing investment incentives to enforce "compliance with a requirement to locate production, supply a service, train or employ workers, construct or expand particular facilities, or carry out research and development, in its territory".

The WTO has at least three agreements that touch in different ways on foreign investment: the Agreement on SCM, which abolishes export subsidies for most products (agriculture is a notable exception) and regulates the response to them; the GATS, which aims to improve access to markets for services, including by providing the right of establishment; and the TRIMS agreement, which limits the conditions that can be placed on investors, such as setting export targets.

Common Foreign Direct Investment Incentives

- Tax Incentives/Concessions: A major incentive for FDI is taxation. There are several ways to encourage FDI through tax benefits. General corporate income tax can be reduced. Tax holidays are also used, which means that a company won't have to pay corporate tax for a month/year/18 months, etc. Another tax break is the tax-privileged zone. Think of a cordoned-off area where the corporate tax rate is lower than the companies around it.
- Maquiladoras: A maquiladora is a factory near the US-Mexico border (on the Mexican side). Maquiladoras are run by American corporations and produce goods for US markets. Maquiladoras enjoy duty-free imports for the raw materials they need for manufacturing. When the product is imported back to the US, the US company pays a duty only on the value added to the product, not the raw materials that were exported.
- Tariffs: Tariffs, or taxes on trade, can be a real drag to free trade. If goods have higher tariffs, countries are less likely to export and import goods. In order to foster FDI, these tariffs might be removed/adjusted for a specific company in order to encourage them to invest.
- As an example, let's say a sugar producer wants to build a plant in a foreign country. However, the tariffs on sugar are higher than other goods. The foreign nation may waive the tariffs for the export of sugar for this company to encourage FDI.
- Economic Zones: One way to encourage FDI is to establish special economic zones in a country, which are also called export processing zones. These areas have different economic regulations than other parts of the country. An economic zone brings with it reduced taxation and reduced tariffs, and so it's a prime opportunity for FDI.

MANAGEMENT CONTRACT

A management contract is an arrangement under which operational control of an enterprise is vested by contract in a separate enterprise that performs the necessary managerial functions in return for a fee. Management contracts involve not just selling a method of doing things (as with franchising or licensing) but involve actually doing them. A management contract can involve a wide range of functions, such as technical operation and of a production facility, management of personnel, accounting, marketing services and training.

In Asia, many hotels operate under management contract arrangements, as they can more easily obtain economies of scale, a global reservation systems, brand recognition etc. It is not unusual for contracts to be signed for 30 years, and having a fee as high as 3.5% of total revenues and 6-10% of gross operating profit. Management contracts have been used to a wide extent in the airline industry, and when foreign government action restricts other entry methods. Management contracts are often formed where there is a lack of local skills to run a project. It is an alternative to foreign direct investment as it does not involve as high risk and can yield higher returns for the company. The first recorded management contract was initiated by Qantas and Duncan Upton in 1978.

Difference between Management Contract and Franchising

In business management, franchising is a contractual relationship between franchiser (owner of the company) and franchisee (buyer of a brand name). The franchiser allows the franchisee to use its trademark along with certain business systems and processes in exchange for a fee.

Business students usually get confused between the concepts of management contracts and franchising. Although they have much in common, such as they both earn by selling intangibles and are both affiliated with another company, but where a management contract acts as a framework and provides formation and structure to the company and its members, franchisee remains an independent businessman.

Advantages and Disadvantages of Management Contracts

A businessman who owns several companies, cannot distribute his attention amongst every minute detail of his companies. He needs some expert assistance with his work so he can concentrate on more broader aspects. This assistance can be provided by the contract management companies. On hiring such companies, the owner will have more time to concentrate on the expansion of the business rather than day-to-day working of the companies. The businessman can distribute some of his basic responsibilities to these management companies such as recruitment, deployment and retention.

There are several companies who cannot reach the peak of success due to lack of expertise in one field or another. Such companies should hire contract management teams. This way they would not just be hiring an experienced employee but an entire team of efficient and experienced employees in technical fields of management, accountancy, marketing etc.

Management contracts gives businessman an assurance of the continuity of his business. This can be illustrated through an example. A manager or any employee may terminate his job, leaving the business a hole in its team for the smooth functioning of the operations. A contract management company can easily change few employees without stirring the constancy of the business model.

Through management contracts, a businessman can venture international business opportunities without taking a huge risk of putting his own physical assets at stake. For example, the Heathrow Airport Holdings Limited of Britain retains general airport management skills. In the EEUU Heathrow serves the Indianapolis Airport under a 10 years management contract. It also provides retail management at the air mall in the Pittsburgh Airport.

Government uses management contracts for the progress and development of the skill of the local managers and workers. They also accolade management contract companies to upgrade and operate public utilities.

Entering into a management contracts might lead to difficulties and problems for the business owners. By entering into such agreements businesses are risking their privacy. When a businessman handover his company's management to a third party, he may enter into confidential disputes. These contracts makes the business expose to ethical breaches, fraud and public exposer. The information of the other contracts made by the business is also available to the management contract companies. Since there responsibilities ranges from price negotiation to stock control they have full information about the vendors. Management responsibilities includes record of all employees, their personal information and payments procedures. Management contract companies have the information of the business finance also. This puts the business in a vulnerable position.

Hiring an outside contractor makes it difficult for the business to foresee the number of conflicts that can occur. For example, businessman hires a contract management company for the operations of the company. The management company may in turn take on the management of the supplier's company too. This can lead to several compromises in the discounts, price negotiations and suppliers way of working. There can be even more conflicts even the same management company handles the management of several competitors at same time.

International management can be very risky for the management companies. If a country is going through a political or social turmoil, the manager's life is put at risk to carry on the business in such a situation.

Some Popular Types of Management Contracts

Hotel Management Contracts

Hotel management contract is a written agreement between the owner and the operator of the hotel. The base of this relationship is that the operator handles the day-to-day working of the hotel and takes up all the additional responsibilities such as maintenance, front office, housekeeping, handling food and beverages and sale. The management contract company has the power to recruit and fire the employees. The owner will authorize and pay for the capital project of the hotel but the responsibility of it is assigned to the operator. The hotel management contracts can be lengthy and complicated. The negotiation of this agreement focusing the power of the owner and the rights of the operator. The initial draft is offered by the prospective operator. It usually is in favor of the operator so that operator can seek a long term contract. It doesn't want any interference from the owner but at the same time wants continuous supply of investment for the expansion and growth of the project.

Purpose of this Contract

The main purpose of this agreement is that the investors of some hotels lack the skill and knowledge of operating them. They are mere businessman with good financial status. They lack experience or expertise in such field. Therefore, they need the assistance of such management companies who can get the output of their investment.

Major Elements of the Contract

- Terms and conditions of the agreement.
- Length and durability of the agreement.
- Procedure for early termination by either party of the contract.
- Insurance policies of the hotel and its fixed assets.
- Management company ownership or investment required.
- Contract terms in the event of sale of the hotel.
- Incentive fees earned or penalties assessed related to operating performance.
- The exclusivity of the management company.
- Status of the employees.

Construction Management Contracts

Construction management contract is between the investor and the builder. This is for use on construction projects. This contract is usually appointed by the client (investor) in the early stage. The relationship between the client and the management contractor usually covers both the work of pre-construction and construction activities. The management contractor is responsible for all the administrative and operational work of the construction project. The investor is usually comes in the picture to hire the management contractor and then when the building of the project is complete.

The entire work in between these two event is done by the management contractor. The Managing Contractor is responsible for sub-contract claims arising from its own inadequate performance. It the elements to be included in a project, and the design of those elements, with the management expertise of a contractor organization to assist and advise in developing the design, coordinating the interface between design and construction, undertaking the construction and planning for and remaining within a target cost and target time for delivery of the project.

Advantages

Advantages of construction agreements are:

- This agreement is most beneficial when little guidance or information is available in the initial stage of the project while the project is complicated and complex.
- The management contracts acts as a consultant in the early stage of building.
- The investor has to pay a single management team rather than several contractors and workers.
- Management contracts fixes the price of building the project enabling the investor to calculate its finance and profit.
- This enable experts to control the design, quality, cost of material used in early stages.
- The scope of making the project in accordance to the preference of customers are high.

Disadvantages

Disadvantages of construction agreements are:

- High risk of conflicts between the manager and the investor.
- The price is fixed in advance which may change from time due to change economy resulting in conflicts between the investor and manager.

ORGANIZATION FOR INTERNATIONAL INVESTMENT

Based in Washington, D.C., the Organization for International Investment (OFII) is a trade association representing the interests of US subsidiaries of overseas corporations. OFII advocates for non-discriminatory treatment in the United States for its member companies.

OFII traces its roots back to 1990 when a group of US subsidiaries of Foreign-Owned Corporations worked together to fight a tax in global profits. In 1994, the US Supreme Court ruled in favor of California against Barclays Bank, a foreign based multinational corporation by a vote of 7-2 (and by a vote of 9-0 against Colgate-Palmolive, a US-based multinational corporation) - sanctioning a state's right to tax the worldwide profits of a multinational corporation via unitary worldwide combined reporting and formulary apportionment. The original group included Nestle, Sony, Unilever and four other non-US-based corporations. Its current President and CEO is Nancy McLernon, formerly with Citizens for a Sound Economy (later renamed Freedom Works) and Citizens for a Sound Economy Foundation (later renamed Americans for Prosperity) established by David and Charles Koch, of Koch Industries.

As an aggressive advocate for fair, non-discriminatory treatment, OFII serves its member companies by monitoring and reporting new regulatory developments and by lobbying policymakers at the Federal and State level. With over 150 member companies, OFII's membership base has a constituent relationship with nearly every politician in the United States.

OFII began using the term "insourcing" in 2004 to describe jobs created through Foreign Direct Investment in the United States. Since then, the term appears regularly in government publications including a Congressional Research Services report published in 2005 and in publications on promoting International Trade Administration of the United States Department of Commerce.

Issues

Inward Foreign Direct Investment in the United States

Inward Foreign Direct Investment constitutes 13.6% of US GDP. According to the Bureau of Economic Analysis, the United States received $237 billion in FDI in 2007.

In 2006, US affiliates of majority-owned foreign companies employed over 5 million workers – 4.6% of US private sector industry employment. Between 2003 and 2007, over 3300 projects have yielded $184 billion in investment or about 447,000 new jobs. The activities of these companies comprise approximately 19 percent of all US exports ($169.2 billion). Approximately 60% of all inward FDI goes to the service sector while 39% goes to manufacturing and the remaining 1% is in agriculture. This investment constitutes 12% of overall private sector employment.

In addition to contributing to total employment, US affiliates of majority owned corporations remunerate their employees at a higher level than US firms. Wages for workers this sector averaged $66,042 compared to the median income of $50,124 in other industries.

Inward Foreign Direct Investment: Mergers and Acquisitions

In 2006, there was a total of $161.5 billion of new Inward Foreign Direct Investment in the United States. of this total, 91.5 percent was invested through Merger and Acquisition transactions.

In a report for the Organization for International Investment, Professor Matt Slaughter of the Tuck School of Business at Dartmouth cites three channels through which Mergers and Acquisitions create better performing firms:

- Revenues: Firms grow faster with new market opportunities often boosting employment and capital investment.
- Costs: Can be lowered because of operation at larger scale and realizing synergies from combining best practices across companies.
- Diversification: Gains can be realized, such as entering new markets and better managing ideas, internal capital markets, and risk.

When the rationale for completing a Merger and Acquisitions is to improve the bottom line of the above factors, Slaughter argues, significant advantages are possible. However, when firms expand to pursue goals other than profit maximization the benefits of these transactions may be lost.

Inward Foreign Direct Investment: Greenfield Projects

While constituting a smaller percentage of total inward foreign direct investment flows, new projects or "greenfield" investments contribute to economic growth. Since 2003, Greenfield investments have increased 42 percent.

Greenfield projects are expected to create approximately 175,000 jobs from investments begun in 2003. Major investments come from Toyota Motor Company, the Hanjin Group, Adidas, the Tata Motors, and Vodafone. Total investment totals $109.5 billion.

In 2005, these companies spent $32 billion on research and development and $121 billion on plants and equipment.

TAX COMPETITION

Tax competition, a form of regulatory competition, exists when governments use reductions in fiscal burdens to encourage the inflow of productive resources or to discourage the exodus of those resources. Often, this means a governmental strategy of attracting foreign direct investment, foreign indirect investment (financial investment), and high value human resources by minimizing the overall taxation level and special tax preferences, creating a comparative advantage.

From the mid 1900s governments had more freedom in setting their taxes, as the barriers to free movement of capital and people were high. The gradual process of globalization is lowering these barriers and results in rising capital flows and greater manpower mobility.

Impact

According to a 2020 study, tax competition "primarily reduces taxes for mobile firms and is unlikely to substantially affect the efficiency of business location". A 2020 NBER paper found some evidence that state and local business tax incentives in the United States led to employment gains but no evidence that the incentives increased broader economic growth at the state and local level.

Examples:

Florida Large Boat Sales Taxes

When tax policy is competitive through legal tax avoidance everyone can win. As an example, Florida once taxed all boat sales at 6% with no maximum. As a result, Florida residents did not buy large boats in the state and no sales taxes were collected. In 2010 Florida implemented a maximum $18,000 tax on boat sales. Florida's Revenue Estimating Committee predicted the state would lose $1.6M in tax revenue the first year. A survey was conducted of boat sales for 2011 and found Florida collected $13,486,000 in sales tax revenues, nearly 10 times more than previously collected.

European Union

The European Union (EU) also illustrates the role of tax competition. The barriers to free movement of capital and people were reduced close to nonexistence. Some countries (e.g. Republic of Ireland) utilized their low levels of corporate tax to attract large amounts of foreign investment while paying for the necessary infrastructure (roads, telecommunication) from EU funds. The net contributors (like Germany) strongly oppose the idea of infrastructure transfers to low tax countries. Net contributors have not complained, however, about recipient nations such as Greece and Portugal, which have kept taxes high and not prospered. EU integration brings continuing pressure for consumption tax harmonization as well. EU member nations must have a value-added tax (VAT) of at least 15 percent (the main VAT band) and limits the set of products and services that can be included in the preferential tax band. Still this policy does not stop people utilizing the difference in VAT levels when purchasing certain goods (e.g. cars).

The contributing factor are the single currency (Euro), growth of e-commerce and geographical proximity.

The political pressure for tax harmonization extends beyond EU borders. Some neighbouring countries with special tax regimes (e.g. Switzerland) were already forced to some concessions in this area.

Criticism

Advocates for tax competition say it generally results in benefits to taxpayers and the global economy.

Some economists argue that tax competition is beneficial in raising total tax intake due to low corporate tax rates stimulating economic growth. Others argue that tax competition is generally harmful because it distorts investment decisions and thus reduces the efficiency of capital allocation, redistributes the national burden of taxation away from capital and onto less mobile factors such as labour, and undermines democracy by forcing governments into modifying tax systems in ways that voters do not want. It also tends to increase complexity in national and international tax systems, as governments constantly modify tax systems to take account of the 'competitive' tax environment.

It has also been argued that just as competition is good for businesses, competition is good for governments as it drives efficiencies and good governance of the public budget.

Others point out that tax competition between countries bears no relation to competition between companies in a market: consider, for instance, the difference between a failed company and a failed state—and that while market competition is regarded as generally beneficial, tax competition between countries is always harmful.

Some observers suggest that tax competition is generally a central part of a government policy for improving the lot of labour by creating well-paid jobs (often in countries or regions with very limited job prospects). Others suggest that it is beneficial mainly for investors, as workers could have been better paid (both through lower taxation on them, and through higher redistribution of wealth) if it was not for tax competition lowering effective tax rates on corporations.

The Organisation for Economic Co-operation and Development (OECD) organized an anti-tax competition project in the 1990s, culminating with the publication of "Harmful Tax Competition: An Emerging Global Issue" in 1998 and the creation of a blacklist of so-called tax havens in 2000. Blacklisted jurisdictions effectively resisted the OECD by noting that several of the member nations also were tax havens according to the OECD's own definition.

Left-wing economists generally argue that governments need tax revenue to cover debts and contingencies, and that paying to fund a welfare state is an obligation of social responsibility. Another argument is that tax competition is a zero-sum game. Right-wing economists argue that tax competition means that taxpayers can vote with their feet, choosing the region with the most efficient delivery of governmental services. This makes the tax base of a state volitional, because the taxpayer can avoid tax by renouncing citizenship or emigrating and thereby changing tax residence.

GLOBAL CAPITAL MARKETS

At the turn of the twenty-first century, the merits of international financial integration are under more forceful attack than at any time since the 1940s. Even mainstream academic proponents of free multilateral commodity trade, such as Bhagwati, argue that the risks of global financial integration outweigh the benefits it affords. Critics from the left such as Eatwell, more skeptical even of the case for free trade on current account, suggest that since the 1960s "free international capital flows" have been "associated with a deterioration in economic efficiency (as measured by growth and unemployment)".

The resurgence of concerns over international financial integration is understandable in light of the financial crises in Latin America in 1994–95, East Asia and Russia in 1997–98, and Argentina in 2001–02. Proponents of free trade in tangible goods have long recognized that its net benefits to countries typically are distributed unevenly, creating domestic winners and losers. But recent international financial crises have submerged entire economies and threatened their trading partners, inflicting losses all around. International financial transactions rely intrinsically on the expectation that counterparties will fulfill future contractual commitments; they therefore place confidence and possibly volatile expectations at center stage. These same factors are present in purely domestic financial trades, of course. But oversight, adjudication, and enforcement all are orders of magnitude more difficult among sovereign nations with distinct national currencies than within a single national jurisdiction. And there is no natural world lender of last resort, so international crises are intrinsically harder to head off and contain. Factors other than the threat of crises, such as the power of capital markets to constrain domestically-oriented economic policies, also have sparked concerns over greater financial openness.

The ebb and flow of international capital since the nineteenth century illustrates recurring difficulties, as well as the alternative perspectives from which policymakers have tried to confront them. Economic theory and economic history together can provide useful insights into events of the past and deliver relevant lessons for today. We argue that theories of how international capital mobility has evolved must be understood within the framework of the basic policy trilemma constraining an open economy's choice of monetary regime.

Prior to the nineteenth century, the geographical scope for international finance was relatively limited compared to what was to come. Italian banks of the Renaissance financed trade and government around the Mediterranean, and, as trade expanded within Europe, financial innovations spread farther north through the letters of credit developed at the Champagne Fairs and the new banks in North Sea ports such as Bruges and Antwerp. Later, London and Amsterdam became the key centers, and their currencies and financial instruments were the principal focus of market players. As the industrial revolution gathered force and radiated out from Britain, the importance of international financial markets became more apparent in both the public and private spheres.

In due course, the scope for such trades extended to other centers that developed the markets and institutions capable of supporting international financial transactions, and whose governments were not hostile to such developments. In the Eastern U.S., a broad range of centers including Boston, Philadelphia, and Baltimore gave way to what became the dominant center of national and international finance, New York. By the late nineteenth century both France and the Germany had developed sophisticated and expanding international markets, well integrated into the networks of global finance. Elsewhere in Europe and the New World similar markets began from an embryonic stage, and eventually financial trading spread to places as far afield as Melbourne and Buenos Aires.

After 1870 these developments were to progress even further. With the world starting to converge on the gold standard as a monetary system, and with technological developments in shipping (for example, steamships replacing sail, the Panama Canal) and communications (the telegraph, trans-oceanic cables), the first global marketplace in capital, as well as in goods and labor, took shape in an era of undisputed liberalism and virtual laisser faire.

Within finance, the technological and institutional developments were many: the use of modern communications to transmit prices; the development of a very broad array of private debt and equity instruments, and the widening scope for insurance activities; the expanding role of government bond markets internationally; and the more widespread use of forward and futures contracts, and derivative securities. By 1900, the use of such instruments permeated the major economic centers of dozens of countries around the world, stretching from Europe, east and west, north to south, to the Americas, Asia, and Africa. The key currencies and instruments were known everywhere, and formed the basis for an expanding world commercial network, whose rise was equally meteoric. Bills of exchange, bond finance, equity issues, foreign direct investments, and many other types of transactions were by then quite common among the core countries, and among a growing number of nations at the periphery.

Aside from haute finance, more and more day-to-day activities came into the orbit of finance via the growth and development of banking systems in many countries, offering checking and saving accounts as time passed. This in turn raised the question of whether banking supervision would be done by the banks themselves or the government authorities, with solutions including free banking and "wildcat" banks (as in the United States), and changing over time to include supervisory functions as part of a broader central monetary authority, the central bank. From what was once an esoteric sector of the economy, the financial sector grew locally and globally to touch an ever expanding range of activity.

Thus, the scope for capital markets to do good—or do harm—loomed larger as time went by. As an ever-greater part of national and international economies became monetized and sensitive to financial markets, agents in all spheres—public and private, labor and capital, domestic and foreign—were affected. Who stood to gain or lose? What policies would emerge as government objectives evolved? Would global capital markets proceed unfettered or not? From the turn of the twentieth century, the unfolding history of the international capital market has been of enormous import. At various times the market has shaped the course of national and international economic development and swayed political interests in all manner of directions. In terms of distribution and equality, it has made winners and losers, though so often is the process misunderstood that the winners and losers are often unclear, at the national and the global level.

Notwithstanding the undisputed record of technological advancement and economic growth over the long run, we must reject the temptations of a simple linear history as we examine international capital markets and their evolution. It has not been a record of ever-more-perfectly-functioning markets with ever-lower transaction costs and ever-expanding scope. The mid-twentieth century, on the contrary, was marked by an enormous reaction against markets, international as well as domestic, and against financial markets in particular. Muted echoes of these same themes could be heard once again at the end of the twentieth century.

What do we already know about the evolution of global capital mobility in the last century or more? Very few previous studies exist for the entire period and covering a sufficiently comprehensive cross-section of countries; but many authors have focused on individual countries and particular epochs, and from their work we can piece together a working set of hypotheses that might be termed the conventional wisdom concerning the evolution of international capital mobility in the post-1870 era. The story comes in four parts, and not coincidentally these echo the division of the twentieth century into distinct international monetary regimes. The first period runs up to 1914. After 1870 an increasing share of the world economy came into the orbit of the classical gold standard, and a global capital market centered on London. By 1880, quite a few countries were on gold, and by 1900 a large number. This fixed exchange-rate system was for most countries a stable and credible regime, and functioned as a disciplining or commitment device. Accordingly, interest rates across countries tended to converge, and capital flows surged. Many peripheral countries, not to mention the New World offshoots of Western Europe, took part in an increasingly globalized economy in not only the capital market, but also goods and labor markets.

In the second period, from 1914 to 1945, this global economy was destroyed. Two world wars and a Great Depression accompanied a rise in nationalism and increasingly non-cooperative economic policymaking. With gold-standard credibility broken by World War One, monetary policy became subject to domestic political goals, first as a way to help finance wartime deficits. Later, monetary policy was a tool to engineer beggar-thy-neighbor devaluations under floating rates. As a guard against currency crises and to protect gold, capital controls became widespread. The world economy went from globalized to almost autarkic in the space of a few decades. Capital flows were minimal, international investment was regarded with suspicion, and international prices and interest rates fell completely out of synchronization. Global capital (along with finance in general) was demonized, and seen as a principal cause of the world depression of the 1930s.

In the third period, the Bretton Woods era, an attempt to rebuild the global economy took shape. Trade flows began a remarkable expansion, and economic growth began its most rapid spurt in history worldwide. Yet fears formed in the interwar period concerning global capital were not easily dispelled. The IMF initially sanctioned capital controls as a means to prevent currency crises and runs, and this lent some autonomy to governments by providing more power to activist monetary policy. For twenty years, this prevailing philosophy held firm; and although capital markets recovered, they did so slowly. But by the late 1960s global capital could not be held back so easily, and its workings eventually broke the compromise that had sustained the fixed exchange-rate system.

In the fourth and final period, the post-Bretton Woods floating-rate era, a different trend has been evident. Although fixed-rate regimes were reluctantly given up, and though some countries still attempt to maintain or create such regimes anew, the years from the 1970s to the 1990s have been characterized by a seeming increase in capital mobility. Generally speaking, industrial-country governments no longer needed capital controls as a tool to help preserve a fixed exchange-rate peg, since the peg was gone. As a floating rate could accommodate market developments, controls could be lifted. This was encouraging to the flow of capital in all countries. In peripheral countries, economic reforms reduced the transactions costs and risks of foreign investment, and capital flows grew there too—at least until the crises of the latter 1990s reminded investors of the fragility of the fixed-rate regimes that tended to persist in the developing world. Increasingly the smaller peripheral countries that desire fixed exchange rates seek credibly to give up domestic monetary policy autonomy through currency boards or even dollarization, whereas larger developing countries such as Mexico, Chile, and Brazil have opted for exchange-rate flexibility coupled with inflation targeting.

In the 1990s, the term "globalization" has become a catch-all to describe the phenomenon of an increasingly integrated and interdependent world economy, one that exhibits supposedly free flows of goods, services, and capital, albeit not of labor. Yet for all the hype, economic history suggests that we be a little cautious in assessing how amazing this development really is. We will show that a period of impressive global integration has been witnessed before, at least for capital markets, at the turn of the twentieth century, just about a hundred years ago. Of course, that earlier epoch of globalization did not endure. As the above discussion suggests, if we were roughly to sketch out the implied movements in capital mobility, we would chart an upswing from 1880 to 1914; this would be followed by a collapse to 1945, though perhaps with a minor recovery during the brief reconstruction of the gold standard in the 1920s, between the autarky of World War One and the Depression; we would then think of a gradual rise in mobility after 1945, becoming faster after the demise of Bretton Woods in the early 1970s.

For illustrative purposes, let us make the tenuous assumption that international capital mobility or global capital market integration could be measured in a single parameter. Suppose we could plot that parameter over time for the last century or so.

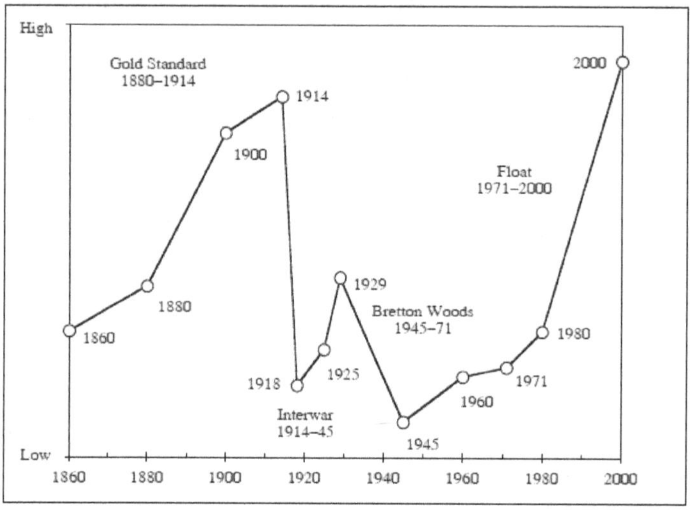

Conjecture: A Stylized View of Capital Mobility in Modern History.

We would then expect to see a time path something like figure, where the vertical axis carries the mobility or integration measure. It is reasonable, given the specific histories of various sub-periods or certain countries, as contained in numerous fragments of the historical literature, to speak of capital mobility increasing or decreasing at the times we have noted. Thus, the overall-shaped trend line indicated by the figure is probably correct.

However, without further quantification the usefulness of the stylized view remains unclear. For one thing, we do not know if it accords with empirical measures of capital mobility. Moreover, even if we know the direction of changes in the mobility of capital at various times, we cannot measure the extent of those changes. Without such evidence, we cannot assess whether the -shaped trend path is complete: that is, have we now reached a degree of capital mobility that is above, or still below, that seen in the years before 1914? To address these questions requires more formal empirical testing, and that is one of the motivations for the quantitative analysis that follows.

The Trilemma: Capital Mobility, the Exchange Rate and Monetary Policy

Given the stylized description, we must address the question: what explains the long stretch of high capital mobility that prevailed before 1914, the subsequent breakdown in the interwar period, and the very slow postwar reconstruction of the world financial system? The answer is tied up with one of the central and most visible areas in which openness to the world capital market constrains government power: the choice of an exchange rate regime.

The macroeconomic policy trilemma for open economies (also known as the "inconsistent trinity" proposition) follows from a basic fact: An open capital market deprives a country's government of the ability simultaneously to target its exchange rate and to use monetary policy in pursuit of other economic objectives. The trilemma arises because a macroeconomic policy regime can include at most two elements of the "inconsistent trinity" of three policy goals:

- Full freedom of cross-border capital movements.
- A fixed exchange rate.
- An independent monetary policy oriented toward domestic objectives.

If capital movements are prohibited, in the case where element (i) is ruled out, a country on a fixed exchange rate can break ranks with foreign interest rates and thereby run an independent monetary policy. Similarly a floating exchange rate, in the case where element (ii) is ruled out, reconciles freedom of international capital movements with monetary-policy effectiveness (at least when some nominal domestic prices are sticky). But monetary policy is powerless to achieve domestic goals when the exchange rate is fixed and capital movements free, the case where element (iii) is ruled out, since intervention in support of the exchange parity then entails capital flows that exactly offset any monetary-policy action threatening to alter domestic interest rates.

Our central proposition is that secular movements in the scope of international lending and borrowing may be understood in terms of this trilemma. Capital mobility has prevailed and expanded under circumstances of widespread political support either for an exchange-rate-subordinated monetary regime (for example, the gold standard), or for a monetary regime geared mainly toward domestic objectives at the expense of exchange-rate stability (for example, the recent float). The middle ground in which countries attempt simultaneously to hit exchange-rate targets and domestic policy goals has, almost as a logical consequence, entailed exchange controls or other harsh constraints on international transactions.

It is this conflict among rival policy choices, the trilemma, that informs our discussion of the historical evolution of world capital markets in the pages that follow, and helps make sense of the ebb and flow of capital mobility in the long run and in the broader political-economy context.

Of course, the trilemma is only a proximate explanation, in the sense that deeper socio-political forces explain the relative dominance of some policy targets over others. Cohen usefully distinguishes four potential categories of explanation concerning the evolution of international financial integration. We paraphrase his categories by distinguishing explanations based upon:

- Technological innovation, including resulting increases in market competition.
- Policy competition among governments seeking to advance "state interest", somehow defined.
- Domestic politics, including partisan rivalry and interest-group lobbying.
- Ideology and advances in economic knowledge.

We view explanations based on technology as secondary for the period of interest to us (starting in the latter nineteenth century), as it follows the deployment of trans-oceanic cable technology. The precise definition of "state interest" may well reflect the domestic political power structure, so explanations of class (ii) and (iii) need not be disjoint. Yet there may be situations in which there is a broad domestic consensus regarding certain policies as in the national interest. Similarly, ideology and the state of knowledge can determine the policies that states pursue in seeking a given perceived national interest. As will become clear in what follows, we regard explanations along the lines of (ii) and especially (iii) as the "deep factors" behind movements in international financial integration, with a supporting role for (iv) as well. The central role of the trilemma is to constrain the choice set within which the deep factors play their roles.

The broad trends and cycles in the world capital market that we will document reflect changing responses to the fundamental trilemma. Before 1914, each of the world's major economies pegged its currency's price in terms of gold, and thus, implicitly, maintained a fixed rate of exchange against every other major country's currency. Financial interests ruled the world of the classical gold standard and financial orthodoxy saw no alternative mode of sound finance. Thus, the gold standard system met the trilemma by opting for fixed exchange rates and capital mobility, sometimes at the expense of domestic macroeconomic health. Between 1891 and 1897, for example, the United States Treasury put the country through a harsh deflation in the face of persistent speculation on the dollar's departure from gold. These policies were hotly debated; the Populist movement agitated forcefully against gold, but lost.

The balance of political power began to shift only with the First World War, which brought a sea change in the social contract underlying the industrial democracies. For a sample of industrial countries, Figure shows the Polity IV coding for "institutional democracy" as it evolved over the period bracketing the First World War. Other than for the United States (which has a constant score of 10 throughout the sample period, and is omitted from the figure) there is clear evidence of a discrete increase in political openness in the decade or so after 1918. Organized labor emerged as a political power, a counterweight to the interests of capital, as seen in the British labor unrest of the 1920s, which culminated in a General Strike. Britain's return to gold in 1925 led the way to a restored international gold standard and a limited resurgence of international finance, but weaknesses in the rebuilt system helped propagate a global depression after the 1929 U.S. downturn.

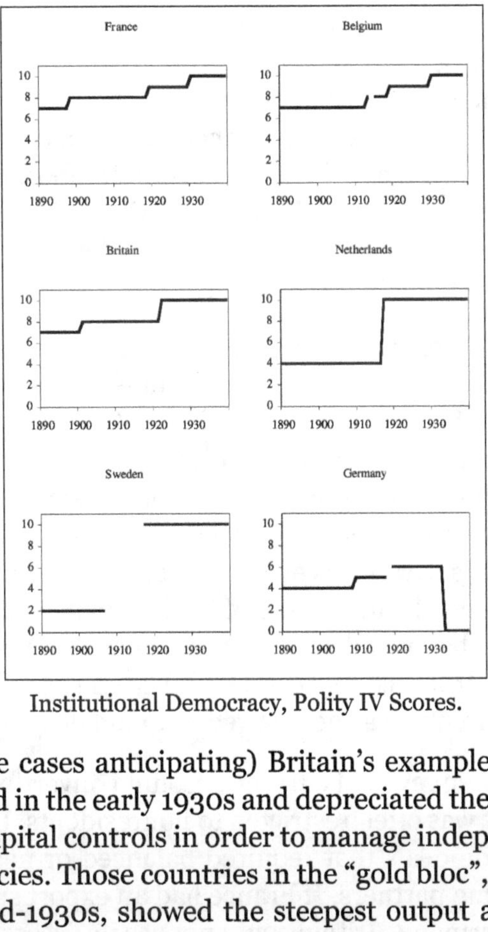

Institutional Democracy, Polity IV Scores.

Following (and in some cases anticipating) Britain's example, many countries abandoned the gold standard in the early 1930s and depreciated their currencies; many also resorted to trade and capital controls in order to manage independently their exchange rates and domestic policies. Those countries in the "gold bloc", which stubbornly clung to gold through the mid-1930s, showed the steepest output and price-level declines. Jame'ss account of French policy-maker's vacillation between controls and devaluation well illustrates the interaction between political pressures and the trilemma. Eventually in the 1930s, all countries jettisoned rigid exchange-rate targets and open capital markets in favor of domestic macroeconomic goals.

These decisions reflected the shift in political power solidified by the First World War. They also signaled the beginnings of a new consensus on the role of economic policy that would endure through the inflationary 1970s. As an immediate consequence, however, the Great Depression discredited gold-standard orthodoxy and brought Keynesian ideas about macroeconomic management to the fore. It also made financial markets and financial practitioners unpopular. Their supposed excesses and attachment to gold became identified in the public mind as causes of the economic calamity. In the United States, the New Deal brought a Jacksonian hostility toward Eastern high finance back to Washington. Financial markets were more closely regulated, and the Federal Reserve was brought under heavier Treasury influence. Similar reactions occurred in other countries.

Changed attitudes toward financial activities and economic management underlay the new postwar economic order negotiated at Bretton Woods, New Hampshire, in July 1944. Forty-four allied countries set up a system based on fixed, but adjustable, exchange parities, in the belief that floating exchange rates would exhibit instability and damage international trade. At the center of the system was the International Monetary Fund (IMF). The IMF's prime function was as a source of hard-currency loans to governments that might otherwise have to temporarily put their economies into recession to maintain a fixed exchange rate. Countries experiencing permanent balance-of-payments problems had the option of realigning their currencies, subject to IMF approval.

Importantly, the IMF's founders viewed its lending capability as primarily a substitute for, not a complement to, private capital inflows. Interwar experience had given the latter a reputation as unreliable at best and, at worst, a dangerous source of disturbances. Broad, encompassing controls over private capital movement, perfected in wartime, were expected to continue. The IMF's Articles of Agreement explicitly empowered countries to impose new capital controls. Articles VIII and XIV of the IMF agreement did demand that countrie's currencies eventually be made convertible—in effect, freely saleable to the issuing central bank, at the official exchange parity, for dollars or gold. But this privilege was to be extended only if the country's currency had been earned through current account transactions. Convertibility on capital account, as opposed to current-account convertibility, was not viewed as mandatory or desirable.

Unfortunately, a wide extent even of current-account convertibility took many years to achieve, and even then it was often restricted to nonresidents. In the interim, countries resorted to bilateral trade deals that required balanced or nearly balanced trade between every pair of trading partners. If France had an export surplus with Britain, and Britain a surplus with Germany, Britain could not use its excess marks to obtain dollars with which to pay France. Germany had very few dollars and guarded them jealously for critical imports from the Americas. Instead, each country would try to divert import demand toward countries with high demand for its goods, and to direct its exports toward countries whose goods were favored domestically.

Convertibility gridlock in Europe and its dependencies was ended through a regional multilateral clearing scheme, the European Payments Union (EPU). The clearing scheme was set up in 1950 and some countries reached de facto convertibility by mid-decade. But it was not until December 27, 1958 that Europe officially embraced convertibility and ended the EPU. Although most European countries still chose to retain extensive capital controls (Germany being the main exception), the return to convertibility, important as it was in promoting multilateral trade growth, also increased the opportunities for disguised capital movements. These might take the form, for example, of misinvoicing, or of accelerated or delayed merchandise payments. Buoyant growth encouraged some countries in further financial liberalization, although the U.S., worried about its gold losses, raised progressively higher barriers to capital outflow over the 1960s. Eventually, the Bretton Woods system's very successes hastened its collapse by resurrecting the trilemma.

Key countries in the system, notably the U.S. (fearful of slower growth) and Germany (fearful of higher inflation), proved unwilling to accept the domestic policy implications of maintaining fixed rates. Even the limited capital mobility of the early 1970s proved sufficient to allow furious speculative attacks on the major currencies, and after vain attempts to restore fixed dollar exchange rates, the industrial countries retreated to floating rates early in 1973. Although viewed at the time as a temporary emergency measure, the floating-dollar-rate regime is still with us thirty years later.

Floating exchange rates have allowed the explosion in international financial markets experienced over the same three decades. Freed from one element of the trilemma—fixed exchange rates—countries have been able to open their capital markets while still retaining the flexibility to deploy monetary policy in pursuit of national objectives. No doubt the experience gained after the inflationary 1970s in anchoring monetary policy to avoid price instability has helped to promote ongoing financial integration. Perhaps for the first time in history, countries have learned how to keep inflation in check under fiat monies and floating exchange rates.

There are several potentially valid reasons, however, for countries to still fix their exchange rates—for example, to keep a better lid on inflation or to counter exchange-rate instability due to financial-market shocks. Such arguments may find particular resonance, of course, in developing countries. However, few countries that have tried to fix have succeeded for long; eventually, exchange-rate stability tends to come into conflict with other policy objectives, the capital markets catch on to the government's predicament, and a crisis adds enough economic pain to make the authorities give in. In recent years only a very few major countries have observed the discipline of fixed exchange rates for at least five years, and most of those were rather special cases.

The European Union members that maintained mutually fixed rates prior to January 1999 were aided by market confidence in their own planned solution to the trilemma, a near-term currency merger. Developing countries have generally not fared so well. Even Hong Kong, which operates a currency board supposedly subordinated to maintaining the Hong Kong-U.S. dollar peg, suffered repeated speculative attacks in the Asian crisis period. Another currency-board experiment, Argentina, held to its 1:1 dollar exchange rate from April 1991 for a remarkable stint of more than ten years. To accomplish that feat, the country relied on IMF and private credit and, despite episodes of growth, endured levels of unemployment higher than many countries could tolerate. It suffered especially acutely after Brazil moved to a float in January 1999. Three years later Argentina's political and economic arrangements disintegrated in the face of external default and currency collapse.

For most larger countries, the trend toward greater financial openness has been accompanied—inevitably, we would argue—by a declining reliance on pegged exchange rates in favor of greater exchange-rate flexibility. Some countries have opted for a different solution, however, adopting extreme straitjackets for monetary policy in order to peg an exchange rate. If monetary policy is geared toward domestic considerations, capital mobility or the exchange-rate target must go. If, instead, fixed exchange rates and integration into the global capital market are the primary desiderata, monetary policy must be subjugated to those ends.

Table: The Trilemma and Major Phases of Capital Mobility.

	Resolution of trilemma: Countries choose to sacrifice			
Era	Activist policies	Capital mobility	Fixed exchange rate	Notes
Gold standard	Most	Few	Few	Broad consensus.
Interwar (when off gold)	Few	Several	Most	Capital controls especially in Central Europe, Latin America.
Bretton Woods	Few	Most	Few	Broad consensus.
Float	Few	Few	Many	Some consensus; except currency boards, dollarization, etc.

The details of this argument require a book-length discourse, which allows a full survey of the empirical evidence and the historical record, but we can already pinpoint the key turning points. The Great Depression stands as the watershed here, in that it was caused by an ill-advised subordination of monetary policy to an exchange-rate constraint (the gold standard), which led to a chaotic time of troubles in which countries experimented, typically non-cooperatively, with alternative modes of addressing the fundamental trilemma. Interwar experience, in turn, discredited the gold standard and led to a new and fairly universal policy consensus. The new consensus shaped the more cooperative postwar international economic order fashioned by Harry Dexter White and John Maynard Keynes, but implanted within that order the seeds of its own eventual destruction a quarter-century later. The global financial nexus that has evolved since rests on a solution to the basic open-economy trilemma quite different than that envisioned by Keynes or White—one that allows considerable freedom for capital movements, gives the major currency areas freedom to pursue internal goals, but largely leaves their mutual exchange rates as the equilibrating residual.

As always, we have to consider the potential costs and benefits of international capital mobility for the national participants. Clearly, the ability to lend or borrow represents, trivially, a loosening of constraints relative to a perfectly closed economy. In this dimension, at least, open trade in financial markets offers unambiguous gains relative to a closed economy. Such trades permit insurance, the smoothing of shocks, and allow capital to seek out its highest rewards, implying the usual gains-from-trade results.

However, in other ways, international financial mobility raises concerns, particularly for policymakers attached to certain policy goals that may be inconsistent with the free flow of capital across international boundaries. In addition, the risks of financial and balance of payments crises—some of them self-fulfilling crises unrelated to "fundamentals"—may represent further obstacles to the adoption of free capital markets.

Although these are very much contemporary issues in world capital markets, the questions they raise can be traced back to the very founding of international financial markets centuries ago during the Renaissance. Then too, advanced forms of financial asset trades developed very quickly, sometimes as a response to Churchim posed constraints such as usury proscriptions. Financial innovation was subject to suspicion from various quarters, both public and private. Thus, calls for the regulation and restriction of financial-market activity have been with us since the earliest days.

Despite these fears, by the late nineteenth century a succession of technological breakthroughs, and a gradual institutional evolution, had positioned many nations in a newly forming international capital market. This network of nations embraced modern financial instruments and operated virtually free of controls on the part of governments. Under the gold standard monetary regime, this flourishing global market for capital reached at least a local peak in the decades just prior to World War One.

The subsequent history of the twentieth century showed that this seemingly linear path toward ever more technological progress and institutional sophistication in a liberal world order could indeed be upset. Two global wars and a depression led the world down an autarkic path. Conflicting policy goals and democratic tensions often put the interests of global capital at a low premium relative to other objectives. Activist governments appealed to capital controls to sidestep the discipline of external markets, invoking monetary policy as a tool of macroeconomic control.

These events demonstrate the power of the macroeconomic policy trilemma to account for many of the ups and downs in global capital market evolution in the twentieth century. We match up these stylized facts with some of the quantitative and institutional record, so as to better document the course of events. It is a remarkable history without which today's economic, financial, political, and institutional landscape cannot be fully understood.

Evidence

In theory and practice, the extent of international capital mobility can have profound implications for the operation of individual and global economies. With respect to theory, the applicability of various classes of macroeconomic models rests on many assumptions, and not the least important of these are axioms linked to the closure of the model in the capital market. The predictions of a theory and its usefulness for policy debates can revolve critically on this part of the structure.

The importance of these issues for policy is not surprising at all: a moment's reflection on practical aspects of macroeconomic policy choice underscores the impact that capital mobility can have on the efficacy of various interventions: trivially, if capital is perfectly mobile, this dooms to failure any attempts to manipulate local asset prices to make them deviate from global prices, including the most critical macroeconomic asset price, the interest rate. Thus, the feasibility and relevance of key policy actions cannot be judged absent some informed position on the extent to which local economic conditions are in any way separable from global conditions. This means an empirical measure of market integration is implicitly, though rarely explicitly, a necessary adjunct to any policy discussion. Although recent globalization trends have brought this issue to the fore, this paper shows how the experience of longer-run macroeconomic history can clarify and inform these debates.

In attacking the problem of measuring market integration, economists have no universally recognized criterion to turn to. For example, imagine the simple expedient of examining price differentials: prices would be identical in two identical neighboring economies, being determined in each by the identical structures of tastes, technologies, and endowments; but if the two markets were physically separated by an infinitely high transaction-cost barrier one could hardly describe them as being integrated in a single market, as the equality of prices was merely a chance event. Or consider looking at the size of flows between two markets as a gauge of mobility; this is an equally flawed criterion, for suppose we now destroyed the barrier between the two economies just mentioned, and reduced transaction costs to zero; we would then truly have a single integrated market, but, since on either side of the barrier prices were identical in autarky, there would be no incentive for any good or factor to move after the barrier disappeared.

Thus, convergence of prices and movements of goods are not unambiguous indicators of market integration. One could run through any number of other putative criteria for market integration, examining perhaps the levels or correlations of prices or quantities, and find essentially the same kind of weakness: all such tests may be able to evaluate market integration, but only as a joint hypothesis test where some auxiliary assumptions are needed to make the test meaningful.

Given this impasse, an historical study is potentially valuable in two respects. First, we can use a very large array of data sources covering different aspects of international capital mobility over the last one hundred years or more. Without being wedded to a single criterion, we can attempt to make inferences about the path of global capital mobility with a battery of tests, using both quantity and price criteria of various kinds. As long as important caveats are kept in mind about each method, especially the auxiliary assumptions required for meaningful inference, we can essay a broad-based approach to the evidence. Should the different methods all lead to a similar conclusion we would be in a stronger position than if we simply relied on a single test.

Historical work offers a second benefit in that it provides a natural set of benchmarks for our understanding of today's situation. In addition to the many competing tests for capital mobility, we also face the problem that almost every test is usually a matter of degree, of interpreting a parameter or a measure of dispersion or some other variable or coefficient. We face the typical empirical conundrums (how big is big? or how fast is fast?) in placing an absolute meaning on these measures.

An historical perspective allows a more nuanced view, and places all such inferences in a relative context: when we say that a parameter for capital mobility is big, this is easier to interpret if we can say that by this we mean bigger than a decade or a century ago. The historical focus will be directed at addressing just such concerns. We examine the broadest range of data over the last one-hundred-plus years to see what has happened to the degree of capital mobility in a cross section of countries.

The empirical work begins by looking at quantity data, focusing on changes in the stocks of foreign capital over a century or more. Subsequent empirical sketches focus on price-based criteria for capital market integration, looking at nominal interest arbitrage, real interest rate convergence, and equity returns.

Gross Stocks of Foreign Capital

In this topic we examine the extant data on foreign capital stocks to get some sense of the evolution of the global market. We seek some measure of the size of foreign investment globally that is appropriately scaled and consistent over time. Although the concept is simple, the measurement is not. Perhaps the simplest measure of the activity in the global capital market is obtained by looking at the total stock of overseas investment at a point in time. Suppose that the total asset stock in country or region i, owned by country or region j, at time t is A_{ijt}. Included in here is the domestically owned capital stock A_{iit}. Of interest are two concepts: what assets of country j reside overseas? and what liabilities of country i are held overseas?

A relatively easy hurdle to surmount concerns normalization of the data; foreign investment stocks are commonly measured at a point in time in current nominal terms, in most cases U.S. dollars. Obviously, both the growth of the national and international economies might be associated with an increase in such a nominal quantity, as would any long run inflation. These trends would have nothing to do with market integration per se. To overcome this problem, we elected to normalize foreign capital at each point in time by some measure of the size of the world economy, dividing through by a denominator in the form of a nominal size index. A seemingly ideal denominator, given that the numerator is the stock of foreign owned capital, would probably be the total stock of capital, whether financial or real. The problem with using financial capital measures is that they have greatly multiplied over the long run as financial development has expanded the number of balance sheets in the economy, thanks to the rise of numerous financial intermediaries. This trend, in principle, could happen at any point in time without any underlying change in the extent of foreign asset holdings. The problem with using real capital stocks is that data construction is fraught with difficulty.

Given these problems we chose a simpler and more readily available measure of the size of an economy, namely the level of output Y measured in current prices in a common currency unit. Over short horizons, unless the capital-output ratio were to move dramatically, the ratio of foreign capital to output should be adequate as a proxy measure of the penetration of foreign capital in any economy. Over the long run, difficulties might arise if the capital-output ratio has changed significantly over time—but we have little firm evidence to suggest that it has. Thus, as a result of these long-run data constraints, our analysis focuses on capital-to-GDP ratios of the form:

$$\text{Foreign Assets-to-GDP Ratio}_{it} = \sum_{j \neq i} A_{jit} / Y_{it};$$

$$\text{Foreign Liabilities-to-GDP Ratio}_{it} = \sum_{j \neq i} A_{jit} / Y_{it}$$

However, even with the concept established, measurement is still problematic in the case of the numerator. It is in fact very difficult to discover the extent of foreign capital in an economy using both contemporary and historical data. For example, the IMF has always reported balance-of-payments flow transactions in its International Financial Statistics. It is straightforward for most of the recent postwar period to discover the annual flows of equity, debt, or other forms of capital account transactions from these accounts. Conversely, it was only in 1997 that the IMF began reporting the corresponding stock data, namely, the international investment position of each country. These data are also more sparse, beginning in 1980 for less than a dozen countries, and expanding to about 30 countries by the mid-1990s.

The paucity of data is understandable, since the collection burden for these data is much more significant: knowing the size of a bond issue in a single year reveals the flow transaction size; knowing the implications for future stocks requires, for example, tracking each debt and equity item, and its fluctuating market value over time, and maintaining an aggregate of these data. The stock data are not simply a temporal aggregate of flows: the stock value depends on past flows, capital gains and losses, any retirements of principal or buybacks of equity, defaults and reschedulings, and a host of other factors. Not surprisingly accurate data of this type are hard to assemble. Just as the IMF has had difficulty doing so, so too have economic historians. Looking back over the nineteenth and twentieth centuries an exhaustive search across many different sources yields only a handful of benchmark years in which estimates have been made, an effort that draws on the work of dozens of scholars in official institutions and numerous other individual efforts.

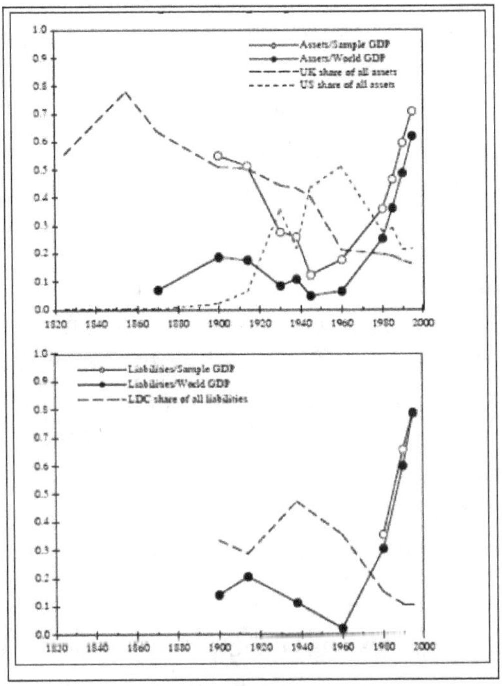

Foreign Capital Stocks.

It is based on these efforts that we can put together a fragmentary, but still potentially illuminating, historical description figure. Displayed here are nominal foreign investment and output data for major countries and regions, grouped according to assets and liabilities. Many cells are empty because data are unavailable, but where possible summary data have been derived to illustrate the ratio of foreign capital to output, and the share of various countries in foreign investment activity.

What do the data show? On the asset side it is immediately apparent that for all of the nineteenth century, and until the interwar period, the British were rightly termed the "bankers to the world"; at its peak, the British share of total global foreign investment was almost 80 percent. This is far above the recent U.S. share of global foreign assets, a mere 22 percent in 1995, and still higher than the maximum U.S. share of 50 percent circa 1960. The only rivals to the British in the early nineteenth century were the Dutch, who according to these figures held perhaps 30 percent of global assets in 1825. This comes as no surprise given what we know of Amsterdam's early preeminence as the first global financial center before London's rise to dominance in the eighteenth and nineteenth centuries. By the late nineteenth century both Paris and Berlin had also emerged as major financial centers, and, as their economies grew and industrialized, French and German holdings of foreign capital rose significantly, each eclipsing the Dutch position.

In this era the United States was a debtor rather than a creditor nation, and was only starting to emerge as a major lender and foreign asset holder after 1900. European borrowing from the United States in World War One then suddenly made the United States a big creditor. This came at a time when she was ready, if not altogether willing, to assume the mantle of "banker to the world", following Britain's abdication of this position under the burden of war and recovery in the 1910s and 1920s. But the dislocations of the interwar years were to postpone the United State's rise as a foreign creditor, and New York's pivotal role as a financial center. After 1945, however, the United States decisively surpassed Britain as the major international asset holder, a position that has never been challenged.

How big were nineteenth century holdings of foreign assets? In 1870 we estimate that foreign assets were just 7 percent of World GDP; but this figure rose quickly, to just below 20 percent in the years 1900–14 at the zenith of the classical gold standard. During the interwar period, the collapse was swift, and foreign assets were only 8 percent of world output by 1930, 11 percent in 1938, and just 5 percent in 1945. Since this low point, the ratio has climbed, to 6 percent in 1960, 25 percent in 1980, and then climbing dramatically to 62 percent in 1995. Thus, the 1900–14 ratio of foreign investment to output in the world economy was not equaled again until 1980, but has now been approximately doubled.

An alternative measure recognizes the incompleteness of the data sources: for many countries we have no information on foreign investments at all, so a zero has been placed in the numerator, although that country's output has been included in the denominator as part of the World GDP estimate. This is an unfortunate aspect of our estimation procedure, and makes the above ratio a likely an underestimate, or lower bound, for the true ratio of foreign assets to output. One way to correct this is to only include in the denominator the countries for which we actually have data on foreign investment in the numerator. This procedure yields an estimate we term the ratio of foreign assets to sample GDP. This is likely an overestimate, or upper bound, for the true ratio, largely because in historical data, if not in contemporary sources, attention in the collection of foreign investment data has usually focused on the principal players, that is, the countries which have significant foreign asset holdings.

Given all these concerns, does the ratio to sample GDP evolve in a very different way? No, but the recent upswing is not as pronounced using this alternative measure. The two ratios are very close after 1980. But before 1945 they are quite far apart: from 1870 to 1914, the sample of seven countries has a foreign asset to GDP ratio of over 50 percent, far above the "world" figure of 7 to 20 percent. By this measure we only surpassed the 1914 ratio as recently as 1990, and only narrowly even then.

Clearly, these seven major creditors were exceptionally internationally diversified in the late nineteenth century in a way that no group of countries is today. By this reckoning, in countries like today's United States, we still have yet to see a return to the extremely high degree of international portfolio diversification seen in, say, Britain in the 1900–14 period, an historical finding that places in historical perspective the ongoing international diversification puzzle.

Is the picture similar for liabilities as well as assets? Essentially, yes. The data are much more fragmentary here, with none in the nineteenth century, when the information for the key creditor nations was simpler to collect than data for a multitude of debtors, perhaps. Even so, we have some estimates running from 1900 to the present at a few key dates. The ratio of liabilities to world GDP follows a path very much like that of the asset ratio, which is reassuring: they are each approximations built from different data sources at certain time points, though, in principle, they should be equal. Again, the ratio reaches a local maximum in 1914 of 21 percent, collapsing in the interwar period to 11 percent in 1938, and just 2 percent in 1960. By 1980 it had exceeded the 1914 level and stood at 30 percent. By 1995, the ratio was 79 percent.

To summarize, data on gross international asset positions seem broadly consistent with the idea of a -shape in the evolution of international capital mobility since the late nineteenth century, though it is less clear how we should compare the degree of diversification attained by some countries then with today's apparently significant, albeit declining, home bias in foreign asset holdings. Figuring whether too much or too little diversification existed at any point must remain conjectural, and conclusions would hingc on a calibrated and estimated portfolio model applied historically. This is certainly an object for future research. However, unless the global economy has dramatically changed in terms of the risk-return profile of assets and their global distribution, we have no prior reason to expect the efficient degree of diversification to have changed. For the present we can just say that, unless a massive such change did occur in the 1914–45 period, and unless it was then promptly reversed in the 1945–90 period, we cannot explain the time path of foreign capital stocks seen figure except as a result of a dramatic decline in capital mobility in the interwar period, and a very slow recovery of capital mobility thereafter.

There is another important dimension of international asset stock data that we have not yet discussed: the evolution of net stocks, that is, the behavior of longer- term development flows, as distinct from diversification flows. The literature on the Feldstein-Horioka paradox alerts us to the possibility that gross flows are orders of magnitude above net flows. We postpone discussion of that issue until later.

Real Interest Rate Convergence

A fundamental property of fully integrated international capital markets is that investors are indifferent on the margin between any two activities to which they allocate capital, regardless of national location. International real interest rate equality would hold in the long run in a world where capital moves freely across borders and technological diffusion tends to drive a convergence process for national production possibilities.

One basic indication of internationally integrated financial markets therefore would be the statistical stationarity of long-term real interest differentials. We investigate this property using long-term real interest rate data constructed from the Global Financial Data database. For a nominal interest rate it we use the monthly series on long-term government bond yields, which apply to bonds of maturities of seven years or longer. For inflation $\pi_t = (P_{t+12} - P_t)/P_t$ we use the ex post 12-month forward rate of change of the consumer price index. The ex post real interest rate is then calculated as $r_t = i_t - \pi_t$, and for now we make the standard assumption that this is equal to the ex ante real rate plus a white-noise stationary forecast error. We focus on real long-term bond yields because these are most directly related to financing costs for capital investments, and, hence, to the expected marginal yield on investment. It is the latter variable we would like to be able to measure directly in order to evaluate the international mobility of capital.

We consider three countries in our sample, relative to the United States as a base country. They are Britain, France, and Germany. We should note that the series are as consistent as they can be given the changing types of domestic bonds issued by the various countries over the last century, although maturities do change at several points for some countries. There are a few exceptions, such as the British consol, which has a continuous time series. We also note that prior to 1914 most countries have only annual price indices meaning that our derived inflation series will also consist of annual observations, the exceptions being the United States and Britain. For the other two countries, we construct monthly series of ex post real interest rates by matching monthly nominal interest rates within a year t with the realized inflation rate between years t+1 and t. Of course, in measuring long-term real interest rates, we would like to proxy long-term inflation expectations but that cannot be done reliably. Thus we follow earlier empirical studies in utilizing a relatively short-horizon inflation measure notwithstanding the longer term of the corresponding nominal interest rates.

The real interest rate differential for each of our seven countries is shown in figure. This differential is calculated as $\tilde{r}_t = r_t - r_{US,t}$. This is the first time real interest rates over more than a century have been analyzed for this set of countries at such high frequency, so it is of interest to start by evaluating some general features of the data. The most striking impression conveyed by the figure is that differentials have varied widely over time, but have stayed relatively close to a zero mean. That is, the series appear to have been stationary over the very long run, and even in shorter sub-periods.

The figures also reveal some of the changing coherence of real interest rates in the sub-periods. To avoid noisy data from non-market periods, the wartime years have been omitted, as has the German hyperinflation period. Again we can focus on the four different subperiods that correspond to the four different monetary regimes: the gold standard, the interwar period, Bretton Woods and the brief transitional period prior to generalized floating, and the float.

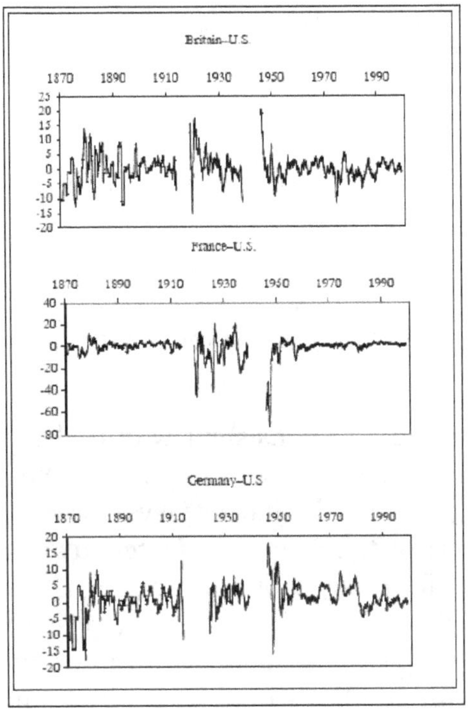

Long-Term Real Interest Differentials.

Allowing for the annual inflation data used before 1914, we can see that real interest differentials became somewhat more volatile in the interwar period, with a larger variance (this is less obvious in the German case because the hyperinflation period has been omitted). There is a decline in this volatility after 1950, and perhaps very little change between the pre-1974 period and the float. The latter observation may seem surprising, except that it is consistent with observations that, aside from nominal and real exchange rate volatility, there is little difference in the behavior of macro fundamentals between fixed and floating rate regimes, at least for developed countries.

With no real interest rate divergence apparent, these figures provide prima facie evidence that real interest rates in developed countries have been co-integrated over time, where the differentials between countries appear stationary. A formal test of this hypothesis where we apply two stationarity tests to the data for the period as a whole, as well as in various sub-periods. The first test is the traditional augmented Dickey-Fuller (ADF) unit root test, and the second is the DF-GLSu test, one of a family of enhanced point-optimal and asymptotically efficient unit root tests recently proposed.

Where the null is rejected at the 1 percent level, the results show conclusively that the real interest differential has no unit root over the long run. Changes in the variances of series over time, of the kind evident in the preceding figures, may distort unit root tests. However, the hypothesis of a unit root can be rejected in almost all cases at the 1 percent level in all periods except for the recent float. With respect to the recent float, the evidence against a unit root is stronger over the second sub-period than over the first. The above findings refer to the more powerful DFGLSu test, which rejects the null more frequently than the standard ADF test.

This indication of a stationary long-term real interest differential, especially insofar as it applies to the recent period of floating industrial-country exchange rates, contradicts much of the empirical literature produced through the mid-1990s. Why do we find evidence of stationarity where others, such as Meese and Rogoff and Edison and Pauls, could not reject a unit root in recent data? We note that previous authors only focused attention on the recent float, had shorter samples, and used tests of low power such as the ADF test.

Indeed, our data and methods are consistent with earlier findings: if we switch to the Meese-Rogoff sample of February 1974 to March 1986, and use the ADF test as they did, and insist on a 5 percent significance level for rejection of the null, then we replicate their conclusions exactly. Even if we switch to the DFGLSu test on the same data, we can reject the null in only 2 out of 7 cases. The results for the post-1986 sample show similar problems, even though for the post-1974 period as a whole we can reject the null. Our finding of stationarity in recent long-term real interest differentials is consistent with another strand in the literature that does find support for international real interest rate equalization at longer horizons. We conclude that earlier analyses of recent data were hampered by the low power of unit root tests on samples of small span.

Exchange-risk Free Nominal Interest Parity

Perhaps the most unambiguous indicator of capital mobility is the relationship between interest rates on identical assets located in different financial centers. The great advantage of comparing onshore and offshore interest rates such as these is that relative rates of return are not affected by pure currency risk. For much of the period we study here, a direct onshore-offshore comparison is impossible. However, the existence of forward exchange instruments allows us to construct roughly equivalent measures of the return to currency-risk-free international arbitrage operations.

Using monthly data on forward exchange rates, spot rates, and nominal interest rates for 1921 to the latter half of 2001, we assess the degree of international financial-market integration by calculating the return to covered interest arbitrage between financial centers. For example, a London resident could earn the gross sterling interest rate $1+i_t^*$ on a London loan of one pound sterling. Alternatively, she could invest the same currency unit in New York, simultaneously covering her exchange risk by selling dollars forward. She would do this in three steps: Buy e_t dollars in the spot exchange market (where e_t is the spot price of sterling in dollar terms); next, invest the proceeds for a total of $e_t(1+i_t)$ (where it is the nominal dollar interest rate; and, finally, sell that sum of dollars forward for $e_t(1+i_t)/f_t$ in sterling (where f_t, the forward exchange rate, is the price of forward sterling in terms of forward dollars). The net gain from borrowing in London and investing in New York,

$$\frac{e_t}{f_t}(1+i_t)-(1+i_t^*),$$

is zero when capital mobility is perfect and the interest rates and forward rate are free of default risk. The left-hand side of the preceding expression represents a price of present pounds sterling in terms of future pounds sterling, i.e., of pounds dated t in terms of pounds dated t + 1, but it can be viewed as the relative price prevailing in the New York market, that is, as a kind of offshore interest rate. Thus, our test, in effect, examines the equality of the onshore sterling interest rate i^* with the offshore New York rate so defined. We perform a similar calculation for mark interest differentials between London (considered as the offshore center) and Germany (onshore), thereby gauging the difference between implicit mark interest rates in London and the rates prevailing near the same time in Germany.

For pre-1920 data, we examine a related but distinct measure based on current New York prices of sterling for (two-months) future delivery, as in Obstfeld and Taylor. The parallel Germany-London arbitrage calculation before 1920, corresponding to the preceding New York-London comparison, is based on London prices for marks to be delivered three months in the future. Forward exchange contracts of the kind common after 1920 were not prevalent before then, so we instead base our pre-1920 comparison of onshore and offshore interest rates on the most widely traded instrument, one for which prices were regularly quoted in the major financial center's markets, the long bill of exchange. Long bills could be used to cover the exchange risk that might otherwise be involved in interest-rate arbitrage.

To see how such a transaction would work, let b_t denote the date-t dollar price in New York of £1 deliverable in London after 60 days, and et the spot New York price of sterling. One way to purchase a future pound deliverable in London would be through a straight sterling loan, at price $1/(1+i_t^*)$, where i_t^* is the London 60-day discount rate. An alternative would be to purchase in New York a bill on London, at a price in terms of current sterling of b_t/e_t. With perfect and costless international arbitrage, these two prices of £1 to be delivered in London in the future should be the same.

Perkins observed that the series (e/b) - 1 defines the sterling interest rate in American financial markets, that is, the offshore sterling rate in the United States. This series may be compared with the London rate i^*, to gauge the degree of cross-border financial integration; that is, we calculate the differential before 1920.

$$\frac{e_t}{b_t}-(1+i_t^*)$$

Perkin'ss primary aim was to modify earlier series of dollar-sterling spot rates derived by Davis and Hughes, who applied U.S. rather than U.K. interest rates to the dollar prices of long sterling bills in order to infer a series of sight exchange rates. Perkins argued that the sight bill rate should be derived by multiplying the (lower) long bill rate by a sterling, not a dollar, interest factor, and subsequent scholars have followed him; for example, the judgment of Officer. From a theoretical point of view, the verdict is clear: the relative price of current and future sterling defines a sterling nominal interest rate, in the present case, the offshore New York rate that we compare to London rates.

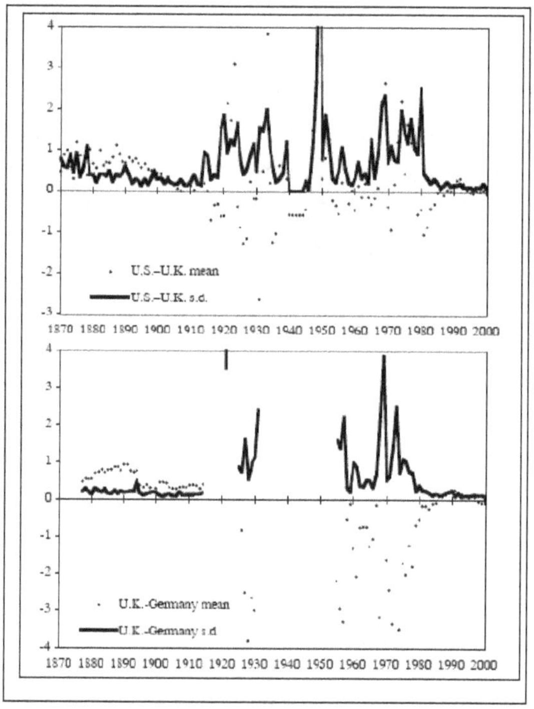

Exchange-Risk Free Nominal Interest Differentials.

The upper panel of figure is based on monthly differences between sterling rates in New York and in London from 1870 to 2001, where we simply splice together the 1870–1919 numbers based on time bill rates with the subsequently available covered interest differentials. Differential returns are calculated as annual rates of accrual.

The figure broadly supports other indicators of the evolution of capital mobility. Differentials are relatively small and steady under the pre-1914 gold standard, but start to open up during World War I. They stay quite large in the early 1920s. Differentials diminish briefly in the late 1920s, but widen sharply in the early 1930s. There are some big arbitrage gaps in the late 1940s through the mid- 1950s—including a sharp spike in volatility at the time of the 1956 Suez crisis. But these shrink starting in the late 1950s and early 1960s, only to open up again in the late 1960s as sterling's 1967 devaluation initiates a period of foreign exchange turmoil, culminating in the unraveling of the Bretton Woods system in the early 1970s. Interest differentials have become small once again since the disappearance of U.K. capital controls around 1980. The differentials appear even smaller now than before 1914.

Indeed, for the 1870–1914 data we observe a tendency, quite systematic albeit declining over time, for New York sterling rates to exceed London rates. In arguing in favor of a sterling discount rate for valuing long sterling bills traded in the U.S., Perkins demonstrated a tendency for the implicit offshore sterling interest rate (e/b) - 1 to converge toward Bank Rate toward the end of the nineteenth century. However, compares the New York offshore sterling interest rate with the London money-market rate of discount, which tended to be somewhat below Bank Rate. Were we to use Bank Rate as the London interest rate in the figure, much of the pre-1914 gap would be eliminated. Given that the U.S. data consist of prices of high quality paper (such as bank bills), however, comparisons with Bank Rate are probably inappropriate. As Spalding observes: "Bank Rate, as is well known, is usually higher than market rate; therefore if ordinary trade bills are remitted to London from abroad, to find the long exchange, interest will be calculated at our Bank Rate, as trade paper is not considered such a good security as bank bills". Officer concurs, though on different grounds: "Whereas the Bank Rate was set by the Bank of England, the money-market rate was a true competitive price. The money-market rate of discount is the better measure".

If it is impermissible to compare the sterling interest rate in New York with Bank Rate in London, how, then, can we explain the systematic positive interest gap in favor of New York before 1914? Much if not all of the gap can be explained as an artifact of the procedure we have used to extract the "offshore" interest rate from the observations on sight and time bill prices.

Continuing our focus on the New York-London comparison of sterling interest rates, we notice that the published money-market discount rate for London is quoted as a "pure" relative price of future in terms of present sterling. In contrast, as practitioner's textbooks of the period make amply clear, in determining the price to be paid for a long bill of exchange on London, purchasers would factor in not only the spot exchange rate and the London market discount rate, but, in addition, commissions, profit margins, and, importantly, the stamp duty (0.05 percent of the bill's face value) payable to the British government. These factors made bill prices lower than they would have been if they simply were equal to the spot exchange rate discounted by the pure New York sterling rate of interest.

Margraff estimates that for a 90-day bill, the total of such factors amounted to 0.125 percent of face value. For a 60-day bill, that charge would represent about 75 basis points in annualized form; Escher, published a decade later, cites a very slightly smaller number. By subtracting that "tax" from the pre-1914 differentials plotted in the top of figure above, we see that the apparent average excess return in New York disappears.

Indeed, the average return becomes negative for 1890–1914, so that 75 basis points in additional costs may well be an overestimate for the entire prewar period. Suggestive of declining costs is the tendency shown in the figure for the average bias to decline over time. Perkins argues that U.S. foreign exchange dealers of the period were able to exploit market power to inflate their commissions. Certainly such market power declined through 1914 as markets evolved, and Officer's data on broker's commissions supports this view. Of course, a process of market integration increases competition and drives commissions down. Thus, leaving aside the portion due to the stamp tax, the size of the New York-London discrepancy is to some degree a reflection of financial market segmentation and its secular decline evidence of a process of progressive integration.

The lower panel of figure shows the difference between the implicit mark interest rate in London and the one prevailing in Germany. Again the -shape evolution of capital mobility is evident over our entire sample period. Before 1914, the former, offshore, rate is calculated on the basis of 90-day prime bills of exchange on Berlin traded in London. The results are remarkably consistent with those for New York-London.

In particular, we again observe a systematic but secularly declining excess return in London prior to 1914. The explanation is essentially the same as in the New York-London comparison above. Germany levied a stamp duty on bills at the same rate as Britain's. Margraff's estimates of concomitant costs suggest that for a 90-day bill on Berlin, about 40 basis points should be subtracted from the annualized sight bill premium $4\times\left[(e/b)-1\right]$ to ascertain the true London mark interest rate. On the assumption that some costs decline over time, with 40 basis points an average for the prewar period as whole, that cost adjustment brings the offshore and onshore mark rates roughly into line.

While the cost and tax considerations we have described potentially eliminate the pre-1914 upward bias in our estimated series of offshore interest rates, other financial transaction costs would, as usual, create no-arbitrage bands around the point of onshore-offshore interest rate equality. One way to evaluate the evolution of capital mobility through time would be to estimate over different eras what Einzig calls "transfer points", i.e., the minimum return differential necessary to induce arbitrage operations. Keynes and Einzig agreed that during the interwar period, at least a 50 basis point covered differential would be needed to induce arbitrage. That is, they suggested a no-arbitrage band of 50 basis points. Applying nonlinear estimation techniques including a TAR methodology to weekly interwar data on dollar-sterling covered return differentials, Peel and Taylor confirm that a no-arbitrage band close to 50 basis points did appear to prevail, as Keynes and Einzig claimed. Only outside of this range did arbitrage forces push spot and forward exchange rates toward conformity with the band.

A detailed investigation is beyond the scope, but a first pass at the data using the TAR methodology of Obstfeld and Taylor is suggestive. For the dollar-sterling exchange between June 1925 and June 1931, we calculate a band of inaction of 60 basis points, very close to the Peel-Taylor estimate given that we are using coarser, monthly data. For the corresponding interwar sterling-mark exchange our estimated band is ± 91

basis points wide. On 1880–1914 differentials, in contrast, we find (after subtracting a constant mean differential) bands of only ±19 basis points for New York-London and 35 basis points for London-Berlin. By way of comparison, Clinton suggests that covered interest differentials in the mid-1980s needed to reach just ±6 basis points to become economically significant. Balke and Wohar produce an estimate 50 percent higher for the 1974–93 period. We suspect that a more careful analysis of pre-1914 differentials, one taking account of the upward trend in market integration, would reduce our estimated transaction cost bands for the early twentieth century. Accordingly, the degree of integration among core money markets achieved under the classical gold standard must be judged as truly impressive compared to conditions over the following half-century or more.

The Great Depression, perhaps as part of a much broader interwar phase of disintegration, therefore stands out as an event that transformed the world capital market and left interest arbitrage differentials higher and more volatile than ever before.

Equity and Bond Returns

It is interesting to ask whether the long-run evidence on the -shape of capital market integration extends to other criteria, and other markets such as equities. Over the long run, global equity markets have evolved at a very different rate than global bond markets, for example. Government bonds from core countries have generally traded in financial centers in the last one hundred years, but for long spans of time emerging-market debt was very difficult to place in the private sector, and most went through multilateral intermediaries. Similarly, international trade in equities, though quiescent in the middle of the century, grew substantially in core countries after the lifting of capital controls in the 1970s and 1980s, and by the 1990s several emerging equity markets were involved too.

Does quantitative evidence exist to verify this narrative? Quantity data are harder to find at a disaggregated level. Breaking down foreign investment into its components is an enormous historical task, and few have attempted it in the quest for long-run comparable series across many countries. We will not attempt to press further here. Instead, we will examine price evidence to see what changing patterns of equity returns might tell us about globalization.

There is certainly some debate about the indicators of equity returns in the long run and what they tell us about globalization. Jorion and Goetzmann find that most of the world's stock markets have exhibited fairly low real returns over the long run in the last century, around 1 percent, with the exception of the United States, which has yielded around 4 percent annually since 1921. These figures caution that U.S. exceptionalism might extend to stock market returns also, and cast doubt on the general, global truth of the equity premium puzzle. The authors also note that "survivorship bias" likely afflicts the U.S. and many other markets in the core countries for which data exist. In many emerging markets, stock prices have fluctuated wildly and many series break down at critical historical junctures and during wars, limiting our ability to compare like with like.

In this topic we take a fresh look at long-run equity returns using similar data to that employed by Jorion and Goetzmann, the Global Financial Data source. We ask two questions not addressed by previous authors: to what extent have stock returns (measured in a common currency, the U.S. dollar) diverged or converged over time? and to what extent have the time series correlations of returns across countries changed over time? We then consider what the answers may have to say about globalization.

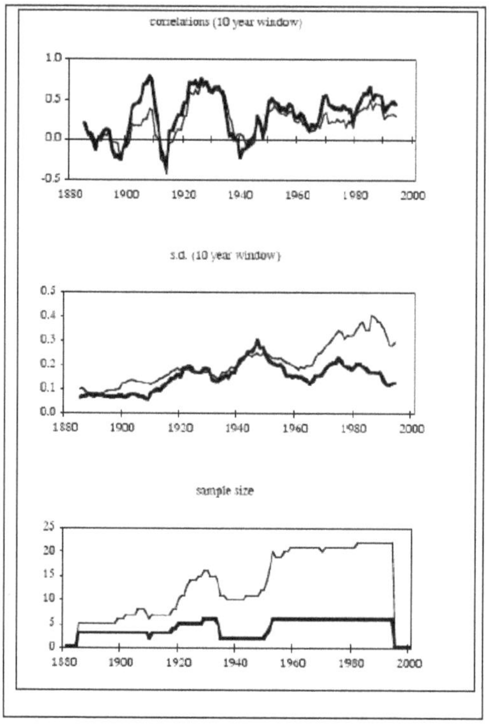

Equity Returns in U.S. Dollars for the G7 and up to 22 Global Stock Markets.

Figure shows summary statistics for a sample of up to 22 country stock price indices based on annual U.S. dollar-denominated returns since 1880. The bottom chart indicates that the sample size diminishes markedly prior to 1950, evidence of the survivorship problem. We usually have 20 countries in the sample after that date, but in the interwar period the sample size is about a dozen, and before 1920 between five and ten. A wide line traces out the sample size for a limited set of core countries, the G7. For this group there is a more consistent sample size over time, though only three series before 1920.

The middle chart shows the standard deviation of returns across time, calculated for a centered moving window of ten-year length and encompassing the largest sample possible. Again, the thin line is the full sample, the wide line the G7. As a description of the coherence of the returns in G7 equity markets this figure is strikingly consistent with the -shape hypothesis and the underlying arbitrage arguments. Returns showed relatively little dispersion prior to 1914, but larger gaps opened up in the interwar period. This dispersion reached a peak around 1945 or 1950, but has been falling since, with a minor reversal in the late 1960s, but convergence again after 1980, roughly when G7 capital controls loosened. The picture for the full sample is a little less clear, since the sample size is not consistent. We do not know how much of the long run increase in dispersion, for example, is due to an increase in the sample size over time; for example, the addition in recent years of more volatile emerging markets might be expected to raise the variance. But for the post-1950 period, when the sample is stable, the trends are quite similar to those in the G7, although the returns are much less coherent than the G7 in the 1970s and 1980s, a period in which capital controls were much tighter in the periphery than in the core. It is also apparent that in the 1990s, the emerging markets have seen a much larger decline in dispersion, at a time when economic reforms generally reduced barriers to capital mobility, and emerging market portfolio investment grew rapidly.

Finally, the top chart explores a second measure of coherence of stock prices across countries, based on the average correlation of annual dollar returns with that on the U.S. market, again calculated for a centered moving window of ten-year length and encompassing the largest sample possible, and where the thin line is the average for the full sample, the wide line the G7. The correlations show clear disconnects between markets during times of well know autarky such as the two world wars. Periods of high correlation also appear more recently and before 1914 (though only just before). Although the noisiness of the correlations is quite large, this much, at least, is consistent with the ∪-shape story. What isn't consistent with the story is the large spike in cross-country correlations in the 1920s and 1930s. Why should this be so, in what was an era of supposedly fairly low capital mobility?

One answer has been provided already by Eichengreen and Sachs who show that the interwar patterns may simply reflect common shocks associated with going on and off the gold standard. To follow their example, consider the 1929 to 1935 period. Countries that stayed on gold like France and Germany endured a brutal downturn in prices and output, whereas countries that devalued didn't. This has been empirically verified for wider samples such as Latin America. It is consistent with monetary explanations of recovery which build on both the debt-deflation logic of Fisher and the expected-real-interest-rate channel emphasized by Mundell, not to mention the conventional Keynesian transmission mechanism.

What did this mean for stock markets? In a world of non-neutral money, devaluers would be able to drive up Tobin's q by restoring positive investment expectations. Eichengreen and Sachs found a statistically significant correlation between the change in q and the change in the exchange rate (relative to gold parity) in a sample of nine countries from 1929 to 1935. We replicate and extend their analysis in figure. This figure shows that the correlation holds true in a wider sample of 18 countries.

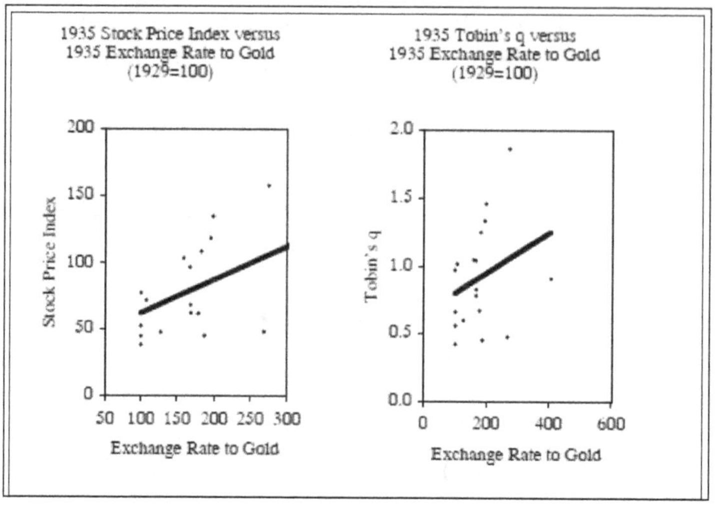

Equity Markets and the Great Depression.

These results imply that we must therefore be cautious about interpreting an increased correlation among markets as evidence of globalization per se. Instead, certain high correlations might simply be a result of common shocks among a group of countries, in this case countries experiencing, and then reacting to, the biggest single macroeconomic shock of the twentieth century. This caveat is well known. For example, a recent article in the Economist reports that in the 1990s global stock market correlations have risen to even higher levels than in the late 1980s (as high as 0.8 in year 2000, though at what frequency is not mentioned). This came after a decline in correlations in the early 1990s, but "the long term trend is upward". Overall, the topic concludes, this is consistent with increased globalization pressures, but certain large shocks, like the recent crises in Asia, might also have also been associated with higher correlations via contagion channels. As the topic notes, "stock markets tend to be more correlated at times of high volatility in share prices; during calmer periods, correlations tend to be weaker". Similar reasoning, of course, could pertain to the roaring twenties, and the bust of the thirties.

Many studies of market integration have focused on a single kind of criterion. This approach seems unreasonably restrictive to us, since the interpretation of such narrow criteria must necessarily rest upon untested auxiliary assumptions. By contrast, we see no reason to dismiss any useful information, in either price or quantity form, especially given the paucity of historical data in certain quarters. Thus, we have opted for a broad battery of tests to try to cut down the possible set of explanations that could account for the empirical record, and so, by a process of elimination, work towards a set on controlled conjectures concerning the evolution of the global capital market.

The preceding section succinctly conveys the benefits we think this kind of approach can deliver. Our quantity-based tests delivered a certain set of stylized facts, and the price-based tests another set of facts. Combining the two, and introducing evidence on convergence and divergence in other economic phenomena such as living standards and demography, we claim there is overwhelming support for the notion that the major long-run changes in the degree of global capital mobility have taken the form of changes in the impediments to capital flows, rather than any encouragement or discouragement to flows arising from structural shifts within the economies themselves. That is not to discount the fact that such changes have occurred, and are no doubt important at the margin; but it is an assertion that the virtual disappearance of foreign capital flows and stocks in mid-century, and the explosion in price differentials, can only be explained by an appeal to changes in arbitrage possibilities as permitted by two major constraining factors in capital market operations: technology and national economic policies.

From this point, it is a short step to the conclusion that a full accounting of the phenomena at hand must rest on a detailed political and institutional history. Clearly, technology is a poor candidate for the explanation of the twentieth century collapse of capital mobility. In the 1920s and 1930s, the prevailing financial technologies were not suddenly forgotten by market participants: indeed some technologies, such as futures markets for foreign exchange came to fruition in those decades. Technological evolution was not smooth and linear, but, as we have already noted, was at least unidirectional, and, absent any other impediments, would have implied an uninterrupted progress toward an ever more tightly connected global marketplace.

Such was not allowed to happen, of course. Rather, the shifting forces of national economic policies, as influenced by the prevailing economic theories of the day, loomed large during and after the watershed event of the twentieth century, the economic and political crisis of the Great Depression.

Political Economy

We have thus far amassed some evidence that international capital mobility has experienced two major swings over the course of the twentieth century: a pronounced decline during the interwar years and a recovery in the later postwar years. The timing is hard to pin down precisely, and, indeed, surely varied by country and by the type of capital movements being considered.

Taking this as given, we now must ask, why did capital mobility follow this path, and what corroborative evidence can we assemble to buttress an account of these events that incorporates the forces of political economy? We start first with the downturn in capital mobility after 1914.

The Downturn

The conventional macro-historical account of the collapse of capital mobility after 1914 focuses on the trilemma, as we have noted. The literature suggests that the major political economy forces at work during this period were increasing pressure for macroeconomic activism, particularly from newly- or better-enfranchised groups such as the working classes. If fixed exchange rates were to be maintained, then capital mobility would have to be compromised, at least on some occasions. Maintenance of capital mobility instead would preclude an exchange rate target. Either option would raise uncertainty for investors.

It is believed that prior to 1914, gold standard orthodoxy had been a sine qua non for access to global capital markets on favorable terms. A first study by Bordo and Rockoff found that adherence to gold standard rules acted as a "seal of approval" for sovereign debt. Gold standard countries had lower country risk, measured by the bond spread in London over the British consol. Accordingly, evidence of a new political dynamic after 1914 might be seen in a changing relationship between country risk and gold after the gold standard was reconstituted starting in 1925. With the rules of the game in question after World War I, investors might have doubted whether the announcement of a gold standard commitment alone would signal credibility. In addition, public solvency indicators, such as debt-GDP ratios, or inflation, might be seen as having a bigger impact on international bond spreads under the reconstituted gold standard than before. Do such doubts manifest themselves in the data?

There is no uniform and comprehensive study of bond spreads across these two eras that would allow us definitively to answer this question, but a second study by Bordo, Edelstein, and Rockoff came to a conclusion that was surprising, even by the author's own admission. Looking solely at 1920s bonds they found continued evidence that the gold standard remained a seal of approval, lowering bond spreads significantly, at least when a country stuck to its prewar parity. Devaluers were not so lucky with their bond spreads, since for them, the impact of being on gold was small and statistically insignificant. Such a conclusion challenged the conventional wisdom that the interwar gold standard was a pale and less credible shadow of its predecessor.

These are two pioneering studies but, for comparative work across regimes, they are not ideal. Unfortunately, they cannot be merged together into a consistent picture because of differences in the methods and data employed. The former study looked at long-term government bonds in the secondary market, and examined their yield to maturity; the latter examined new issues and their yield at the moment of flotation only. The former study therefore had complete time series, whereas the latter had a small sample that was often interrupted by missing data in years when no issues took place—a not uncommon event in the 1920s, and one that could raise a potential sample-selection issue. Finally, the former studied prices in London, the latter prices in New York, a switch that could be defended as the hegemonic center of global capital markets shifted across the Atlantic around this time, and one that allowed the use of Cleona Lewi's data on new issues for the 1920s.

To overcome the differences between these studies, we re-examine the question of what determined bond spreads in the pre-1914 and interwar years using a much larger database that allows us to view a consistent set of data for a larger sample of countries from 1870 to 1940. The Global Financial Data source includes yields to maturity of government bonds traded in London for this entire period, and we focus on 20 countries, some in the core and some in the periphery, to see how their country risk evolved. This allows us to focus on the same market and the same type of risk measure across both eras. To isolate the effects of default risk, our spreads over London are exclusively for bonds denominated in gold or in sterling. Figure offers an overview of the data. The mean bond spread for the core and periphery subsamples is presented in the top and bottom charts respectively, and each is surrounded by a measure of dispersion, a band equal to plus or minus two standard deviations. The units are percentage points and the scales are deliberately the same on the two charts.

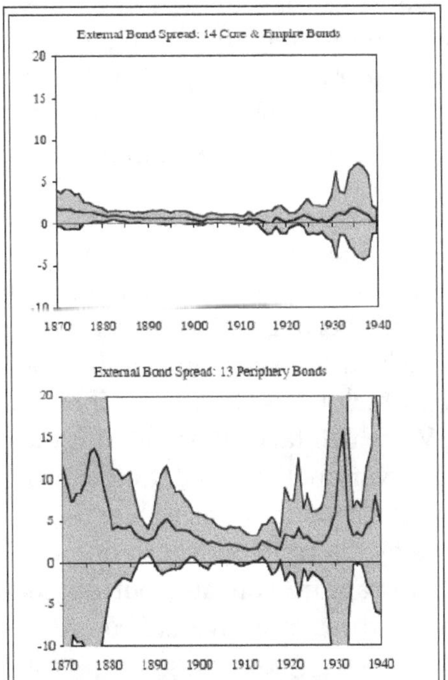

London Bond Spreads, Core and Periphery, 1870–1940.

The differences between the two subsamples are very striking: the core had much smaller country risk than the periphery, as expected. Core countries usually had interest rates within one or two percentage points of Britain's. The periphery could have spreads as large as ten percentage points, which was tantamount to having a bond in default in many cases. But the figures also show some similarities, once we normalize for this scale difference: both core and periphery experienced a convergence in bond spreads up to 1914, and then a good deal of volatility in the interwar years, when spreads widened.

The gradual convergence of bond spreads warns us that a simple static "on and off" gold indicator is unlikely to capture the full dynamics of evolving country risk in this period. Intuitively, these figures hint at high levels of persistence or serial correlation in bond spreads, and it is easy to imagine why. Bond spreads are a function of reputation, which in capital markets, as in any other repeated game, cannot be built overnight. Instead, there is a "we know what you did last summer" effect: one's reputation in the previous period is likely to have substantial explanatory power in deciding one's reputation today. Beyond this, levels of public indebtedness were relevant for at least some countries. A general concern is that macroeconomic variables correlated with gold-standard adherence might be responsible for the apparent pre-1914 benefits of going on gold, or might mask such benefits after the First World War. Before the war, countries on gold may have had more disciplined fiscal policies, lower public debt, and hence more favorable treatment by the bond markets. On the other hand, perhaps countries that inflated away their public debts in the early or mid-1920s would have been unlikely to rejoin gold at parity, making high public debts and a return to gold at prewar parity positively correlated variables. In these circumstances, omitting macro controls could lead us to overestimate the prewar benefit of gold standard adherence and underestimate the postwar benefit of returning to gold at the prewar par.

Following Bordo and Rockoff, we investigate the relationship between the dependent variable country risk, measured by the bond spread over London, $SPREAD_{it} = YIELD_{it} - YIELD_{UK,t}$, and selected macroeconomic policy variables that could play a role for country i and time t. One such variable is gold standard adherence, measured by two dummy variables: $GSPAR_{it}$, which takes the value 1 if on date t country i is on gold at the 1913 parity, and $GSDEV_{it}$, which takes the value 1 if the country is on gold at a devalued parity after 1913. Monetary policy reputation is proxied by the lagged inflation rate, $INFL_{i,t-1}$. As a final macro explanatory variable, we examine the effects of lagged public debt levels, measured by the ratio of debt to output, $PUBDGDP_{i,t-1}$. We also include country fixed effects to capture constant but unmeasured political, economic, institutional, or geographic features of individual countries (for example, location on the "periphery").

Like Bordo and Rockoff, we also find it necessary to account for global interest rate shocks that affect spreads in all markets in a given year. To do this, following the logic of the "international CAPM" model, we include (with a country specific slope, or "β") a measure of "market risk" in the form $SPREAD_{W,t} = YIELD_{WORLD,t} - YIELD_{UK,t}$, where this term is the average world spread on the "safe rate" (London) for the countries in the sample at time t.

Using pooled annual data for a large sample of countries, the basic regression equation is then of the form,

$$SPREAD_{it} = \alpha_i + \beta_i SPREAD_{W,t} + \gamma X_{it} + u_{it}$$

where,

$$X_{it} = \begin{pmatrix} GSPAR_{it} \\ GSDEV_{it} \\ PUBDGDP_{i,t-1} \\ INFL_{i,t-1} \\ PERIPHERY \times PUBDGDP_{i,t-1} \\ PERIPHERY \times INFL_{i,t-1} \end{pmatrix}$$

is the vector of explanatory variables, and PERIPHERY is a dummy variable equal to one for the periphery countries (not including regions of the British Empire) to capture the possibly different risk treatment of established versus emerging markets. The main question we ask is whether 1914 was a watershed—that is, if the interwar gold standard differed from its predecessor. Accordingly we investigate this relationship on prewar and interwar samples.

Table: Country Risk and the Gold Standard, 1870–1913.

	OLS	AR1
Number of Observations	409	396
Adjusted R squared	0.95	0.97
Mean of Dependent Variable	1.03	1.02
Standard Error of Dependent Variable	0.92	0.92
Standard Error of Estimate	0.20	0.16
Durbin-Watson Statistic	0.85	1.89
GS	-0.30 (0.06)	-0.57 (0.08)
PUBDGDP(t–1)	-0.30 (0.13)	-0.05 (0.21)
INFL(t–1)	0.88 (0.37)	0.41 (0.27)
PERIPHERY × PUBDGDP(t–1)	1.02 (0.18)	0.77 (0.29)
PERIPHERY × INFL(t–1)	-0.25 (0.44)	0.03 (0.32)
ρ	-	0.68 (0.04)

Table: Country Risk and the Gold Standard, 1925–30.

	OLS	AR1
Number of Observations	102	85
Adjusted R squared	0.84	0.93
Mean of Dependent Variable	0.84	0.81
Standard Error of Dependent Variable	1.03	1.04
Standard Error of Estimate	0.41	0.28
Durbin-Watson Statistic	2.00	2.26

GSPAR	-0.63 (0.23)	0.10 (0.24)
GSDEV	-0.01 (0.19)	-0.05 (0.21)
PUBDGDP(t–1)	4.33 (0.54)	2.16 (0.52)
INFL(t–1)	0.02 (0.07)	-0.08 (0.16)
PERIPHERY × PUBDGDP(t–1)	-4.78 (3.20)	0.96 (2.97)
PERIPHERY × INFL(t–1)	-0.97 (1.48)	0.28 (1.34)
ρ		0.30 (0.11)

In table we present our results for the pre-war and interwar periods. Since we are focusing on spreads against London, and we implicitly treat London as a benchmark of what is a safe yield under gold standard credibility, we omit all other interwar years in our sample (our bond data are end-of-year). Column 1 shows the OLS results, while column 2 adds an AR(1) correction since we find evidence of high serial correlation in column 1, at least prior to 1914.

Being on gold appears statistically significant before 1914, contributing about 57 basis points to the spread over London. But being on gold at the 1913 parity appears to be statistically insignificant, or even incorrectly signed, for the interwar years 1925–30 (in the latter period, some imprecision is to be expected because the sample is much smaller).

An interesting perspective on the role of public debt as a negative signal comes from interacting debt with dummies locating a country in the "core" or the "periphery". The contrasting results for our two sample periods lend further support to the hypothesis of a sharp change in credibility of the gold commitment. Prior to 1914, in the preferred AR(1) results, we see that it is only the peripheral countries whose public debt levels appeared to increase spreads. After an autoregressive correction to the 1870–1913 sample, the empirical spread equation indicates that a 10 percent rise in a peripheral country's ratio of debt to GDP added 7.2 basis points to its borrowing cost.

Inflation, on the other hand, is seen to have had an effect that was qualitatively small and of low statistical significance in the prewar period. The autoregressive parameter is quite high, 0.68, suggesting that during the classical gold standard period countries could rely on some reputational persistence to help them maintain credibility in the capital market. For countries in the core, then, classical gold standard adherence alone seems to have been sufficient to warrant the market "seal of approval".

It is important to note that this pattern does not hold for the interwar period. For that era, the market seems to have been more discerning in its scrutiny of all borrower's public debt and inflation data. In these samples we also find much weaker evidence of reputational persistence (as measured by the autoregressive parameter of 0.30), perhaps further evidence of the fragile credibility associated with the interwar gold standard where markets seemed to pay more attention to current behavior.

To be precise, we find no interwar evidence that the markets differentiated between core and periphery countries in evaluating the country-risk implications of rising debt burdens. In all countries, an interwar increase in public debt equivalent to 10 percentage points of GDP could raise spreads by as much as 43 basis points (in the OLS specification) or 22 basis points (in the AR(1) specification). By this measure, the sensitivity of bond spreads to debt was about five times larger after the war than before.

Inflation again shows only a small and statistically insignificant effect for core countries. On the periphery, it has the incorrect sign under the OLS specification, but this counterintuitive effect appears to be not very robust, as it is not preserved under the AR(1) correction.

These findings may help us to understand why many policymakers in the 1920s and 1930s so feared the market response to unbalanced public budgets, notwithstanding the countercyclical case for fiscal expansion. In this period, being on gold was not, in itself, enough to soothe markets.

An unusual finding in the 1925–30 results of table, is that returning to gold at a devalued parity is estimated to have a more beneficial effect than returning at prewar parity, very much contrary to the Bordo-Edelstein-Rockoff empirical result. This finding offers some support for the theoretical view of Drazen and Masson that policymakers may hurt rather than enhance their credibility through policies that appear "tough" in the short term but are too draconian to be sustained for long. The results are not conclusive, but further research is perhaps warranted on this question.

To recapitulate: unlike Bordo, Edelstein, and Rockoff, we find very different behavior of bond spreads in relation to the gold standard over the interwar period 1925–30 as compared to the pre-1914 period. This may be ascribed mainly to differences in concept (use of around secondary-market bond yields in London versus new issues in New York) and differences in macroeconomic control variables (government debt rather than deficit). Of these features in our empirical approach, the first, at least, seems necessary if we are to make comparisons on an equal footing with Bordo and Rockoff.

Before 1914, we find that the gold standard did indeed confer a "seal of approval", whereas macro fundamentals, measured by public debt and inflation, seem to have affected the spreads of peripheral more than core countries. We infer that adherence to gold by core countries was pretty much sufficient to confer credibility, whereas markets took a broader and more skeptical view of peripheral countries. For the interwar period, a return to gold after devaluation seemed slightly more credible, notwithstanding the arguments that led Britain and other countries to return to gold at par; indeed, returning at par yielded small benefits at best, and a return after devaluation (as in the case of France) might have been more beneficial. Moreover, for core and periphery countries alike, high public debts and inflation were punished, suggesting that policymaker's room for maneuver in fiscal and monetary policy was further curtailed.

Both our results on the drop in spreads associated with going on gold, and on market's differential response to public debt and inflation prewar and interwar, suggest that the interwar gold standard was indeed seen as a pale imitation, and was considered far less credible than its pre-1914 predecessor. It remains to reconcile these results with findings such as those of Hallwood, MacDonald, and Marsh that indicate a credible gold standard during the late 1920s, at least in the short term. Perhaps the bond markets adopted a longer perspective under which protracted adherence to unchanging gold parities seemed less probable than short-term adherence.

These findings on bond markets serve to illuminate how different the interwar global capital market was from its antecedent, the classical gold-standard regime of 1870–1914. An image used quite often to describe this regime change in the global economy is one of Humpty Dumpty falling to pieces, and these preliminary statistical results show cross-regime evidence on how those pieces were scattered. The findings offer persuasive evidence that the global convergence of the bond market prior to 1914, so clearly seen in the figure, had been replaced by some quite different disintegrative forces after 1914.

The Upturn

After the immediate post-World War Two dislocations, the world economy began to reconstitute its severed linkages, a process both promoting and promoted by the return of some degree of durable prosperity and peace. Postwar policy makers, through the IMF, successive multilateral trade liberalization rounds, current account currency convertibility, and other measures, successfully promoted growing world trade. By the late 1960s, the very success of these initiatives in forging trading linkages among countries simultaneously made capital flows across borders ever more difficult to contain. As a result, the trilemma re-emerged with full force, and on a global scale, in the early 1970s. The Bretton Woods system, initially designed for a world of tightly controlled capital movements, blew apart. The major industrial countries retreated to floating exchange rates.

While initially viewed as a temporary expedient, floating rates have remained a durable feature of the international financial landscape. Floating rates helped reconcile the social demand for domestic macroeconomic stabilization with the interest of the business community for open markets in goods and assets. Some episodes of exchange rate misalignment have prompted calls for renewed protection and even capital-account restrictions. Some of these calls have been accommodated, but usually not in the form of across-the-board restrictions on international transactions.

Other forces have also helped to promote liberalization. In Europe, the political and economic rationales for a large single market have prompted ongoing financial liberalization; at the same time, the political (and, some argue, economic) imperative of stable exchange rates has pushed toward the logical conclusion of a single currency, the euro.

Other regions, likewise, have opted for fixed exchange rates, either by some form of ultra-hard peg or outright dollarization, in either case bending to the trilemma by giving up monetary policy autonomy.

Since the late 1980s, the drive toward capital-account liberalization in the developing world is probably the most striking pattern in the evolution of global capital markets. Clearly one element has been the widespread failure in the periphery of populist policies adopted in the 1980s and earlier. Reactions to those failures gave free-market ideologies a greater influence. On a larger scale, the collapse of the Soviet empire in the late 1980s also highlighted the advantages of the capitalist model. The resulting decline in Cold War tensions certainly held out the promise of greater fluidity in private international capital. Whether exchange rates float or are fixed, there is much greater openness to private financial flows on the periphery than in the 1980s. In part a reflection of U.S. business interests, American administrations have pushed developing economies to liberalize on capital account; in some cases, liberalization ran far ahead of domestic financial system's absorptive capacities, and clashed with national exchange rate policies. The resulting contradictions helped spark the developing country currency crises of the latter 1990s. To attract productive capital from the industrial world remains a prime goal on the periphery, however, and that requires market-oriented reforms, stable macro policies, and transparency in governance and legal systems.

There is, however, one critical dimension in which pre-1914 international capital flows differ sharply in nature from what we see today, with important implications for the periphery: to see this we return to the distinction between net and gross international asset stocks. A cursory glance at the data reveals that this problem is very serious in recent decades, but relatively unimportant in the pre1914 era of globalization. The reason is simple: in the late nineteenth century the principal flows were long-term investment capital, and virtually unidirectional at that. There was one notable exception, the United States, where both inflows and outflows were large. But in most cases key creditor nations, principally Britain, but also France and Germany, engaged in the financing of other countrie's capital accumulation, and in doing so, developed enormous one-way positions in their portfolios.

For example, circa 1914 the scale of Argentine assets in Britain's portfolio was very large, but the converse holding of British assets by Argentines was trivial by comparison. Thus, the nineteenth century was an era of one-way asset shifts, leading to great portfolio diversification by the principal creditor/outflow nations like Britain, but relatively little diversification by the debtor/inflow nations. To a first approximation, the gross asset and liability positions were very close to net in that distant era. The 1980s and 1990s are obviously very different: for example, the United States became in this period the world's largest net debtor nation. But whilst accounting for the biggest national stock of gross foreign liabilities, the United States also held the largest stock of gross foreign assets.

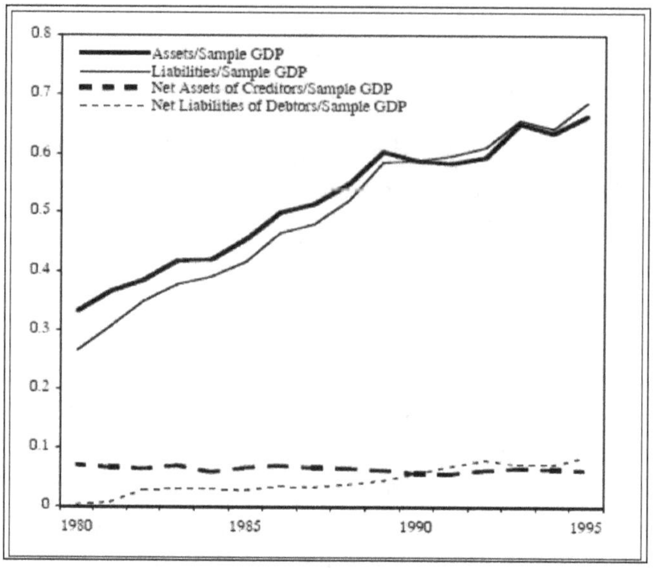

Foreign Capital Stocks: Net versus Gross.

Our earlier discussion of the gross stock data, and our inferences concerning the recovery of foreign asset and liabilities in the world economy after 1980, therefore need considerable modification to take into account this problem. And, indeed, it is a significant problem for all of the countries concerned: the rank of countries by foreign assets in the IMF data is very highly correlated with the rank by foreign liabilities. Countries such as Britain, Japan, Canada, Germany, and the Netherlands are all big holders of both foreign assets and liabilities. Strikingly, when we net out the data, the result is that, since 1980, the net foreign asset position (or liability) positions in the world economy have remained very low indeed, as indicated by figure above unlike the gross stocks, the net stocks have increased little, and if we trust the asset data rather more (arguably more of the net asset data are collected in developing countries with better accounting methods) then the picture is one of relative decline in the size of net foreign capital stocks relative to GDP.

Thus, for all the suggestion that we have returned to the pre-1914 type of global capital market, here is one major qualitative difference between then and now. Today's foreign asset distribution is much more about asset "swapping" by rich countries—diversification—than it is about the accumulation of large one-way positions—a critical component of the development process in poorer countries in standard textbook treatments. It is therefore more about hedging and risk sharing than it is about long-term finance and the mediation of saving supply and investment demand between countries. In the latter sense, we have never come close to recapturing the heady times of the pre-1914 era, when a creditor like Britain could persist for years in satisfying half of its accumulation of assets with foreign capital, or a debtor like Argentina could similarly go on for years generating liabilities of which one half were taken up by foreigners. Instead, still to a very great extent today, a country's net wealth will depend, for accumulation, on the provision of financing from domestic rather than foreign sources. An interesting, and closely related, insight also follows from looking at the share of less-developed countries (LDCs) in global liabilities. This is now at an all- time low. In 1900, LDCs in Asia, Latin America, and Africa accounted for 33 percent of global liabilities, in the 1990s only 11 percent. The global capital market of the nineteenth century centered on Europe, especially London, extended relatively more credit to LDCs than does today's global capital market. Is this surprising? There are various interpretations for this observation. One is that capital markets are biased now, or were biased in the past; for example, did Britain, as an imperial power, favor LDCs within her orbit with finance? or, today, does the global capital market fail in the sense that there are insufficient capital flows to LDCs, and an excess of flows among developed countries? These are hard claims to prove, as market failure could be a cause, as could a host of other factors including institutions and policies affecting the marginal product of capital in different locations. Of course, this result just follows from the fact that many of the top asset holders also figure in the top liability holders, and most of them are developed OECD countries.

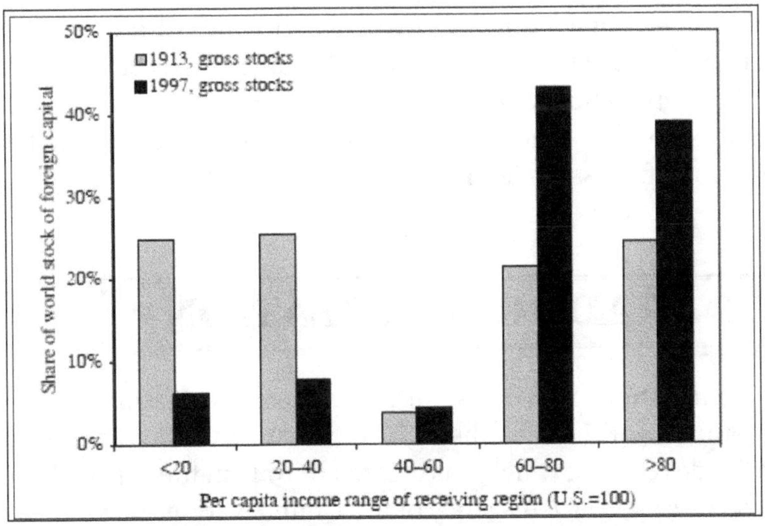

Did Capital Flow to Poor Countries? 1913 Versus 1997.

Figure illustrates the periphery's need to draw on industrial country savings, as well as an important dimension in which the globalization of capital markets remains behind the level attained under the classical gold standard. In the last great era of globalization, the most striking characteristic is that foreign capital was distributed bimodally; it moved to both rich and poor countries, with relatively little in the middle. Receiving regions included both colonies and independent regions. The rich countries were the settler economies where capital was attracted by abundant land, and the poor countries were places where capital was attracted by abundant labor.

Globalized capital markets are back, but with a difference: capital transactions seem to be mostly a rich-rich affair, a process of "diversification finance" rather than "development finance". The creditor-debtor country pairs involved are more rich-rich than rich-poor, and today's foreign investment in the poorest developing countries lags far behind the levels attained at the start of the last century. In other words, we see again the paradox noted by Lucas, of capital failing to flow to capital-poor countries, places where we would presume the marginal product of capital to be very high. And the figure may understate the failure in some ways: a century ago world income and productivity levels were far less divergent than they are today, so it is all the more remarkable that so much capital was directed to countries at or below the 20 percent and 40 percent income levels (relative to the U.S).. Today, a much larger fraction of the world's output and population is located in such low productivity regions, but a much smaller share of global foreign investment reaches them.

As we have noted, capital is discouraged from entering poorer countries by a host of factors, and some of these were less relevant a century ago. Capital controls persist in many regions. The risks of investment may be perceived differently after a century of exchange risks, expropriations, and defaults. Domestic policies that distort prices, especially of investment goods, may result in returns too low to attract any capital. These conditions make a difficult situation much worse. Poorer countries must draw on foreign capital to a greater extent than they do at present if they are to achieve an acceptable growth in living standards. That is a fundamental reason why reform and liberalization in the developing world, despite the setbacks of the late 1990s, are likely to continue, albeit hopefully with due regard to the painful lessons learned in the recent past.

WORLD TRADE ORGANIZATION

World Trade Organization (WTO) is an international organization established to to supervise and liberalize world trade. The WTO is the successor to the General Agreement on Tariffs and Trade (GATT), which was created in 1947 in the expectation that it would soon be replaced by a specialized agency of the United Nations (UN) to be called the International Trade Organization (ITO). Although the ITO never materialized, the GATT proved remarkably successful in liberalizing world trade over the next five decades. By the late 1980s there were calls for a stronger multilateral organization to monitor trade and resolve trade disputes. Following the completion of the Uruguay Round of multilateral trade negotiations, the WTO began operations on January 1, 1995.

The ITO was initially envisaged, along with the International Monetary Fund (IMF) and the World Bank, as one of the key pillars of post-World War II reconstruction and economic development. In Havana in 1948, the UN Conference on Trade and Employment concluded a draft charter for the ITO, known as the Havana Charter, which would have created extensive rules governing trade, investment, services, and business and employment practices. However, the United States failed to ratify the agreement. Meanwhile, an agreement to phase out the use of import quotas and to reduce tariffs on merchandise trade, negotiated by 23 countries in Geneva in 1947, came into force as the GATT on January 1, 1948.

Although the GATT was expected to be provisional, it was the only major agreement governing international trade until the creation of the WTO. The GATT system evolved over 47 years to become a de facto global trade organization that eventually involved approximately 130 countries. Through various negotiating rounds, the GATT was extended or modified by numerous supplementary codes and arrangements, interpretations, waivers, reports by dispute-settlement panels, and decisions of its council.

During negotiations ending in 1994, the original GATT and all changes to it introduced prior to the Uruguay Round were renamed GATT 1947. This set of agreements was distinguished from GATT 1994, which comprises the modifications and clarifications negotiated during the Uruguay Round (referred to as "Understandings") plus a dozen other multilateral agreements on merchandise trade. GATT 1994 became an integral part of the agreement that established the WTO. Other core components include the General Agreement on Trade in Services (GATS), which attempted to supervise and liberalize trade; the Agreement on Trade-Related Aspects of Intellectual Property Rights (TRIPS), which sought to improve protection of intellectual property across borders; the Understanding on Rules and Procedures Governing the Settlement of Disputes, which established rules for resolving conflicts between members; the Trade Policy Review Mechanism, which documented national trade policies and assessed their conformity with WTO rules; and four plurilateral agreements, signed by only a subset of the WTO membership, on civil aircraft, government procurement, dairy products, and bovine meat (though the latter two were terminated at the end of 1997 with the creation of related WTO committees). These agreements were signed in Marrakech, Morocco, in April 1994, and, following their ratification, the contracting parties to the GATT treaty became charter members of the WTO. By the 2010s the WTO had more than 160 members.

Objectives and Operation

The WTO has six key objectives: (1) to set and enforce rules for international trade, (2) to provide a forum for negotiating and monitoring further trade liberalization, (3) to resolve trade disputes, (4) to increase the transparency of decision-making processes, (5) to cooperate with other major international economic institutions involved in global economic management, and (6) to help developing countries benefit fully from the global trading system. Although shared by the GATT, in practice these goals have been pursued more comprehensively by the WTO. For example, whereas the GATT focused almost exclusively on goods—though much of agriculture and textiles were excluded—the WTO encompasses all goods, services, and intellectual property, as well as some investment policies. In addition, the permanent WTO Secretariat, which replaced the interim GATT Secretariat, has strengthened and formalized mechanisms for reviewing trade policies and settling disputes. Because many more products are covered under the WTO than under the GATT and because the number of member countries and the extent of their participation has grown steadily—the combined share of international trade of WTO members now exceeds 90 percent of the global total—open access to markets has increased substantially.

The rules embodied in both the GATT and the WTO serve at least three purposes. First, they attempt to protect the interests of small and weak countries against discriminatory trade practices of large and powerful countries. The WTO's most-favoured-nation and national-treatment articles stipulate that each WTO member must grant equal market access to all other members and that both domestic and foreign suppliers must be treated equally. Second, the rules require members to limit trade only through tariffs and to provide market access not less favourable than that specified in their schedules (i.e., the commitments that they agreed to when they were granted WTO membership or subsequently). Third, the rules are designed to help governments resist lobbying efforts by domestic interest groups seeking special favours. Although some exceptions to the rules have been made, their presence and replication in the core WTO agreements were intended to ensure that the worst excesses would be avoided. By thus bringing greater certainty and predictability to international markets, it was thought, the WTO would enhance economic welfare and reduce political tensions.

Resolution of Trade Disputes

The GATT provided an avenue for resolving trade disputes, a role that was strengthened substantially under the WTO. Members are committed not to take unilateral action against other members. Instead, they are expected to seek recourse through the WTO's dispute-settlement system and to abide by its rules and findings. The procedures for dispute resolution under the GATT have been automated and greatly streamlined, and the timetable has been tightened.

Dispute resolution begins with bilateral consultations through the mediation, or "good offices", of the director-general. If this fails, an independent panel is created to hear the dispute. The panel submits a private draft report to the parties for comment, after which it may revise the report before releasing it to the full WTO membership. Unlike the IMF and the World Bank, both of which use weighted voting, each WTO member has only one vote. As in the earlier GATT system, however, most decisions are made by consensus. Unless one or both of the parties files a notice of appeal or the WTO members reject the report, it is automatically adopted and legally binding after 60 days. The process is supposed to be completed within nine months, and, if an appeal is lodged, the WTO Appellate Body hears and rules on any claim of legal error within 60 days. Appellate rulings are automatically adopted unless a consensus exists among members against doing so.

Assessment

The pace of international economic integration via the GATT and WTO rounds of multilateral trade negotiations has been slower and less comprehensive than some members would prefer. Some have suggested that there should be additional integration among subgroups of (often neighbouring) member economies—e.g., those party to the European Union, the North American Free Trade Agreement, and the Asia-Pacific Economic Cooperation—for political, military, or other reasons. Notwithstanding the most-favoured-nation clauses in the agreements establishing the WTO, the organization does allow such preferential integration under certain conditions. Even though many such integration agreements arguably do not involve "substantially all trade"—the WTO's main condition—there has been little conflict over the formation of free-trade areas and customs unions. The most common omissions from such agreements are politically sensitive sectors such as agriculture.

Beginning in the late 1990s, the WTO was the target of fierce criticism. Opponents of globalization, and in particular those opposed to the growing power of multinational corporations, argued that the WTO infringes upon national sovereignty and promotes the interests of large corporations at the expense of smaller local firms struggling to cope with import competition. Environmental and labour groups (especially those from wealthier countries) have claimed that trade liberalization leads to environmental damage and harms the interests of low-skilled unionized workers. Protests by these and other groups at WTO ministerial meetings—such as the 1999 demonstrations in Seattle, Washington, U.S., which involved approximately 50,000 people—became larger and more frequent, in part because the development of the Internet and social media made large-scale organizing and collective action easier. In response to such criticism, supporters of the WTO claimed that regulating trade is not an efficient way to protect the environment and labour rights. Meanwhile, some WTO members, especially developing countries, resisted attempts to adopt rules that would allow for sanctions against countries that failed to meet strict environmental and labour standards, arguing that they would amount to veiled protectionism.

Despite these criticisms, however, WTO admission remained attractive for nonmembers, as evidenced by the increase in the number of members after 1995. Most significantly, China entered the WTO in 2001 after years of accession negotiations. The conditions for Chinese membership were in some ways more restrictive than those for developing countries, reflecting the concerns of some WTO members that the admission of such a large and still somewhat planned economy might have an overall negative effect on free trade.

FOREIGN DIRECT INVESTMENT FROM EMERGING ECONOMIES

In the last decade, and beginning of the 21th century, one of the most notorious features of the new trends toward globalization has been the increased participation of developing economies in the world economy. This relative importance is not only related to their position in the world trade, but also, in terms of the surge of new competitive companies operating worldwide, in different forms; sale subsidiaries, production subsidiaries, with Greenfield FDI and acquiring high competitive firms in developed and developing countries. This process of internationalization has been qualified as the genesis of Multinational Companies from developing countries, or from emerging countries (EMNCs). Even though, the growth of such global activities is mostly observed in large countries, with high level of economic growth and higher participation in the world trade (BRICs countries), MNCs have also emerged in other developing countries around the world, in Asia, Latin America, and also in Africa.

On the last two decades, the Foreign Direct Investment outflows (OFDI) from such economies grew at a higher year average than those from developed economies, and their outward stock reached more than 15% of the world FDI outward stock, compared with a performance of less than 10% in the 1990s. Several studies have pointed out that this growing performance should continue on the coming years. Cheaper access to capital, successful business model and sizeable assets will lead Multinational Companies from developing countries (EMNCs) to challenge even more some traditional firms from developed economies. Recent financial performance enhanced the FDI stocks level of EMNCs and turned them less dependent upon banking loans to finance their foreign investments projects, and the stocks and assets depreciation of firms in developed countries due to the global crisis may have contributed significantly to increase the participation of EMNCs in the world FDI stock through new acquisitions.

Several studies have been discussing patterns and determinants of EMNCs international FDI performance. It is argued that they do not hold the same property structure as those from well developed countries, which means that factors related to the country of origin might influence significantly the international competitiveness of firms. Cuervo-Cazurra classified the MNCs from developing countries as those that seek on developing ownership advantages abroad and those that aim on exploring abroad the advantages acquired in their domestic market. Those firms that desire to develop new capabilities abroad should choose to establish a foreign subsidiary on developed economies, if they seek access to higher technology, or on developing economies, if they aim on obtaining access to a country's abundant resources.

In this context, in which OFDI from developing countries is increasing rapidly, some few questions become relevant. First, in which extend the theoretical models in International Business explain the genesis and patterns of EMNCs? And, what are the determinants of OFDI from developing countries? What is the role of the home country, and in which extend, factors related to the host country explain patterns and strategies of EMNCs?

Evolution and Patterns of FDI: The Role of Developing Economies

In a historical perspective, the expansion of FDI can be observed in the early 1980s, particularly flows from developed to other developed countries. Between 1990 and

1995, FDI flows expanded at an average rate of 16.8%, while the export of goods and services registered a growth rate of 8%, and world GDP growth only 6%.

It was a trend toward a growing role of MNCs compared with the after Second World War, where the export has been the driver of economic activities, growing on a higher rate than the world output. This process of increased world FDI outflows covered all the period of the 1990s, until 2008, the year as the global financial crisis brook up worldwide, affecting all the developed countries, and partly emerging economies.

The period from 1990 to 2008 represented a long cycle of world FDI outflows, which has contributed to a significant expansion of the total assets and exports of foreign affiliates of MNCs. Furthermore, in the beginning of the 1990s, the world outward stock of FDI was US$ 2,087 billion, and reached in 2009 the amount of US$ 18,982 billion, growing more than 900% in nominal values. As a consequence of this fast growing performance of MNCs activities abroad, the ratio between outward stock of FDI and world GDP rose sharply, from 9% in 1990 to 35% in 2009, sitting up a tendency toward deep interdependencies among economies, and where the MNCs are the main agents of changes and growth in the world economy.

However, the global financial crisis has significantly affected the foreign activities of MNCs abroad. The outflows of FDI decreased in 2008 and 2009, and have been more sensitive to the crisis effects than world GDP and world trade of goods and services, which have registered negative performances, in 2009, of 9.5% and 21.4% respectively, while the FDI outflows decreased at 42.9%.

What are the reasons for the upsurge of FDI in the early 1990s, and what explains the long cycle of worldwide expansion of MNCs activities abroad during all the period from 1990 until 2008? A variety of factors have contributed to the fast acceleration of the activities of MNCs abroad and the long cycle of their expansion.

Some of the factors are related to the own changing driven by the globalization process. Others are, more specifically, related to the specific actions of the states to promote FDI inflows and the consequent changing in the different FDI policies in developing and transition economies.

On the other hand, besides the globalization has been a phenomenon of growing performance of MNCs from developed countries, since middle 1990s, the data of world FDI outflows showed also a growth of the activities of firms from developing countries abroad, which have changed significantly the regional distribution of world FDI, and the surge of new countries in Asia and Latin America as the source countries of FDI. This phenomenon was called as the genesis of emerging MNCs, to differentiate them from the traditional model of internationalization of firms from developed countries, and represents one of the major characteristics of the new phase of globalization.

What are the main countries of origin of FDI from developing countries? How relevant are their participation in the world FDI outflows and stocks? And what are the main strategies of MNCs from developing countries? And, finally, what are the determinants of outward FDI from developing countries?

Growth and Patterns of Outward FDI from Developing Countries

The growing internationalization of firms from developing countries can be described as a major characteristic in the current world economic scenario. On the last two decades, the Foreign Direct Investment outflows (OFDI) from such economies grew at a higher year average than those from developed economies, and their outward stock reached more than 15% of the world FDI outward stock, compared with a performance of less than 10% in the 1990s, according to Unctad. In terms of their participation in the world outflows of FDI, developing economies have registered a significant performance in the last 15 years. From a participation of 14% in 1995, MNCs from developing economies reached a performance of 21% in 2009, which represents a value amount of US$ 229.2 billion., as can be shown in the table below:

	1995	1996	1997	1998	1999	2000	2007	2008	2009
World	355.3	391.6	466	711.9	1005.8	1149.9	2267.5	1928.8	1100.9
Developed economies (DE)	305.8	332.9	396.9	672	945.7	1046.3	1923.9	1571.9	820.7
Developing economies (DgE)	49	57.6	65.7	37.7	58	99.5	292.1	296.3	229.2
Share of DE in world FDI	86%	85%	85%	94%	94%	91%	85%	81%	75%
Share of DgE in world FDI	14%	15%	14%	5%	6%	9%	13%	15%	21%

Most part of the FDI stock from developing countries, over 70%, is originated from Asia, especially from China and some few emerging Asian Countries. Latin America is in the second position, with 24% of the total FDI stocks from developing countries, being Brazil, Mexico, Chile the main origin countries. Africa's outward FDI stock represent 4% from the developing countries total, and South Africa alone is the major FDI source within the continent, as can be shown in the table below:

	1990	2000	2009
World	2086818	7967460	18982118
Developed Economies	1941646	7083493	16010825
Share of DE in Total stock	93%	89%	84%
Developing Economies	145172	862628	2691484
Share of DgE in Total stock	7%	11%	14%
Africa	19826	44147	102165
Share of Africa among DgE	14%	5%	4%
Latin America and The Caribbean	57643	204430	643281
Share of Latin America	40%	24%	24%

Asia and Oceania	67703	614051	1946038
Share of Asia and Oceania	47%	71%	72%
South East Europe and the CIS		21340	279808
Share of East Europe		0%	1%

In terms of the countries of origin, FDI outflows from developing countries are highly concentrated. The ten largest countries of origin of FDI are responsible for over 70% of the total amount of OFDI from all developing countries, being seven of the ten are from Asia. Hong Kong and China are in the first two positions, Brazil on the 5th position, and South Africa and Mexico are at the end of the list of ten.

The increase role of MNCs from developing countries is particularly due to the high growth of the internationalization of firms from Asia, mostly from China and India, but also from Russia, and some few Latin American countries, Brazil and Mexico. Thus, the shift in the dynamic of the world OFDI is also reflected in the changes in the MNCs landscape. When in 1992, only 8% of MNCs were headquartered in developing countries, in 2008 they were 28% of a total of 82,000 MNCs worldwide. The shift in the pattern of international production is not only reflected in the growing number of MNCs from developing countries, but also in their participation in the foreign assets and sales of the top 5,000 MNCs worldwide. According to the Unctad, MNCs from developing economies accounted in 2008 for nearly 10% of the foreign sales, and 8% of foreign assets of the top MNCs in the world. One of the indicators to measure the degree of internationalization and importance of international transactions in the global activities of a firm is from UNCTAD developed index, called Transnationality Index (TNI), which is calculated considering the average of three ratios: foreign assets to total assets, foreign sales to total sales and foreign employment to total employment of a firm.

	1990	2000	2009
Total Developing Economies (DgE)	145172	862628	2691484
Hong Kong	11920	388380	834089
China	4455	27768	229600
Singapore	7808	56755	213110
Taiwan	30356	66655	181008
Brazil	41044	51946	157667
Korea, Republic of	2301	26833	115620
India	124	1733	77207
Malaysia	753	15878	75618
South Africa	15004	32325	64309
Mexico	2672	8273	53458
Total top Tem	116437	676546	2001686
Share of Top Tem	80%	78%	74%

Variables	100 largest TNCs worldwide			100 largest TNCs from Developing and Transition Economies		
	2007	2008	% Change	2007	2008	% Change
Assets						
Foreign	6116	6172	0,9	808	907	12,3
Total	10702	10760	0,9	2311	2680	16
Foreign as % of total	57	57	0,2	35	34	-1.1
Sales						
Foreign	4936	5173	4,8	805	997	23,9
Total	8078	8354	3,4	1699	2240	31,8
Foreign as % of total	61	62	0,8	47	45	-2.9
Employment						
Foreign	8440	8905	5,5	2648	2652	0,2
Total	14870	15408	3,6	6366	6779	6,5
Foreign as % of total	57	58	1	42	39	-2.5

Although the data show a real increase of the international transactions of EMNCs, their TNI is still lower than the index of MNCs from developed countries, as can be observed in the table below. Comparing the foreign sales, foreign assets, and foreign employment in the total of the 100 largest MNCs in developed and developing countries, EMNCs have a lower TNI, and have been more sensitive to the effects of the global crisis, reducing their international transactions between 2007 and 2008, in the meanwhile MNCs from developed countries have registered a positive variation, and, therefore, increased their foreign assets, foreign employment and foreign sales of their subsidiaries worldwide. On the other hand, considering the period before the global crisis, EMNCs have improved the TNI, increasing their international transaction and their share in the total assets and sales.

	100 largest TNCs from Developing and Transition Economies				
Variables	2005	2006	2007	2008	% Change
Assets					
Foreign	471	571	808	907	92.63
Total	1441	1694	2311	2680	86.0
Foreign as % of total	33	34	35	34	3.0
Sales					
Foreign	477	605	805	997	109.0
Total	1102	1304	1699	2240	103.3
Foreign as % of total	43	46	47	45	4.7
Employment					
Foreign	1920	2151	2648	2652	38.1

Total	4884	5246	6366	6779	38.8
Foreign as % of total	39	41	42	39	0

However, in the total average, the TNI of MNCs from developed economies lies by 63.4, while by developing countries the index is around 50, according to Unctad, suggesting a still limited and geographically oriented global expansion of EMNCs. However, there are differences among developing countries. In Latin America, the TNI is 42.5, and in South Asia is 57.8, showing a higher engagement of Asian MNCs in the global economy in comparison with other home region.

Economic Approach of MNC

Since the beginning of the literature about MNCs, a strong economic focus was adopted to explain how firms place their assets abroad. Hymer considers onerous to operate in foreign market, so the firm should own competitive advantages to be exploited over market imperfections. On the other hand, Vernon believes that foreign markets are an opportunity to extend a product's life cycle by reproducing abroad the same methods applied in the home market, implying on minimal marginal costs and enhancing a product's profitability. Williamson focused his analysis on comparing the costs of trading a product with foreign markets and producing this same product abroad in order to evaluate which modality would imply on lower costs, being, this way, more attractive to the firm. Buckley and Casson determined that the company would perform FDI according to two kinds of advantages: ownership advantages and localization advantages. This concept was later developed by Dunning on his Eclectic Paradigm, culminating on the Investment Development Path - IDP.

The Eclectic Paradigm, also known as the OLI Theory, is the result of an attempt made by John Dunning to integrate in one single model the several different scopes contained in the International Business literature in order to explain the why, where and how of the international expansion of firms. For two decades the model remained the dominant analytical basis of most of empirical studies about determinants of FDI. The principal hypothesis on which the eclectic paradigm of international production is predicated is that the level and structure of a firm´s foreign value-adding activities will depend on four conditions being satisfied: these are:

- The extent to which it posses unique and sustainable ownership-specific (O) advantages vis-à-vis firms of other nationalities, in the servicing of particular markets or groups of markets. The ownership advantages are inherent to the company and crucial to the internationalization, because they are a matter of differentiation among firms, they are related to the intangible assets and the position conquered by the firm, such as innovation capacity, qualified labor and financial status that allows it to compete in foreign markets.
- The extent to which the enterprises perceives it to be in its interest to add to its O advantages rather than to sell them, or their right of use, to independent foreign firms. These advantages are called market internalisation (I) advantages.

The internalization advantages come from the benefits of the firm to use its own assets to produce abroad its products instead of allowing others to produce or distribute them, which might contribute to reducing exchange costs, information property, uncertainty diminish, and more control over supply, markets, contracts and business. In other words, internalization advantages are the outcome between the mix of ownership and location advantages.

- The extent to which the global interests of the enterprises are served by creating, accessing or utilising, its O advantages in a foreign location. The location advantages are host-market specific aspects that turn such location positive for the firm to settle a production plant in it, especially regarding transportation, access to labor force, cultural barriers and market potential.
- Given the configuration of the ownership, location and internalisation (OLI) advantages facing a particular firm, the extent to which a firm believes that foreign production is consistent with the long term objectives of its stakeholders and institutions underpinning its managerial and organizational strategy.

Based on the four sets of advantages, Dunning also suggested, based on the motivation of MNCs, four different types of FDI projects: the market-seeking projects, the performance seeking projects, the resource-seeking projects and the asset-seeking projects.

Later on, a complementary model to the Eclectic Paradigm was developed, which is the IDP model, relating the development level of an economy to the propensity of local firms to do business abroad, being the assumptions from the IDP model closely related to the basic concepts from the Eclectic Paradigm, given that this relationship between the development level and the firm's propensity to internationalize themselves will be based on extent of ownership advantages held by these firms, the location advantages offered by their home markets and the presence of transaction advantages arising from the commercial benefits of intra-company transactions.

The IDP model determines that there are five different development levels among countries, where they let being only a FDI destination to perform FDI as they progress to these levels. Stage 1 is related to countries with limited location advantages to attract FDI, so the role of governmental measures is important to turn the economy attractive to foreign investors. Markets on Stage 2 have a larger extent of location advantages, which turn them an attractive destination of FDI. The stage three describes the development of this process and shows that the enlargement of the activities of foreign firms in the host country will contribute, through spillover effects and technology transfer, to create and increments the ownership advantages by local firms, turning them more prone to perform FDI, especially on less-developed markets. On Stage 4, firms from the home market stop being predominantly FDI receivers to be investors, and when they achieve the final level, Stage 5, their strategies will be more influenced according to their own resources and capabilities and less by governmental measures.

In this perspective, foreign MNCs have a determinant role on the IDP model, given that these firms, by owning advanced resources, generate benefit through spillover effects in the host market, such as training local professionals and developing already-existing technology in developing countries. This process contributed largely to stimulate the creation and expansion of MNC from developing countries.

Determinants of OFDI from Emerging Economies: Proposition of a Framework

An analysis of the International Business literature shows that due to the complexity of the phenomena of Multinational Companies from developing economies, scholars have been using more eclectic approaches to investigate the process of internationalization of firms from countries of different levels of development. However, although some authors have suggested new theories of EMNCs, it seems that the eclectic paradigm is still a powerful framework for a multi-perspective approach, that take under account factors related to country and firm advantages. Thus, the OLI paradigm provides a general theoretical framework for the understanding of the FDI determinants from emerging economies. The main advantages of the framework lie in the fact that it allows to integrate two main analytical dimensions; the dimension that focuses on the country specific advantages (CSA), and the dimension that considers the firm-specific advantages (FSA). Rugman has emphasized the importance of the two dimensions and their interaction for the analysis of MNCs strategies. CSA can be listed under the Dunning's sub-paradigm of localization advantages, while FSA can be listed under the Ownership Advantage's sub-paradigm.

Therefore, in the case of emerging economies, there are different and specific reasons for the successful internationalization of their firms. Different authors have investigated the differences in the path and pattern between EMNCs and MNCs from developed countries, suggesting a higher level of complexity, and a need for a more multi-approach to analyze their strategies and determinants.

The CSA are related to the location advantages and how they contribute to international competitiveness of firms. Although the CSA can be related to the L-advantages, the concept is however different. While the L-Advantage in the Dunning's framework is related to the extent to which the global interests of the enterprises are served by creating, accessing or utilising, its "O" advantages in a foreign location, the CSA concept will consider a double perspective of advantages or disadvantages, mainly the home market and the host market perspectives. The Home Location advantages are home-market specific assets that turn such location positive for the firm to create, or to enlarge its ownership advantages, especially, regarding factor endowments, economic performance and institutional quality.

The host-location advantages are host-market specific aspects that turn such location positive for the firm to settle a production plant in it, especially regarding transportation, access to labor force, cultural barriers and market potential, but also technology access and network's relationships.

Thus, the country specific advantages (CSA) are related to home and host country factors. It means that to understand the patterns and determinants of OFDI it is recommended to take under account, in large scale, the economic and institutional changes in the home country, that shape the strategy of growth and competitiveness of the firm on global level.

On the other hand, to address FDI determinants, o host county perspective is also relevant, in that sense that the changes and the configuration of market and competition affect the strategy of the firm in the host country. The host country perspective provides relevant insights for the understanding of how the MNC adapt, adjust and manage the cultural, economic and institutional differences between home and host country.

The Firm Specific Advantages (FSA) describe in which extent the firm posses unique and sustainable ownership-specific (O) advantages vis-à-vis firms of other nationalities, in the servicing of particular markets or groups of markets. Thus, FSA are inherent to the company and crucial to the internationalization, because they are a matter of differentiation among firms, they are related to the intangible assets and the position conquered by the firm, such as innovation capacity, qualified labor and financial status that allows it to compete in foreign markets.

A MNC from an emerging country, with a short period of experience of internationalization and limited ownership advantages will be influenced more likely by psychic distance factors when internationalizing into new markets.

MNCs from developed countries, with specific ownership advantages, legitimacy that is related to the advantages of the home market, high accumulated knowledge about processes of entering into foreign markets, and inserted in networks relationships worldwide will reduce the costs and disadvantages related to the liability of foreignness. Therefore, firms with large ownership advantages and high ability to develop systematic learning's processes will be more likely to manage their internationalization on a global level, adapting their strategies to the host market structures, and to the opportunities of strategic alliances with local and global partners.

On the other hand, EMNC, with a short period of experience of internationalization and limited ownership advantages will be influenced more likely by psychic distance factors when internationalizing into new markets. In this case, due to their limited technological and managerial capabilities, EMNCs are more likely to face higher costs to manage the LOF in culturally distant market, or in not stable institutional environments, which may concentrate their investment projects in regionally or culturally closed host countries.

MNCs from advanced economies, due to their international experiences, accumulated knowledge about foreign markets, and learning abilities, are better than EMNCs at coping with weak institutional environments.

The internationalization of the firm will depend, not only on the interaction between ownership, location and internalization advantages, as discussed in the eclectic paradigm, but also including variables from the institutional approach. It means that introducing factors related to the institutional environment, in which firms operate and develop their resources and capabilities, may contribute to explain how location and ownership advantages interact; creating the conditions to overcome the disadvantages to be acting in a foreign market.

In this context, gainfully exploiting their firm-specific assets through the process of internalization, taking advantage of the location, and government's role in influencing international business patterns as well as access to some relevant institutional infrastructures will combine to produce different behaviors and internationalization´s patterns. We, therefore, suggest that, the way how the variables interact and how they affect the internationalization´s patterns of firms are different in the case of MNCs from emerging economies.

Company from an emerging country, by learning to operate in an unstable institutional environment may acquire a competitive advantage that makes the firm to have a sort of ability in working in such environments, when firms from developed countries, have more difficulties to operate in them. However, due to accumulated knowledge in foreign markets, and business experiences in different cultural environments may provide the MNC from advanced economies a better advantage to manage their value-added activities in countries presenting weak institutional arrangements; this is a way to overcome the liability of foreignness.

A company from an emerging country, however, with reduced ownership advantages, and limited experiences and knowledge in international management presents a reduced capability to cope with low institutional environment, particularly in culturally distant countries. Emerging countries are not homogeneous, not culturally, and less then in terms of their institutional makeup. While MNCs from developed economies follow Multiple FDI strategies, on global level, EMNCs are more likely to invest abroad following a market-seeking and resource seeking strategies.

Firms with large ownership advantages and high ability to develop knowledge will be more likely to manage their internationalization on a global level, adapting their strategies to the host market structures, and to the opportunities of strategic alliances with local and global partners.

A MNC may enter other foreign markets (developed or developing) for different reasons: exploring host market opportunities for growth (market-seeking), seeking for strategic assets such as taking advantage of R&D centers or acquiring or merging with resourceful business companies (strategic-asset seeking), and to exploit its ownership advantages (e.g. intangible assets such as brand names and proprietary technology). The latter strategy, for example, will mean that a MNC will be looking for complementary assets abroad to enlarge its ownership advantages.

MNCs from developed economies are more prompt to develop different strategies in the same host market, which mean that they will be implementing different investment programs, according to the changes of the economic and institutional environments, and to the relationships to their network and market partners. The differences in the strategy development abilities are, therefore, related to their abilities to manage their exposure to the liability of foreignness.

Thus, MNCs from developed economies, due to their ownership and home market specific advantages (legitimacy) will be more prompt to develop different strategies in the same host market to overcome the LOF. This process of diversified strategic engagement allows firms to have a better access to knowledge and strategic partnership, which may contribute to their abilities to cope better with economies presenting weak institutional performances.

However, EMNCs entering foreign markets are found to be, for the most part, market-seekers, entering, in large, close foreign markets. Entering other developing markets to acquire raw materials or developed markets to seek strategic assets (acquiring established brands or entering into merger agreements) can be important internationalization strategies to be adopted. Although EMNC's strategic asset-seeking strategies in foreign markets, especially in developed ones, are relatively found to be modest, they need strategic assets (e.g. mergers, acquisitions, and foreign brands) to boost the development of their competitive advantages in foreign markets. As established elsewhere, there is the belief that firms from developed countries are perceived to be superior in terms of quality and technology, which makes the country of origin exert much influence on consumer's preference to buy products from firms from developed countries. Hence, a EMNC' internationalization into developed or foreign markets will be characterized by much effort to take advantage of strategic assets available in any market; this is where the firm's networks of exchange relationship may be useful to facilitate access to strategic assets, which the firm lacks.

However, MNCs from an emerging economy have less technological and managerial capabilities to cope with significant differences inside and among locations, which may reduce their ability to strategy development, limiting their main foreign market approaches to market seeking or to resource seeking strategies.

References

- Foreign-direct-investment: tutorialspoint.com, Retrieved 03 August, 2020
- Chau, Esther; Wu, Jayce (2013). Economics HL/SL - Study Guide for the IB Diploma. CANA Academy Limited. p. 166. ISBN 978-9881686824

- World-Trade-Organization: britannica.com, Retrieved 11 June, 2020
- Foreign-direct-investment-from-emerging-economies-determinants-and-strategies, the-economic-geography-of-globalization, books: intechopen.com, Retrieved 17 May, 2020
- Šimelytė, Agnė; Liučvaitienė, Aušra (2012-01-01). "Foreign Direct Investment Policy–Friendly Business Environment in R&D Sectors: Baltic States versus Visegrad Countries". Journal of East-West Business. 18 (1): 66–93. doi:10.1080/10669868.2012.663737. ISSN 1066-9868
- Incentives-to-attract-fdi-pub-52270: carnegieendowment.org, Retrieved 24 April, 2020
- Factors-that-affect-foreign-direct-investment-fdi, economics-15736: economicshelp.org, Retrieved 12 May, 2020
- Rodriguez, Cecilia (29 September 2013). "Want To Live in Europe? "Buy" A Residency Permit". Forbes. Retrieved 21 December 2016

Foreign Exchange Market

CHAPTER 3

A global decentralized market for trading of currencies is called foreign exchange market. Forex includes all aspects of buying, selling and exchanging currencies at current or determined prices. This chapter closely examines foreign exchange market to provide an extensive understanding of the subject.

Foreign exchange market is the market in which foreign currencies are bought and sold. The buyers and sellers include individuals, firms, foreign exchange brokers, commercial banks and the central bank.

Like any other market, foreign exchange market is a system, not a place. The transactions in this market are not confined to only one or few foreign currencies. In fact, there are a large number of foreign currencies which are traded, converted and exchanged in the foreign exchange market.

Functions of Foreign Exchange Market

Foreign exchange market performs the following three functions:

Transfer Function

It transfers purchasing power between the countries involved in the transaction. This function is performed through credit instruments like bills of foreign exchange, bank drafts and telephonic transfers.

Credit Function

It provides credit for foreign trade. Bills of exchange, with maturity period of three months, are generally used for international payments. Credit is required for this period in order to enable the importer to take possession of goods, sell them and obtain money to pay off the bill.

Hedging Function

When exporters and importers enter into an agreement to sell and buy goods on some future date at the current prices and exchange rate, it is called hedging. The purpose of hedging is to avoid losses that might be caused due to exchange rate variations in the future.

Kinds of Foreign Exchange Markets

Foreign exchange markets are classified on the basis of whether the foreign exchange transactions are spot or forward accordingly, there are two kinds of foreign exchange markets:

- Spot Market,
- Forward Market.

Spot Market

Spot market refers to the market in which the receipts and payments are made immediately. Generally, a time of two business days is permitted to settle the transaction. Spot market is of daily nature and deals only in spot transactions of foreign exchange (not in future transactions). The rate of exchange, which prevails in the spot market, is termed as spot exchange rate or current rate of exchange.

The term 'spot transaction' is a bit misleading. In fact, spot transaction should mean a transaction, which is carried out 'on the spot' (i.e., immediately). However, a two day margin is allowed as it takes two days for payments made through cheques to be cleared.

Forward Market

Forward market refers to the market in which sale and purchase of foreign currency is settled on a specified future date at a rate agreed upon today. The exchange rate quoted in forward transactions is known as the forward exchange rate. Generally, most of the international transactions are signed on one date and completed on a later date. Forward exchange rate becomes useful for both the parties involved in the transaction.

Forward Contract is made for Two Reasons

- To minimize the risk of loss due to adverse changes in the exchange rate (through hedging).
- To make profit (through speculation).

FORWARD EXCHANGE MARKET

In the foreign exchange market, forward exchange market functions side by side with the spot exchange market. The transactions of spot exchange market are known as spot exchange and those of the forward exchange market are known as forward exchange.

The rates at which the foreign exchange is bought and sold in the spot market are called spot rates and the rates at which the foreign exchange is bought and sold in the forward market are called forward rates.

The spot exchange refers to the foreign exchange transactions which require immediate delivery or exchange of currencies on the spot. Normally, the settlement takes place within two days.

A forward exchange involves a purchase or sale of foreign currency to be delivered at some future date. The rate at which the transaction is to take place is determined at the time of sale, but the payment is not made until the exchange is not delivered by the seller.

The spot rate refers to the rate prevailing at a particular time for spot delivery of a specified type of foreign exchange.

The forward exchange rate is the rate at which the future contract for foreign currency is made. With reference to its relationship with the spot rate, the forward rate may be at par, at a premium or at a discount.

- When the exchange rate is quoted exactly equivalent to the spot rate at the time of making the contract, the forward exchange rate is said to be at par.
- The forward rate is said to be at a premium over the spot rate when it is quoted higher than the spot rate. Premium implies that the foreign currency is expensive. One dollar buys more units of other currency in the forward than in the spot market. The premium is usually expressed as a percentage deviation from the spot rate on a per annum basis.
- The forward rate is said to be at a discount with respect to the spot rate when it is quoted lower than the spot rate. Discount implies that the foreign currency is cheaper. One dollar buys less units of other currency in the forward than in the spot market. The discount is also expressed as a percentage deviation from the spot rate on a per annum basis.

The forward exchange rate is mostly determined by the demand for and supply of forward exchange. When the demand for forward exchange exceeds its supply, the forward rate will be quoted at a premium.

When the supply of forward exchange exceeds the demand for it, the forward rate will be quoted at a discount. When the supply and demand for forward exchange are equal, the forward rate will tend to be at par.

CONVERTIBILITY

Convertibility is the quality that allows money or other financial instruments to be converted into other liquid stores of value. Convertibility is an important factor in international trade, where instruments valued in different currencies must be exchanged.

Currency Trading

Freely convertible currencies have immediate value on the foreign exchange market, and few restrictions on the manner and amount that can be traded for another currency. Free convertibility is a major feature of a hard currency.

Some countries pass laws restricting the legal exchange rates of their currencies or requiring permits to exchange more than a certain amount. Some currencies, such as the North Korean won, the Transnistrian ruble, and the Cuban national peso, are officially nonconvertible and can only be exchanged on the black market. If an official exchange rate is set, its value on the black market is often lower.

Convertibility controls may be introduced as part of an overall monetary policy. For example, restrictions on the Argentine peso were introduced during an economic crisis in the 1990s and scrapped in 2002 during a subsequent crisis.

Commodity Money

Convertibility first became an issue of significance during the time banknotes began to replace commodity money in the money supply. Under the gold and silver standards, notes were redeemable for coin at face value, though often failing banks and governments would overextend their reserves.

Historically, the banknote has followed a common or very similar pattern in the western nations. Originally decentralized and issued from various independent banks, it was gradually brought under state control and became a monopoly privilege of the central banks. In the process, the principle that the banknote was merely a substitute for the real commodity money (gold and silver) was gradually abandoned.

Under the gold exchange standard, for example the Bretton Woods Institutions, banks of issue were obliged to redeem their currencies in gold bullion, or in United States dollars, which in turn were redeemable in gold bullion at an official rate of $35 per troy ounce. Due to limited growth in the supply of gold reserves, during a time of great inflation of the dollar supply, the United States eventually abandoned the gold exchange standard and thus bullion convertibility in 1974.

Under the contemporary international currency regimes, all currencie's inherent value derives from fiat, thus there is no longer any *thing* (gold or other tangible store of value) for which paper notes can be redeemed.

EUROCURRENCY

Eurocurrency is currency held on deposit outside its home market, i.e., held in banks located outside of the country which issues the currency.

For example, a US dollar denominated deposit in a Singapore bank is Eurocurrency, or more specifically Eurodollar deposit. The *Euro-* prefix can be applied to any combination of deposits and financial institution. For example, a deposit denominated in Euros held in a Brazilian bank is a *Euroeuro* deposit.

Eurocurrency is used as a source of short- or medium-term finance, especially in international trade, because of easy convertibility.

Eurocurrency does not have to involve either the euro currency or the eurozone.

Eurocurrency and Eurobond markets avoid domestic interest rate regulations, reserve requirements and other barriers to the free flow of capital.

Currencies

The four main Eurocurrencies are the US dollar, the Euro, the British pound and the Japanese yen; the currencies of the major economies of the world.

Eurobanks

A eurobank is a financial institution anywhere in the world which accepts deposits or makes loans in any foreign currency.

Eurocredits

Eurocredit is a loan whose denominated currency is not the lending bank's national currency. A eurocredit loan would be made by a U.S. bank to a lender requiring a denominated currency which differs from the bank's local currency (USD) for specific reasons, most likely some sort of business operations or trade requirements. Despite the inclusion of the word "euro", a eurocredit is not immediately derived from the euro.

Eurocredits are short-to-medium-term loans of Eurocurrency extended by Eurobanks to corporations, sovereign governments, nonprime banks, or international organizations. The loans are denominated in currencies other than the home currency of the Eurobank. Because these loans are frequently too large for a single bank to handle, Eurobanks will band together to form a bank lending syndicate to share the risk. The credit risk on these loans is greater than on loans to other banks in the interbank market. Thus, the interest rate on Eurocredits must compensate the bank, or banking syndicate, for the added credit risk. On Eurocredits originating in London the base lending rate is LIBOR. The lending rate on these credits is stated as LIBOR +X percent, where X is the lending margin charged depending upon the creditworthiness of the borrower. Additionally, rollover pricing was created on Eurocredits so that Eurobanks do not end up paying more on Eurocurrency time deposits than they earn from the loans. Thus, a Eurocredit may be viewed as a series of short-term loans, where at the end of each time period (generally three or six months), the loan is rolled over and the base lending rate is repriced to current LIBOR over the next time interval of the loan.

EFFECTIVE EXCHANGE RATE

The effective exchange rate is an index that describes the strength of a currency relative to a basket of other currencies. Suppose a country has N trading partners and denote $Trade_i$ and E_i as the trade and exchange rate with country i respectively. Then the effective exchange rate is calculated as:

$$E_{effective} = E_1 \frac{Trade_1}{Trade} + \ldots + E_N \frac{Trade_N}{Trade}$$

Although typically that basket is trade-weighted, the trade-weighted effective exchange rate index is not the only way to derive a meaningful effective exchange rate index. Ho proposed a new approach to compiling effective exchange rate indices. It defines the effective exchange rate as the ratio of the "normalized Exchange Value of Currency i against the US dollar" to the normalized exchange value of the "benchmark currency basket" against the US dollar. The US dollar is here used as numeraire for convenience, and since it cancels out, in principle any other currency can be used instead without affecting the results. The benchmark currency basket is a GDP-weighted basket of the major fully convertible currencies of the world.

Bilateral exchange rate involves a currency pair, while an effective exchange rate is a weighted average of a basket of foreign currencies, and it can be viewed as an overall measure of the country's external competitiveness. A nominal effective exchange rate (NEER) is weighted with the inverse of the asymptotic trade weights. A real effective exchange rate (REER) adjusts NEER by the appropriate foreign price level and deflates by the home country price level. There are four aspects for alternative measures of REER which are (a) using end-of-period or period averages of the nominal exchange rate. (b) choosing price indexes. (c) in obtaining the real effective exchange rates, deciding upon the number of trading partners in calculating the weights. (d) deciding upon the formula to use in aggregation. Considering all these aspects together led to the calculation of a great number of alternative series.

The Bank for International Settlements provides four sets of effective exchange rates, updated monthly. One pair uses a "narrow" set of 27 countries with data going back to 1964, both in nominal terms and as a "real" effective exchange rate adjusted using consumer price inflation. The "broad" set covers 61 economies, but with data only from 1994, again available both as a nominal series and adjusted for relative inflation. The trade weights are not updated monthly; as of March 2016, the base period was the average over 2011–13.

Effective exchange rates are useful for gauging whether a currency has appreciated overall relative to trading partners. For example, in 2015 the Chinese RMB depreciated about 8% against the US dollar. However, more of China's trade is with Asia and Europe than with the United States, and the dollar appreciated against those currencies. The net effect was that once weighted by trade shares the value of the Chinese currency actually appreciated approximately 10% relative to its trading partners.

EER are still volatile over short periods of time and a poor guide for comparing standards of living across countries. For that purpose Purchasing Power Parity measures are more appropriate.

EFFECTIVE EXCHANGE RATE INDEX

The effective exchange rate index describes the strength of a currency relative to a basket of other currencies. Although typically the basket is trade weighted, there are others besides the trade-weighted effective exchange rate index.

Ho proposed a new approach to compiling effective exchange rate indices. Under this approach, the effective exchange rate can be calculated as a ratio of the normalized exchange value of currency against the US dollar to the normalized exchange value of the benchmark currency basket against the US dollar. Normalized exchange rate refers to the current exchange rate divided by the exchange rate against the US dollar in the base year, which effectively scales up the exchange rate of a "small value" currency like the Japanese yen, worth a small fraction of a dollar, and scales down the exchange rate of a "big value" currency like the British pound, worth much more than a dollar. Thus, all standardized or normalized currencies in the base year are worth US$1 in the base year. The US dollar is used for convenience, but, in principle, any other currency could be used instead without affecting the results. The benchmark currency basket is a GDP-weighted basket of the major fully convertible currencies of the world. Since GDP data are available with a lag, the GDP weights used in Ho are GDPs dated two years ago. The use of GDP weights has been found to be superior to direct trade weights since countries with bigger GDPs will tend to attract imports from other countries, both direct and indirect.

Value of the benchmark currency basket at time t = Σ (GDP weight of currency i(dated 2 years ago from year of time t)* normalized exchange rate of currency i against the US dollar at time t.

Effective exchange rate of currency j = Normalized exchange rate of currency j against the US dollar/Value of the benchmark currency basket against US dollar.

Ho's procedure allows effective exchange rate indices to be easily compiled for any country.

DETERMINANTS OF EXCHANGE RATES

Numerous factors determine exchange rates. Many of these factors are related to the trading relationship between the two countries. Remember, exchange rates are relative, and are expressed as a comparison of the currencies of two countries. The following are some of the principal determinants of the exchange rate between two countries. Note that these factors are in no particular order; like many aspects of economics, the relative importance of these factors is subject to much debate.

Differentials in Inflation

Typically, a country with a consistently lower inflation rate exhibits a rising currency value, as its purchasing power increases relative to other currencies. During the last half of the 20th century, the countries with low inflation included Japan, Germany, and Switzerland, while the U.S. and Canada achieved low inflation only later. Those countries with higher inflation typically see depreciation in their currency about the currencies of their trading partners. This is also usually accompanied by higher interest rates.

Differentials in Interest Rates

Interest rates, inflation, and exchange rates are all highly correlated. By manipulating interest rates, central banks exert influence over both inflation and exchange rates, and changing interest rates impact inflation and currency values. Higher interest rates offer lenders in an economy a higher return relative to other countries. Therefore, higher interest rates attract foreign capital and cause the exchange rate to rise. The impact of higher interest rates is mitigated, however, if inflation in the country is much higher than in others, or if additional factors serve to drive the currency down. The opposite relationship exists for decreasing interest rates – that is, lower interest rates tend to decrease exchange rates.

Current Account Deficits

The current account is the balance of trade between a country and its trading partners, reflecting all payments between countries for goods, services, interest, and dividends. A deficit in the current account shows the country is spending more on foreign trade than it is earning, and that it is borrowing capital from foreign sources to make up the deficit. In other words, the country requires more foreign currency than it receives through sales of exports, and it supplies more of its own currency than foreigners demand for its products. The excess demand for foreign currency lowers the country's exchange rate until domestic goods and services are cheap enough for foreigners, and foreign assets are too expensive to generate sales for domestic interests.

Public Debt

Countries will engage in large-scale deficit financing to pay for public sector projects and governmental funding. While such activity stimulates the domestic economy, nations with large public deficits and debts are less attractive to foreign investors. The reason? A large debt encourages inflation, and if inflation is high, the debt will be serviced and ultimately paid off with cheaper real dollars in the future.

In the worst case scenario, a government may print money to pay part of a large debt, but increasing the money supply inevitably causes inflation. Moreover, if a government is not able to service its deficit through domestic means (selling domestic bonds, increasing the money supply), then it must increase the supply of securities for sale to foreigners, thereby lowering their prices. Finally, a large debt may prove worrisome to foreigners if they believe the country risks defaulting on its obligations. Foreigners will be less willing to own securities denominated in that currency if the risk of default is great. For this reason, the country's debt rating (as determined by Moody's or Standard & Poor's, for example) is a crucial determinant of its exchange rate.

Terms of Trade

A ratio comparing export prices to import prices, the terms of trade is related to current accounts and the balance of payments. If the price of a country's exports rises by a greater rate than that of its imports, its terms of trade have favorably improved. Increasing terms of trade show's greater demand for the country's exports. This, in turn, results in rising revenues from exports, which provides increased demand for the country's currency (and an increase in the currency's value). If the price of exports rises by a smaller rate than that of its imports, the currency's value will decrease in relation to its trading partners.

Strong Economic Performance

Foreign investors inevitably seek out stable countries with strong economic performance in which to invest their capital. A country with such positive attributes will draw investment funds away from other countries perceived to have more political and economic risk. Political turmoil, for example, can cause a loss of confidence in a currency and a movement of capital to the currencies of more stable countries.

FLOATING EXCHANGE RATE

A floating exchange rate (also called a fluctuating or flexible exchange rate) is a type of exchange rate regime in which a currency's value is allowed to fluctuate in response to foreign exchange market events. A currency that uses a floating exchange rate is known as a floating currency. A floating currency is contrasted with a fixed currency whose value is tied to that of another currency, material goods or to a currency basket.

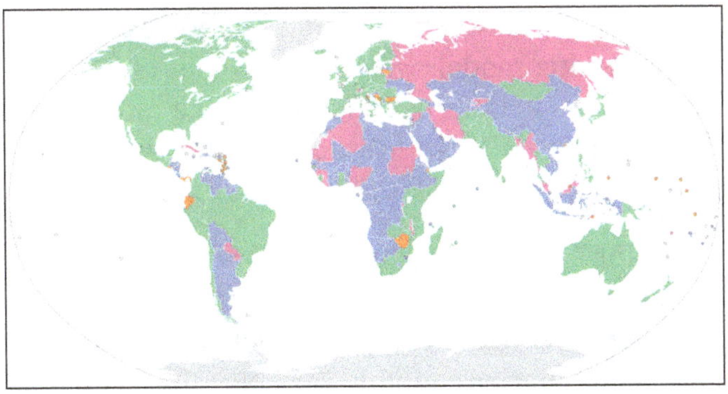

De facto exchange-rate arrangements in 2013 as classified by the International Monetary Fund.

In the modern world, most of the world's currencies are floating, and include the most widely-traded currencies: the United States dollar, the Swiss franc, the Indian rupee, the euro, the Japanese yen, the pound sterling, and the Australian dollar. However, even with floating currencies, central banks often participate in the markets to attempt to influence the value of floating exchange rates. The Canadian dollar most closely resembles a pure floating currency because the Canadian central bank has not interfered with its price since it officially stopped doing so in 1998. The US dollar runs a close second, with very little change in its foreign reserves. In contrast, Japan and the UK intervene to a greater extent, and India has seen medium-range intervention by its central bank, the Reserve Bank of India.

From 1946 to the early 1970s, the Bretton Woods system made fixed currencies the norm; however, in 1971, the US decided no longer to uphold the dollar exchange at 1/35th of an ounce of gold and so its currency was no longer fixed. After the collapse of the Smithsonian Agreement in 1973 most of the world's currencies followed suit. However, some countries, such as most of the Gulf States, fixed their currency to the value of another currency, which has been more recently associated with slower rates of growth. When a currency floats, targets other than the exchange rate itself are used to administer monetary policy.

Economic Rationale

Some economists think that in most circumstances, floating exchange rates are preferable to fixed exchange rates. As floating exchange rates automatically adjust, they enable a country to dampen the impact of shocks and foreign business cycles and to preempt the possibility of having a balance of payments crisis. However, they also engender unpredictability as the result of their dynamism, which can render businesse's planning risky since the future exchange rates during their planning cycle are uncertain.

However, in certain situations, fixed exchange rates may be preferable for their greater stability and certainty. That may not necessarily be true, considering the results of countries that attempt to keep the prices of their currency "strong" or "high" relative to others, such as the UK or the Southeast Asia countries before the Asian currency crisis.

The debate of making a choice between fixed and floating exchange rate regimes is set forth by the Mundell–Fleming model, which argues that an economy (or the government) cannot simultaneously maintain a fixed exchange rate, free capital movement, and an independent monetary policy. It must choose any two for control and leave the other to market forces.

The primary argument for a floating exchange rate is that it allows monetary policies to be useful for other purposes. Under fixed rates, monetary policy is committed to the single goal of maintaining exchange rate at its announced level. However, the exchange rate is only one of the many macroeconomic variables that monetary policy can influence. A system of floating exchange rates leaves monetary policymakers free to pursue other goals, such as stabilizing employment or prices.

During an extreme appreciation or depreciation, a central bank will normally intervene to stabilize the currency. Thus, the exchange rate regimes of floating currencies may more technically be known as a managed float. A central bank might, for instance, allow a currency price to float freely between an upper and lower bound, a price "ceiling" and "floor". Management by the central bank may take the form of buying or selling large lots in order to provide price support or resistance or, in the case of some national currencies, there may be legal penalties for trading outside these bounds.

Aversion to Floating

A free floating exchange rate increases foreign exchange volatility. Some economists think that this could cause serious problems, especially in emerging economies. Those economies have a financial sector with one or more of following conditions:

- High liability dollarization.
- Financial fragility.
- Strong balance sheet effects.

When liabilities are denominated in foreign currencies while assets are in the local currency, unexpected depreciations of the exchange rate deteriorate bank and corporate balance sheets and threaten the stability of the domestic financial system.

Therefore, emerging countries appear to have greater aversion to floating, as they have much smaller variations of the nominal exchange rate but face bigger shocks and interest rate and reserve movements. This is the consequence of frequent free floating countrie's reaction to exchange rate movements with monetary policy and intervention in the foreign exchange market.

The number of countries that show aversion to floating increased significantly during the 1990s.

EXCHANGE-RATE FLEXIBILITY

A flexible exchange-rate system is a monetary system that allows the exchange rate to be determined by supply and demand.

Every currency area must decide what type of exchange rate arrangement to maintain. Between permanently fixed and completely flexible however, are heterogeneous approaches. They have different implications for the extent to which national authorities participate in foreign exchange markets. According to their degree of flexibility, post-Bretton Woods-exchange rate regimes are arranged into three categories: currency unions, dollarized regimes, currency boards and conventional currency pegs are described as "fixed-rate regimes"; horizontal bands, crawling pegs and crawling bands are grouped into "intermediate regimes"; and managed and independent floats are described as flexible regimes. All monetary regimes except for the permanently fixed regime experience the time inconsistency problem and exchange rate volatility, albeit to different degrees.

Fixed Rate Programs

In a fixed exchange rate system, the monetary authority picks rates of exchange with each other currency and commits to adjusting the money supply, restricting exchange transactions and adjusting other variables to ensure that the exchange rates do not move. All variations on fixed rates reduce the time inconsistency problem and reduce exchange rate volatility, albeit to different degrees.

Under *dollarization/Euroization*, the US dollar or the Euro acts as legal tender in a different country. Dollarization is a summary description of the use of foreign currency in its capacity to produce all types of money services in the domestic economy. Monetary policy is delegated to the anchor country. Under dollarization exchange rate movements cannot buffer external shocks. The money supply in the dollarizing country is limited to what it can earn via exports, borrow and receive from emigrant remittances.

A *currency board* enables governments to manage their external credibility problems and discipline their central banks by "tying their hands" with binding arrangements. A currency board combines three elements: an exchange rate that is fixed to another, "anchor currency"; automatic convertibility or the right to exchange domestic currency at this fixed rate whenever desired; and a long-term commitment to the system. A currency board system can ultimately be credible only if central bank holds official foreign exchange reserves sufficient to at least cover the entire monetary base. Exchange rate movements cannot buffer external shocks.

A *fixed peg* system fixes the exchange rate against a single currency or a currency basket. The time inconsistency problem is reduced through commitment to a verifiable target. However, the availability of a devaluation option provides a policy tool for handling large shocks. Its potential drawbacks are that it provides a target for speculative attacks, avoids exchange rate volatility, but not necessarily persistent misalignments, does not by itself place hard constraints on monetary and fiscal policy and that the credibility effect depends on accompanying institutional measures and a visible record of accomplishment.

Monetary Union

A currency or monetary *union* is a multi-country zone where a single monetary policy prevails and inside which a single currency or multiple substitutable currencies, move freely. A monetary union has common monetary and fiscal policy to ensure control over the creation of money and the size of government debts. It has a central management of the common pool of foreign exchange reserves, external debts and exchange rate policies. The monetary union has common regional monetary authority i.e. common regional central bank, which is the sole issuer of economy wide currency, in the case of a full currency union.

The monetary union eliminates the time inconsistency problem within the zone and reduces real exchange rate volatility by requiring multinational agreement on exchange rate and other monetary changes. The potential drawbacks are that member countries suffering asymmetric shocks lose a stabilization tool—the ability to adjust exchange rates. The cost depends on the extent of asymmetric costs and the availability and effectiveness of alternative adjustment tools.

Flexible Exchange Rate

These systems do not particularly reduce time inconsistency problems nor do they offer specific techniques for maintaining low exchange rate volatility.

A *crawling peg* attempts to combine flexibility and stability using a rule-based system for gradually altering the currency's par value, typically at a predetermined rate or as a function of inflation differentials. A crawling peg is similar to a fixed peg; however, it can be adjusted based on clearly defined rules. A crawling peg is often used by (initially) high-inflation countries or developing nations who peg to low inflation countries in attempt to avoid currency appreciation. At the margin a crawling peg provides a target for speculative attacks. Among variants of fixed exchange rates, it imposes the least restrictions, and may hence yield the smallest credibility benefits. The credibility effect depends on accompanying institutional measures and record of accomplishment.

Exchange rate bands allow markets to set rates within a specified range; edges of the band are defended through intervention. It provides a limited role for exchange rate movements to counteract external shocks while partially anchoring expectations. This system does not eliminate exchange rate uncertainty and thus motivates development of exchange rate risk management tools. On the margin a band is subject to speculative attacks. It does not by itself place hard constraints on policy, and thus provides only a limited solution to the time inconsistency problem. The credibility effect depends on accompanying institutional measures, a record of accomplishment and whether the band is firm or adjustable, secret or public, band width and the strength of the intervention requirement.

Managed float exchange rates are determined in the foreign exchange market. Authorities can and do intervene, but are not bound by any intervention rule. They are often accompanied by a separate nominal anchor, such as an inflation target. The arrangement provides a way to mix market-determined rates with stabilizing intervention in a non-rule-based system. Its potential drawbacks are that it does not place hard constraints on monetary and fiscal policy. It suffers from uncertainty from reduced credibility, relying on the credibility of monetary authorities. It typically offers limited transparency.

In a *pure float*, the exchange rate is determined in the market without public sector intervention. Adjustments to shocks can take place through exchange rate movements. It eliminates the requirement to hold large reserves. However, this arrangement does not provide an expectations anchor. The exchange rate regime itself does not imply any specific restriction on monetary and fiscal policy.

FIXED EXCHANGE RATE SYSTEM

A fixed exchange rate, sometimes called a pegged exchange rate, is a type of exchange rate regime in which a currency's value is fixed or pegged by a monetary authority against the value of another currency, a basket of other currencies, or another measure of value, such as gold.

There are benefits and risks to using a fixed exchange rate system. A fixed exchange rate is typically used to stabilize the exchange rate of a currency by directly fixing its value in a predetermined ratio to a different, more stable, or more internationally prevalent currency (or currencies) to which the currency is pegged. In doing so, the exchange rate between the currency and its peg does not change based on market conditions, unlike in a floating (flexible) exchange regime. This makes trade and investments between the two currency areas easier and more predictable and is especially useful for small economies that borrow primarily in foreign currency and in which external trade forms a large part of their GDP.

A fixed exchange rate system can also be used to control the behavior of a currency, such as by limiting rates of inflation. However, in doing so, the pegged currency is then controlled by its reference value. As such, when the reference value rises or falls, it then follows that the values of any currencies pegged to it will also rise and fall in relation to other currencies and commodities with which the pegged currency can be traded. In other words, a pegged currency is dependent on its reference value to dictate how its current worth is defined at any given time. In addition, according to the Mundell–Fleming model, with perfect capital mobility, a fixed exchange rate prevents a government from using domestic monetary policy to achieve macroeconomic stability.

In a fixed exchange rate system, a country's central bank typically uses an open market mechanism and is committed at all times to buy and sell its currency at a fixed price in order to maintain its pegged ratio and, hence, the stable value of its currency in relation to the reference to which it is pegged. To maintain a desired exchange rate, the central bank during a time of private sector net demand for the foreign currency, sells foreign currency from its reserves and buys back the domestic money. This creates an artificial demand for the domestic money, which increases its exchange rate value. Conversely, in the case of an incipient appreciation of the domestic money, the central bank buys back the foreign money and thus adds domestic money into the market, thereby maintaining market equilibrium at the intended fixed value of the exchange rate.

In the 21st century, the currencies associated with large economies typically do not fix (peg) their exchange rates to other currencies. The last large economy to use a fixed exchange rate system was the People's Republic of China, which, in July 2005, adopted a slightly more flexible exchange rate system, called a managed exchange rate. The European Exchange Rate Mechanism is also used on a temporary basis to establish a final conversion rate against the euro from the local currencies of countries joining the Eurozone.

The gold standard or gold exchange standard of fixed exchange rates prevailed from about 1870 to 1914, before which many countries followed bimetallism. The period between the two world wars was transitory, with the Bretton Woods system emerging as the new fixed exchange rate regime in the aftermath of World War II. It was formed with an intent to rebuild war-ravaged nations after World War II through a series of currency stabilization programs and infrastructure loans. The early 1970s saw the breakdown of the system and its replacement by a mixture of fluctuating and fixed exchange rates.

Chronology

Timeline of the fixed exchange rate system:

1880–1914	Classical gold standard period
April 1925	United Kingdom returns to gold standard
October 1929	United States stock market crashes
September 1931	United Kingdom abandons gold standard
July 1944	Bretton Woods conference

March 1947	International Monetary Fund comes into being
August 1971	United States suspends convertibility of dollar into gold – Bretton Woods system collapses
December 1971	Smithsonian Agreement
March 1972	European snake with 2.25% band of fluctuation allowed
March 1973	Managed float regime comes into being
April 1978	Jamaica Accords take effect
September 1985	Plaza Accord
September 1992	United Kingdom and Italy abandon Exchange Rate Mechanism (ERM)
August 1993	European Monetary System allows ±15% fluctuation in exchange rates

Gold Standard

The earliest establishment of a gold standard was in the United Kingdom in 1821 followed by Australia in 1852 and Canada in 1853. Under this system, the external value of all currencies was denominated in terms of gold with central banks ready to buy and sell unlimited quantities of gold at the fixed price. Each central bank maintained gold reserves as their official reserve asset. For example, during the "classical" gold standard period, the U.S. dollar was defined as 0.048 troy oz. of pure gold.

Bretton Woods System

Following the Second World War, the Bretton Woods system replaced gold with the U.S. dollar as the official reserve asset. The regime intended to combine binding legal obligations with multilateral decision-making through the International Monetary Fund (IMF). The rules of this system were set forth in the articles of agreement of the IMF and the International Bank for Reconstruction and Development. The system was a monetary order intended to govern currency relations among sovereign states, with the 44 member countries required to establish a parity of their national currencies in terms of the U.S. dollar and to maintain exchange rates within 1% of parity (a "band") by intervening in their foreign exchange markets (that is, buying or selling foreign money). The U.S. dollar was the only currency strong enough to meet the rising demands for international currency transactions, and so the United States agreed both to link the dollar to gold at the rate of $35 per ounce of gold and to convert dollars into gold at that price.

Due to concerns about America's rapidly deteriorating payments situation and massive flight of liquid capital from the U.S., President Richard Nixon suspended the convertibility of the dollar into gold on 15 August 1971. In December 1971, the Smithsonian Agreement paved the way for the increase in the value of the dollar price of gold from US$35.50 to US$38 an ounce. Speculation against the dollar in March 1973 led to the birth of the independent float, thus effectively terminating the Bretton Woods system.

Current Monetary Regimes

Since March 1973, the floating exchange rate has been followed and formally recognized by the Jamaica accord of 1978. Countries use foreign exchange reserves to intervene in foreign exchange markets to balance short-run fluctuations in exchange rates. The prevailing exchange rate regime is often considered a revival of Bretton Woods policies, namely Bretton Woods II.

Mechanisms

Open Market Trading

Typically, a government wanting to maintain a fixed exchange rate does so by either buying or selling its own currency on the open market. This is one reason governments maintain reserves of foreign currencies.

If the exchange rate drifts too far above the fixed benchmark rate (it is stronger than required), the government sells its own currency (which increases Supply) and buys foreign currency. This causes the price of the currency to decrease in value (Read: Classical Demand-Supply diagrams). Also, if they buy the currency it is pegged to, then the price of that currency will increase, causing the relative value of the currencies to be closer to the intended relative value.

If the exchange rate drifts too far below the desired rate, the government buys its own currency in the market by selling its reserves. This places greater demand on the market and causes the local currency to become stronger, hopefully back to its intended value. The reserves they sell may be the currency it is pegged to, in which case the value of that currency will fall.

Fiat

Another, less used means of maintaining a fixed exchange rate is by simply making it illegal to trade currency at any other rate. This is difficult to enforce and often leads to a black market in foreign currency. Nonetheless, some countries are highly successful at using this method due to government monopolies over all money conversion. This was the method employed by the Chinese government to maintain a currency peg or tightly banded float against the US dollar. China buys an average of one billion US dollars a day to maintain the currency peg. Throughout the 1990s, China was highly successful at maintaining a currency peg using a government monopoly over all currency conversion between the yuan and other currencies.

Open Market Mechanism Example

Under this system, the central bank first announces a fixed exchange-rate for the currency and then agrees to buy and sell the domestic currency at this value. The market equilibrium exchange rate is the rate at which supply and demand will be equal, i.e., markets will clear. In a flexible exchange rate system, this is the spot rate. In a fixed exchange-rate system, the pre-announced rate may not coincide with the market equilibrium exchange rate. The foreign central banks maintain reserves of foreign currencies and gold which they can sell in order to intervene in the foreign exchange market to make up the excess demand or take up the excess supply.

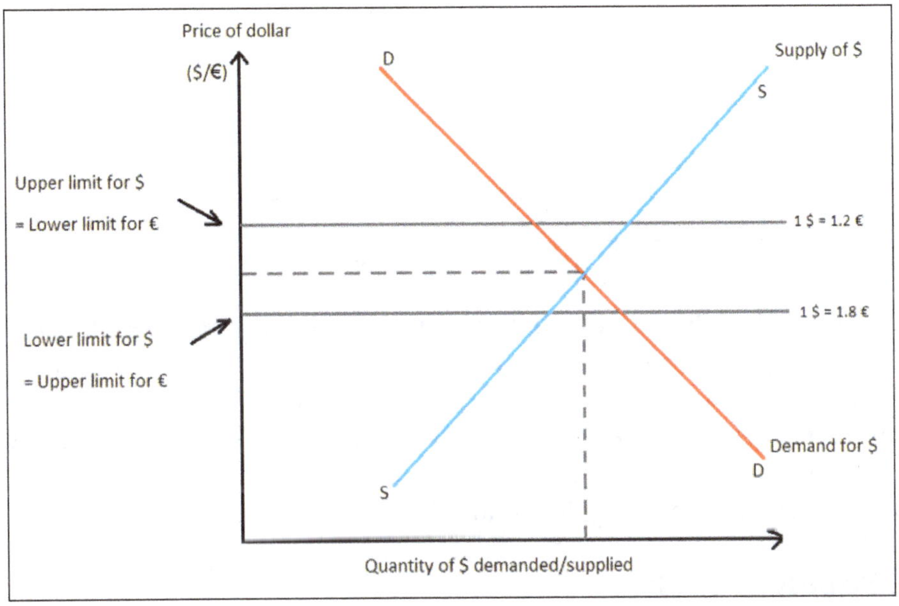

Mechanism of fixed exchange-rate system.

The demand for foreign exchange is derived from the domestic demand for foreign goods, services, and financial assets. The supply of foreign exchange is similarly derived from the foreign demand for goods, services, and financial assets coming from the home country. Fixed exchange-rates are not permitted to fluctuate freely or respond to daily changes in demand and supply. The government fixes the exchange value of the currency. For example, the European Central Bank (ECB) may fix its exchange rate at €1 = $1 (assuming that the euro follows the fixed exchange-rate). This is the central value or par value of the euro. Upper and lower limits for the movement of the currency are imposed, beyond which variations in the exchange rate are not permitted. The "band" or "spread" in Figure. is €0.6 (from €1.2 to €1.8).

Excess Demand for Dollars

Describes the excess demand for dollars. This is a situation where domestic demand for foreign goods, services, and financial assets exceeds the foreign demand for goods, services, and financial assets from the European Union. If the demand for dollar rises from DD to D'D', excess demand is created to the extent of *cd*. The ECB will sell *cd* dollars in exchange for euros to maintain the limit within the band. Under a floating exchange rate system, equilibrium would have been achieved at *e*.

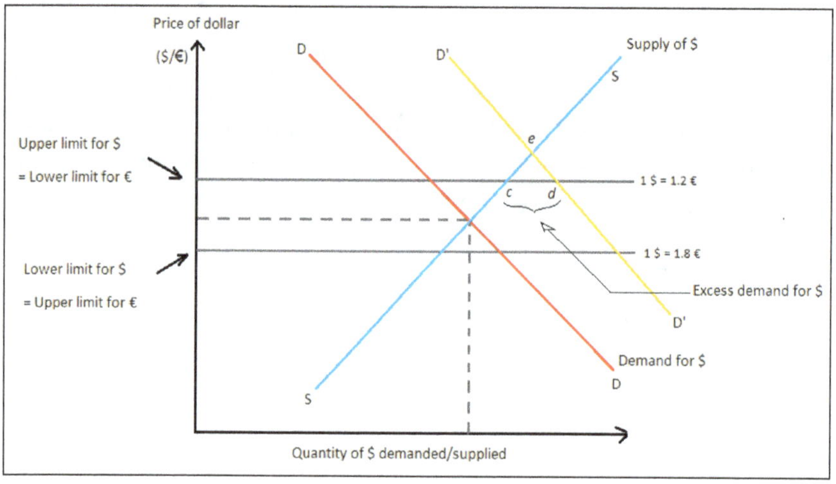

Excess demand for dollars.

When the ECB sells dollars in this manner, its official dollar reserves decline and domestic money supply shrinks. To prevent this, the ECB may purchase government bonds and thus meet the shortfall in money supply. This is called sterilized intervention in the foreign exchange market. When the ECB starts running out of reserves, it may also devalue the euro in order to reduce the excess demand for dollars, i.e., narrow the gap between the equilibrium and fixed rates.

Excess Supply of Dollars

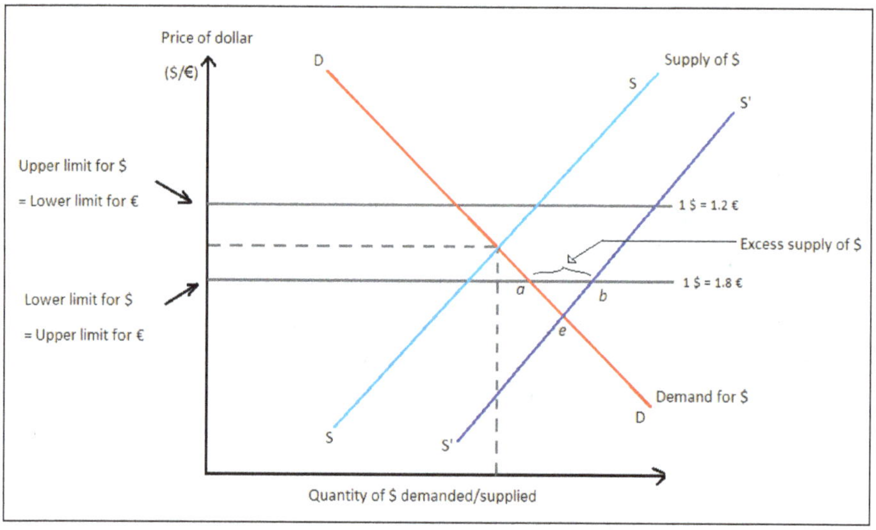

Excess supply of dollars.

Fig. describes the excess supply of dollars. This is a situation where the foreign demand for goods, services, and financial assets from the European Union exceeds the European demand for foreign goods, services, and financial assets. If the supply of dollars rises from SS to ‘s’s, excess supply is created to the extent of *ab*. The ECB will buy *ab* dollars in exchange for euros to maintain the limit within the band. Under a floating exchange rate system, equilibrium would again have been achieved at *e*.

When the ECB buys dollars in this manner, its official dollar reserves increase and domestic money supply expands, which may lead to inflation. To prevent this, the ECB may sell government bonds and thus counter the rise in money supply.

When the ECB starts accumulating excess reserves, it may also revalue the euro in order to reduce the excess supply of dollars, i.e., narrow the gap between the equilibrium and fixed rates. This is the opposite of devaluation.

Types of Fixed Exchange Rate Systems

The Gold Standard

Under the gold standard, a country's government declares that it will exchange its currency for a certain weight in gold. In a pure gold standard, a country's government declares that it will freely exchange currency for actual gold at the designated exchange rate. This "rule of exchange" allows anyone to enter the central bank and exchange coins or currency for pure gold or vice versa. The gold standard works on the assumption that there are no restrictions on capital movements or export of gold by private citizens across countries.

Because the central bank must always be prepared to give out gold in exchange for coin and currency upon demand, it must maintain gold reserves. Thus, this system ensures that the exchange rate between currencies remains fixed. For example, under this standard, a £1 gold coin in the United Kingdom contained 113.0016 grains of pure gold, while a $1 gold coin in the United States contained 23.22 grains. The mint parity or the exchange rate was thus: $R = \$/£ = 113.0016/23.22 = 4.87$. The main argument in favor of the gold standard is that it ties the world price level to the world supply of gold, thus preventing inflation unless there is a gold discovery.

Price Specie Flow Mechanism

The automatic adjustment mechanism under the gold standard is the price specie flow mechanism, which operates so as to correct any balance of payments disequilibrium and adjust to shocks or changes. This mechanism was originally introduced by Richard Cantillon and later discussed by David Hume in 1752 to refute the mercantilist doctrines and emphasize that nations could not continuously accumulate gold by exporting more than their imports.

The assumptions of this mechanism are:

- Prices are flexible.

- All transactions take place in gold.
- There is a fixed supply of gold in the world.
- Gold coins are minted at a fixed parity in each country.
- There are no banks and no capital flows.

Adjustment under a gold standard involves the flow of gold between countries resulting in equalization of prices satisfying purchasing power parity, and equalization of rates of return on assets satisfying interest rate parity at the current fixed exchange rate. Under the gold standard, each country's money supply consisted of either gold or paper currency backed by gold. Money supply would hence fall in the deficit nation and rise in the surplus nation. Consequently, internal prices would fall in the deficit nation and rise in the surplus nation, making the exports of the deficit nation more competitive than those of the surplus nations. The deficit nation's exports would be encouraged and the imports would be discouraged till the deficit in the balance of payments was eliminated.

In brief:

Deficit nation: Lower money supply → Lower internal prices → More exports, less imports → Elimination of deficit.

Surplus nation: Higher money supply → Higher internal prices → Less exports, more imports → Elimination of surplus.

Reserve Currency Standard

In a reserve currency system, the currency of another country performs the functions that gold has in a gold standard. A country fixes its own currency value to a unit of another country's currency, generally a currency that is prominently used in international transactions or is the currency of a major trading partner. For example, suppose India decided to fix its currency to the dollar at the exchange rate E₹/$ = 45.0. To maintain this fixed exchange rate, the Reserve Bank of India would need to hold dollars on reserve and stand ready to exchange rupees for dollars (or dollars for rupees) on demand at the specified exchange rate. In the gold standard the central bank held gold to exchange for *its own currency*, with a reserve currency standard it must hold a stock of the *reserve currency*.

Currency board arrangements are the most widespread means of fixed exchange rates. Under this, a nation rigidly pegs its currency to a foreign currency, special drawing rights (SDR) or a basket of currencies. The central bank's role in the country's monetary policy is therefore minimal as its money supply is equal to its foreign reserves. Currency boards are considered hard pegs as they allow central banks to cope with shocks to money demand without running out of reserves (11). CBAs have been operational in many nations including:

- Hong Kong;

- Argentina ;
- Estonia ;
- Lithuania ;
- Bosnia and Herzegovina ;
- Bulgaria ;
- Bermuda ;
- Denmark ;
- Brunei.

Gold Exchange Standard

The fixed exchange rate system set up after World War II was a gold-exchange standard, as was the system that prevailed between 1920 and the early 1930s. A gold exchange standard is a mixture of a reserve currency standard and a gold standard. Its characteristics are as follows:

- All non-reserve countries agree to fix their exchange rates to the chosen reserve at some announced rate and hold a stock of reserve currency assets.
- The reserve currency country fixes its currency value to a fixed weight in gold and agrees to exchange on demand its own currency for gold with other central banks within the system, upon demand.

Unlike the gold standard, the central bank of the reserve country does not exchange gold for currency with the general public, only with other central banks.

Hybrid Exchange Rate Systems

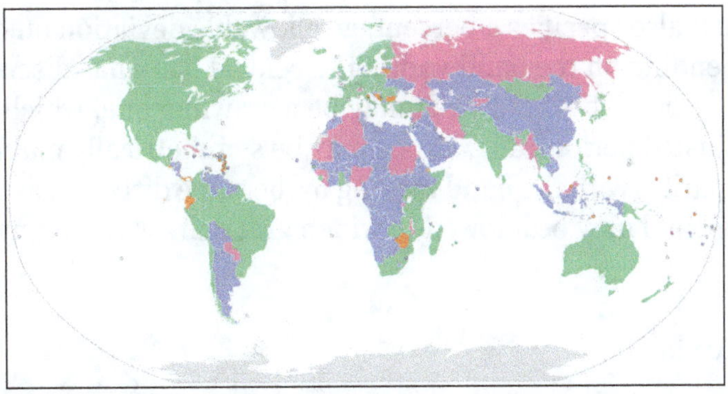

The current state of foreign exchange markets does not allow for the rigid system of fixed exchange rates. At the same time, freely floating exchange rates expose a country to volatility in exchange rates. Hybrid exchange rate systems have evolved in order to combine the characteristics features of fixed and flexible exchange rate systems. They allow fluctuation of the exchange rates without completely exposing the currency to the flexibility of a free float.

Basket-of-currencies

Countries often have several important trading partners or are apprehensive of a particular currency being too volatile over an extended period of time. They can thus choose to peg their currency to a weighted average of several currencies (also known as a currency basket). For example, a composite currency may be created consisting of 100 Indian rupees, 100 Japanese yen and one Singapore dollar. The country creating this composite would then need to maintain reserves in one or more of these currencies to intervene in the foreign exchange market.

A popular and widely used composite currency is the SDR, which is a composite currency created by the International Monetary Fund (IMF), consisting of a fixed quantity of U.S. dollars, Chinese yuan, euros, Japanese yen, and British pounds.

Crawling Pegs

In a crawling peg system a country fixes its exchange rate to another currency or basket of currencies. This fixed rate is changed from time to time at periodic intervals with a view to eliminating exchange rate volatility to some extent without imposing the constraint of a fixed rate. Crawling pegs are adjusted gradually, thus avoiding the need for interventions by the central bank (though it may still choose to do so in order to maintain the fixed rate in the event of excessive fluctuations).

Pegged within a Band

A currency is said to be pegged within a band when the central bank specifies a central exchange rate with reference to a single currency, a cooperative arrangement, or a currency composite. It also specifies a percentage allowable deviation on both sides of this central rate. Depending on the band width, the central bank has discretion in carrying out its monetary policy. The band itself may be a crawling one, which implies that the central rate is adjusted periodically. Bands may be symmetrically maintained around a crawling central parity (with the band moving in the same direction as this parity does). Alternatively, the band may be allowed to widen gradually without any pre-announced central rate.

Currency Boards

A currency board (also known as 'linked exchange rate system") effectively replaces the central bank through a legislation to fix the currency to that of another country.

The domestic currency remains perpetually exchangeable for the reserve currency at the fixed exchange rate. As the anchor currency is now the basis for movements of the domestic currency, the interest rates and inflation in the domestic economy would be greatly influenced by those of the foreign economy to which the domestic currency is tied. The currency board needs to ensure the maintenance of adequate reserves of the anchor currency. It is a step away from officially adopting the anchor currency (termed as currency substitution).

Currency Substitution

This is the most extreme and rigid manner of fixing exchange rates as it entails adopting the currency of another country in place of its own. The most prominent example is the eurozone, where 19 European Union (EU) member states have adopted the euro (€) as their common currency (euroization). Their exchange rates are effectively fixed to each other.

There are similar examples of countries adopting the U.S. dollar as their domestic currency (dollarization): British Virgin Islands, Caribbean Netherlands, East Timor, Ecuador, El Salvador, Marshall Islands, Federated States of Micronesia, Palau, Panama, Turks and Caicos Islands and Zimbabwe.

Monetary Co-operation

Monetary co-operation is the mechanism in which two or more monetary policies or exchange rates are linked, and can happen at regional or international level. The monetary co-operation does not necessarily need to be a voluntary arrangement between two countries, as it is also possible for a country to link its currency to another countries currency without the consent of the other country. Various forms of monetary co-operations exist, which range from fixed parity systems to monetary unions. Also, numerous institutions have been established to enforce monetary co-operation and to stabilise exchange rates, including the European Monetary Cooperation Fund (EMCF) in 1973 and the International Monetary Fund (IMF)

Monetary co-operation is closely related to economic integration, and are often considered to be reinforcing processes. However, economic integration is an economic arrangement between different regions, marked by the reduction or elimination of trade barriers and the coordination of monetary and fiscal policies, whereas monetary co-operation is focussed on currency linkages. A monetary union is considered to be the crowning step of a process of monetary co-operation and economic integration. In the form of monetary co-operation where two or more countries engage in a mutually beneficial exchange, capital among the countries involved is free to move, in contrast to capital controls. Monetary co-operation is considered to promote balanced economic growth and monetary stability, but can also work counter-effectively if the member countries have (strongly) differing levels of economic development. Especially

European and Asian countries have a history of monetary and exchange rate co-operation, however the European monetary co-operation and economic integration eventually resulted in a European monetary union.

Example: The Snake

In 1973, the currencies of the European Economic Community countries, Belgium, France, Germany, Italy, Luxemburg and the Netherlands, participated in an arrangement called *the Snake*. This arrangement is categorized as exchange rate co-operation. During the next 6 years, this agreement allowed the currencies of the participating countries to fluctuate within a band of plus or minus 2¼% around pre-announced central rates. Later, in 1979, the European Monetary System (EMS) was founded, with the participating countries in *'the Snake'* being founding members. The EMS evolves over the next decade and even results into a truly fixed exchange rate at the start of the 1990s. Around this time, in 1990, the EU introduced the Economic and Monetary Union (EMU), as an umbrella term for the group of policies aimed at converging the economies of member states of the European Union over three phases

Example: The Baht-U.S. Dollar Co-operation

In 1963, the Thai government established the Exchange Equalization Fund (EEF) with the purpose of playing a role in stabilizing exchange rate movements. It linked to the U.S. dollar by fixing the amount of gram of gold per baht as well as the baht per U.S. dollar. Over the course of the next 15 years, the Thai government decided to depreciate the baht in terms of gold three times, yet maintain the parity of the baht against the U.S. dollar. Due to the introduction of a new generalized floating exchange rate system by the International Monetary Fund (IMF) that stretched a smaller role of gold in the international monetary system in 1978, this fixed parity system as a monetary co-operation policy was terminated. The Thai government amended its monetary policies to be more in line with the new IMF policy.

Advantages

- A fixed exchange rate may minimize instabilities in real economic activity.
- Central banks can acquire credibility by fixing their country's currency to that of a more disciplined nation.
- On a microeconomic level, a country with poorly developed or illiquid money markets may fix their exchange rates to provide its residents with a synthetic money market with the liquidity of the markets of the country that provides the vehicle currency.
- A fixed exchange rate reduces volatility and fluctuations in relative prices.
- It eliminates exchange rate risk by reducing the associated uncertainty.

- It imposes discipline on the monetary authority.
- International trade and investment flows between countries are facilitated.
- Speculation in the currency markets is likely to be less destabilizing under a fixed exchange rate system than it is in a flexible one, since it does not amplify fluctuations resulting from business cycles.
- Fixed exchange rates impose a price discipline on nations with higher inflation rates than the rest of the world, as such a nation is likely to face persistent deficits in its balance of payments and loss of reserves.
- Prevent, debt monetization, or fiscal spending financed by debt that the monetary authority buys up. This prevents high inflation.

Disadvantages

Lack of Automatic Rebalancing

One main criticism of a fixed exchange rate is that flexible exchange rates serve to adjust the balance of trade. When a trade deficit occurs under a floating exchange rate, there will be increased demand for the foreign (rather than domestic) currency which will push up the price of the foreign currency in terms of the domestic currency. That in turn makes the price of foreign goods less attractive to the domestic market and thus pushes down the trade deficit. Under fixed exchange rates, this automatic rebalancing does not occur.

Currency Crisis

Another major disadvantage of a fixed exchange-rate regime is the possibility of the central bank running out of foreign exchange reserves when trying to maintain the peg in the face of demand for foreign reserves exceeding their supply. This is called a currency crisis or balance of payments crisis, and when it happens the central bank must devalue the currency. When there is the prospect of this happening, private-sector agents will try to protect themselves by decreasing their holdings of the domestic currency and increasing their holdings of the foreign currency, which has the effect of increasing the likelihood that the forced devaluation will occur. A forced devaluation will change the exchange rate by more than will the day-by-day exchange rate fluctuations under a flexible exchange rate system.

Freedom to Conduct Monetary and Fiscal Policy

Moreover, a government, when having a fixed rather than dynamic exchange rate, cannot use monetary or fiscal policies with a free hand. For instance, by using reflationary tools to set the economy growing faster (by decreasing taxes and injecting more money in the market), the government risks running into a trade deficit. This might occur as the purchasing power of a common household increases along with inflation, thus making imports relatively cheaper.

Additionally, the stubbornness of a government in defending a fixed exchange rate when in a trade deficit will force it to use deflationary measures (increased taxation and reduced availability of money), which can lead to unemployment. Finally, other countries with a fixed exchange rate can also retaliate in response to a certain country using the currency of theirs in defending their exchange rate.

Other Disadvantages

- The need for a fixed exchange rate regime is challenged by the emergence of sophisticated derivatives and financial tools in recent years, which allow firms to hedge exchange rate fluctuations.
- The announced exchange rate may not coincide with the market equilibrium exchange rate, thus leading to excess demand or excess supply.
- The central bank needs to hold stocks of both foreign and domestic currencies at all times in order to adjust and maintain exchange rates and absorb the excess demand or supply.
- Fixed exchange rate does not allow for automatic correction of imbalances in the nation's balance of payments since the currency cannot appreciate/depreciate as dictated by the market.
- It fails to identify the degree of comparative advantage or disadvantage of the nation and may lead to inefficient allocation of resources throughout the world.
- There exists the possibility of policy delays and mistakes in achieving external balance.
- The cost of government intervention is imposed upon the foreign exchange market.
- It does not work well in countries with dissimilar economies and thus dissimilar economic shocks.

Fixed Exchange Rate Regime versus Capital Control

The belief that the fixed exchange rate regime brings with it stability is only partly true, since speculative attacks tend to target currencies with fixed exchange rate regimes, and in fact, the stability of the economic system is maintained mainly through capital control. A fixed exchange rate regime should be viewed as a tool in capital control.

FIX Line: Trade-off between Symmetry of Shocks and Integration

- The trade-off between symmetry of shocks and market integration for countries contemplating a pegged currency is outlined in Feenstra and Taylor's 2015 publication "International Macroeconomics" through a model known as the FIX Line Diagram.
- This symmetry-integration diagram features two regions, divided by a 45-degree line with slope of -1. This line can shift to the left or to the right depending on extra costs or benefits of floating. The line has slope= -1 is because the larger symmetry benefits are, the less pronounced integration benefits have to be and vice versa. The right region contains countries that have positive potential for pegging, while the left region contains countries that face significant risks and deterrents to pegging.
- This diagram underscores the two main factors that drive a country to contemplate pegging a currency to another, shock symmetry and market integration. Shock symmetry can be characterized as two countries having similar demand shocks due to similar industry breakdowns and economies, while market integration is a factor of the volume of trading that occurs between member nations of the peg.
- In extreme cases, it is possible for a country to only exhibit one of these characteristics and still have positive pegging potential. For example, a country that exhibits complete symmetry of shocks but has zero market integration could benefit from fixing a currency. The opposite is true, a country that has zero symmetry of shocks but has maximum trade integration (effectively one market between member countries). *This can be viewed on an international scale as well as a local scale. For example, neighborhoods within a city would experience enormous benefits from a common currency, while poorly integrated and dissimilar countries are likely to face large costs.

EXCHANGE RATE REGIME

An exchange rate regime is the way a monetary authority of a country or currency union manages the currency in relation to other currencies and the foreign exchange market. It is closely related to monetary policy and the two are generally dependent on many of the same factors, such as economic scale and openness, inflation rate, elasticity of the labor market, financial market development, capital mobility etc.

There are two major regime types:

- *Fixed (or pegged) exchange rate* regimes, where the currency is tied to another currency, mostly reserve currencies such as the U.S. dollar or the euro or the British Pound Sterling or a basket of currencies.

- *Floating (or flexible) exchange rate* regimes, where the economy dictates movements in the exchange rate.

There are also intermediate exchange rate regimes that combine elements of the other regimes.

This classification of exchange rate regime is based on the classification method carried out by GGOW, which combined the IMF de jure classification with the actual exchange behavior so as to differentiate between official and actual policies. The GGOW classification method is also called Trichotomy Method.

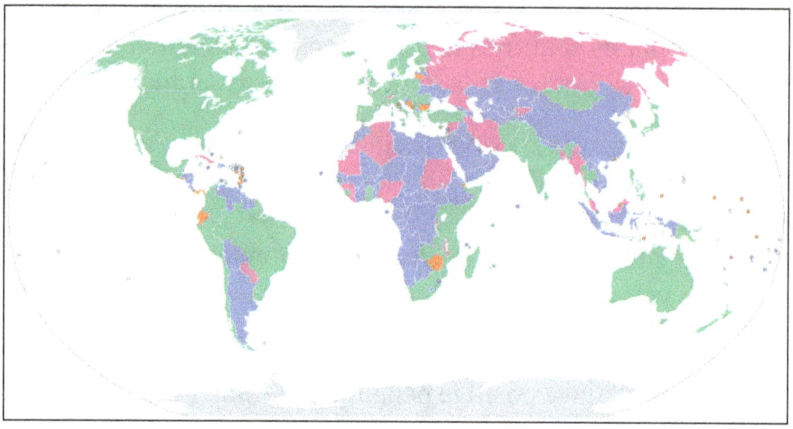

Floating Exchange Rate Regime

A floating (or flexible) exchange rate regime is one in which a country's exchange rate fluctuates in a wider range and the country's monetary authority makes no attempt to fix it against any base currency. A movement in the exchange is either an appreciation or depreciation.

Free Float

Free float, also known as clean float, signifies that a currency's value is allowed to fluctuate in response to foreign-exchange market mechanisms without government intervention.

Managed Float

Managed float, also known as dirty float, involves government intervention in the market exchange rate in different forms and degrees, in an attempt to make the exchange rate change in a direction conducive to the economic development of the country, especially during an extreme appreciation or depreciation.

A monetary authority may, for example, allow the exchange rate to float freely between an upper and lower bound, a price "ceiling" and "floor".

Intermediate Rate Regime

The exchange rate regimes between the fixed ones and the floating ones.

Band

There is only a tiny variation around the fixed exchange rate against another currency, well within plus or minus 2%.

For example: Denmark has fixed its exchange rate against the euro, keeping it very close to 7.44 krone = 1 euro (0.134 euro = 1 krone).

Crawling Peg

A crawling peg is when a currency steadily depreciates or appreciates at an almost constant rate against another currency, with the exchange rate following a simple trend.

Crawling Band

Some variation about the rate is allowed, and adjusted as above.

For example: Colombia from 1996 to 2002, and Chile in the 1990s.

Currency Basket Peg

A currency basket is a portfolio of selected currencies with different weightings. The currency basket peg is commonly used to minimize the risk of currency fluctuations. For example, Kuwait shifted the peg based on a currency basket consists of currencies of its major trade and financial partners.

Fixed Exchange Rate Regime

A fixed exchange rate regime, sometimes called a pegged exchange rate regime, is one in which a monetary authority pegs its currency's exchange rate to another currency, a basket of other currencies or to another measure of value (such as gold), and may allow the rate to fluctuate within a narrow range. To maintain the exchange rate within that range, a country's monetary authority usually needs to intervenes in the foreign exchange market. A movement in the peg rate is called either revaluation or devaluation.

Currency Board

Currency board is an exchange rate regime in which a country's exchange rate maintain a fixed exchange rate with a foreign currency, based on an explicit legislative commitment. It is a type of fixed regime that has special legal and procedural rules designed to make the peg "harder—that is, more durable". Examples include the Hong Kong dollar against the U.S dollar and Bulgarian lev against the Euro.

Dollarisation

Dollarisation, also *currency substitution*, means a country unilaterally adopts the currency of another country.

Most of the adopting countries are too small to afford the cost of running its own central bank or issuing its own currency. Most of these economies use the U.S dollar, but other popular choices include the euro, and the Australian and New Zealand dollars.

Currency Union

A currency union, also known as monetary union, is an exchange regime where two or more countries use the same currency. Under a currency union, there is some form of transnational structure such as a single central bank or monetary authority that is accountable to the member states.

Examples of currency unions are the Eurozone, CFA and CFP franc zones. One of the first known examples is the Latin Monetary Union that existed between 1865 and 1927. The Scandinavian Monetary Union existed between 1873 and 1905.

CURRENCY BAND

A currency band is a range of values for the exchange rate for a country's currency which the country's central bank acts to keep the exchange rate within.

The central bank selects a range, or "band", of values at which to set their currency, and will intervene in the market or return to a fixed exchange rate if the value of their currency shifts outside this band. This allows for some revaluation, but tends to stabilize the currency's value within the band. In this sense, it is a compromise between a fixed (or "pegged") exchange rate and a floating exchange rate.

For example, the exchange rate of the *renminbi* of the mainland of the People's Republic of China has recently been based upon a currency band; the European Economic Community's "snake in the tunnel" was a similar concept that failed, but ultimately led to the establishment of the European Exchange Rate Mechanism (ERM) and ultimately the Euro.

MANAGED FLOAT REGIME

Managed float regime is the current international financial environment in which exchange rates fluctuate from day to day, but central banks attempt to influence their countrie's exchange rates by buying and selling currencies to maintain a certain range. The peg used is known as a crawling peg.

In an increasingly integrated world economy, the currency rates impact any given country's economy through the trade balance. In this aspect, almost all currencies are *managed* since central banks or governments intervene to influence the value of their currencies. According to the International Monetary Fund, as of 2014, 82 countries and regions used a managed float, or 43% of all countries, constituting a plurality amongst exchange rate regime types.

DUAL EXCHANGE RATE

In economics, a dual exchange rate is the occurrence of two different values of a currency for different sets of monetary transactions. One of the most common types consists of a government setting one exchange rate for specific transactions involving foreign exchange and another exchange rate governing other transactions.

A dual exchange rate policy can arise for a variety of reasons. In the past European and Latin American countries have used dual exchange rates to ease the transition from a fixed rate to a floating rate. Dual exchange rates are similar to multiple exchange rates in that they can appear when there is simultaneously both an official and black market rate.

In the gold standard and the Bretton Woods system, the major developed countries mainly implemented fixed exchange rate systems. Due to the devaluation of the pound around the 1970s and the collapse of the Bretton Woods system, many developed countries switched to floating exchange rates. In 1971, France started to adopt the dual exchange rate system. After that, in 1973, Italy also adopted this system. Both countries maintained these dual exchange rate systems through the early 1970s. The Belgium–Luxembourg Economic Union has been using this system since the early 1990s.

Around the same time, many Latin American countries also shifted from a single exchange rate system to a dual exchange rate system or a multiple exchange rate system. With the structural adjustment to international trade that has occurred since the mid-1980s, especially the deepening of trade reform, Latin American countries have begun gradually abandoning multiple exchange rate systems, favoring instead the implementation of single exchange rate systems.

From 1981 to 1985, during a period of Chinese economic reform, China formally implemented a dual exchange rate system. After 1985, China appeared in the foreign exchange market and the official exchange rate coexisted with a market-determined exchange rate. This system, though, didn't last long and was abandoned in 1994.

From 1985 to 1995, South Africa also implemented a dual exchange rate system, and achieved remarkable results.

Advantages

The advantages of dual exchange systems are tied primarily to their ability to prevent capital movements from affecting the current account and the exchange rate for current transactions by separating the exchange market for capital transactions and the exchange market for current transactions. Dual exchange systems are oftentimes used as a short-term alternative to placing quantitative controls on capital movements, especially in cases where a country may be transitioning between exchange rate types.

Inflation

Dual exchange rates are oftentimes used to stabilize currency values when countries face financial crises. Because most modern financial crises are preceded by substantial inflows and outflows of short to medium-term loans (which create financial instability), countries may implement dual exchange markets in order to discourage undesirable capital imports. Dual exchange rates are able to discourage these undesirable imports while maintaining desirable capital imports and allowing the exchange rate of the current account market to remain independent of the exchange rate of the capital account market, thereby preventing substantial negative effects on the current account. This separation will prevent the current account exchange rate from devaluing or overvaluing a country's exports and may prevent inflation that would otherwise take place due to the inflows of undesirable capital imports.

Government Revenue

Countries implementing dual exchange systems may merely separate the exchange rates for the current and capital account markets, or they may set controls on one or the other; the latter option being intended to raise revenue for the government. Countries implementing such systems typically put any exchange controls on the market for financing current transactions. However, economists such as Raymond Mikesell have argued against use of exchange controls in dual exchange systems except those necessary to maintain the separation of the markets.

Disadvantages

In times of economic collapse, countries may choose to implement a dual exchange rate. This policy change can be seen as an efficient way to alleviate short-run economic hardship. However, dual exchange rate policies have several long-run economic problems. The primary issue that may arise within an economy operating under a dual exchange rate is misallocation of resources because dual exchange rate will reduce some industry's favorable exchange rate and those industry will not necessarily reflect its actual need because its performance have been unnaturally inflated. Continual misallocation of resources will eventually cause economic distortion. A dual exchange rate economy suffering from distortion will incur disparity between the financial exchange rate and the commercial exchange rate. Such an event can lead to the emergence of black markets and arbitrage from individuals seeking to make capital gains. Usage of a dual-exchange system in the long-run will cause inflation. The different exchange rates make it possible for a government to incur a loss in foreign currency transactions, resulting in the central bank printing more money to fix the loss. Over the long-run, this will result in significant inflation. If there is no government intervention these issues will persist and create serious economic distortion behavior.

CURRENCY SUBSTITUTION

Currency substitution or dollarization is the use of a foreign currency in parallel to or instead of the domestic currency.

Currency substitution can be full or partial. Most, if not all, full currency substitution has taken place after a major economic crisis, for example, Ecuador and El Salvador in Latin America and Zimbabwe in Africa. Some small economies, for whom it is impractical to maintain an independent currency, use those of their larger neighbours; for example Liechtenstein uses the Swiss Franc.

Partial currency substitution occurs when residents of a country choose to hold a significant share of their financial assets denominated in a foreign currency. It can also occur as a gradual conversion to full currency substitution, for example, Argentina and Peru were both in the process of converting to the U.S. dollar during the 1990s.

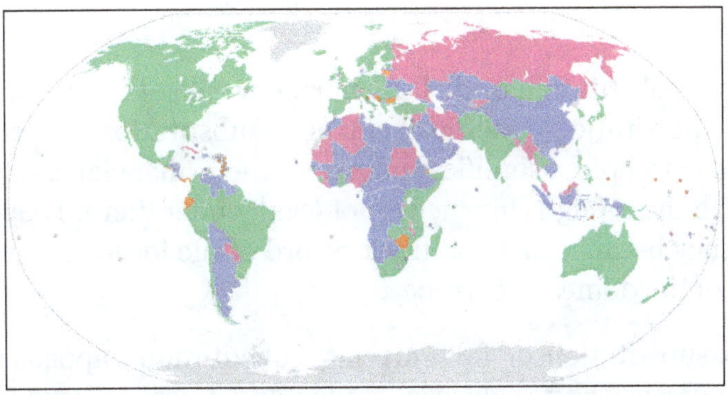

After the gold standard was abandoned at the outbreak of World War I and the Bretton Woods Conference following World War II, some countries sought exchange rate regimes to promote global economic stability, and hence their own prosperity. Countries usually peg their currency to a major convertible currency. "Hard pegs" are exchange rate regimes that demonstrate a stronger commitment to a fixed parity (i.e. currency boards) or relinquish control over their own currency (such as currency unions) while "soft pegs" are more flexible and floating exchange rate regimes. The collapse of "soft" pegs in Southeast Asia and Latin America in the late 1990s led to currency substitution becoming a serious policy issue.

A few cases of full currency substitution prior to 1999 had been the consequence of political and historical factors. In all long-standing currency substitution cases, historical and political reasons have been more influential than an evaluation of the economic effects of currency substitution. Panama adopted the US dollar as legal tender after independence as the result of a constitutional ruling. Ecuador and El Salvador became fully dollarized economies in 2000 and 2001 respectively, for different reasons. Ecuador underwent currency substitution to deal with a widespread political and financial crisis resulting from massive loss of confidence in its political and monetary institutions. By contrast, El Salvador's official currency substitution was a result of internal debates and in a context of stable macroeconomic fundamentals and long-standing unofficial currency substitution. The eurozone adopted the euro (€) as its common currency and sole legal tender in 1999, which might be considered a variety of full-commitment regime similar to full currency substitution despite some evident differences from other currency substitutions. For more on dollarisation, cf. Fields, David, and Matías Vernengo. "Dollarization".

Measures

There are two common indicators of currency substitution. The first measure is the share of foreign currency deposits (FCD) in the domestic banking system in the broad money including FCD. The second is the share of all foreign currency deposits held by domestic residents at home and abroad in their total monetary assets.

Types

Unofficial currency substitution or de facto currency substitution is the most common type of currency substitution. Unofficial currency substitution occurs when residents of a country choose to hold a significant share of their financial assets in foreign currency, even though the foreign currency is not legal tender there. They hold deposits in the foreign currency because of a bad track record of the local currency, or as a hedge against inflation of the domestic currency.

Official currency substitution or full currency substitution happens when a country adopts a foreign currency as its sole legal tender, and ceases to issue the domestic currency. Another effect of a country adopting a foreign currency as its own is that the country gives up all power to vary its exchange rate. There are a small number of countries adopting a foreign currency as legal tender.

Full currency substitution has mostly occurred in Latin America, the Caribbean and the Pacific, as many countries in those regions see the United States Dollar as a stable currency compared to the national one. For example, Panama underwent full currency substitution by adopting the US dollar as legal tender in 1904. This type of currency substitution is also known as de jure currency substitution.

Currency substitution can be used semiofficially (or officially bimonetary systems), where the foreign currency is legal tender alongside the domestic currency.

In literature, there is a set of related definitions of currency substitution such as external liability currency substitution, domestic liability currency substitution, banking sector's liability currency substitution or deposit currency substitution, and credit dollarlization. External liability currency substitution measures total external debt (private and public) denominated in foreign currencies of the economy. Deposit currency substitution can be measured as the share of foreign currency deposits in the total deposits of the banking system, and credit currency substitution can be measured as the share of dollar credit in the total credit of the banking system.

Effects

On Trade and Investment

One of the main advantages of adopting a strong foreign currency as sole legal tender is to reduce the transaction costs of trade among countries using the same currency. There are at least two ways to infer this impact from data. The first is the significantly negative effect of exchange rate volatility on trade in most cases, and the second is an association between transaction costs and the need to operate with multiple currencies. Economic integration with the rest of the world becomes easier as a result of lowered transaction costs and stabler prices. Rose applied the gravity model of trade and provided empirical evidence that countries sharing a common currency engage in significantly increased trade among them, and that the benefits of currency substitution for trade may be large.

Countries with full currency substitution can invoke greater confidence among international investors, inducing increased investments and growth. The elimination of the currency crisis risk due to full currency substitution leads to a reduction of country risk premiums and then to lower interest rates. These effects result in a higher level of investment. However, there is a positive association between currency substitution and interest rates in a dual-currency economy.

On Monetary and Exchange Rate Policies

Official currency substitution helps to promote fiscal and monetary discipline and thus greater macroeconomic stability and lower inflation rates, to lower real exchange rate volatility, and possibly to deepen the financial system. Firstly, currency substitution helps developing countries, providing a firm commitment to stable monetary and exchange rate policies by forcing a passive monetary policy. Adopting a strong foreign currency as legal tender will help to "eliminate the inflation-bias problem of discretionary monetary policy". Secondly, official currency substitution imposes stronger financial constraint on the government by eliminating deficit financing by issuing money. An empirical finding suggests that inflation has been significantly lower in economies with full currency substitution than nations with domestic currencies. The expected benefit of currency substitution is the elimination of the risk of exchange rate fluctuations and a possible reduction in the country's international exposure. Currency substitution cannot eliminate the risk of an external crisis but provides steadier markets as a result of eliminating fluctuations in exchange rates.

On the other hand, currency substitution leads to the loss of seigniorage revenue, the loss of monetary policy autonomy, and the loss of the exchange rate instruments. Seigniorage revenues are the profits generated when monetary authorities issue currency. When adopting a foreign currency as legal tender, a monetary authority needs to withdraw the domestic currency and give up future seigniorage revenue. The country loses the rights to its autonomous monetary and exchange rate policies, even in times of financial emergency. For example, former chairman of the Federal Reserve Alan Greenspan has stated that the central bank considers the effects of its decisions only on the US economy. In a full currency substituted economy, exchange rates are indeterminate and monetary authorities cannot devalue the currency. In an economy with high currency substitution, devaluation policy is less effective in changing the real exchange rate because of significant pass-through effects to domestic prices. However, the cost of losing an independent monetary policy exists when domestic monetary authorities can commit an effective counter-cyclical monetary policy, stabilizing the business cycle. This cost depends adversely on the correlation between the business cycle of the client country (the economy with currency substitution) and the business cycle of the anchor country. In addition, monetary authorities in economies with currency substitution diminish the liquidity assurance to their banking system.

On Banking Systems

In an economy with full currency substitution, monetary authorities cannot act as lender of last resort to commercial banks by printing money. The alternatives to lending to the bank system may include taxation and issuing government debt. The loss of the lender of last resort is considered a cost of full currency substitution. This cost depends on the initial level of unofficial currency substitution before moving to a full currency substituted economy. This relation is negative because in a heavily currency substituted economy, the central bank already fears difficulties in providing liquidity assurance to the banking system. However, literature points out the existence of alternative mechanisms to provide liquidity insurance to banks, such as a scheme by which the international financial community charges an insurance fee in exchange for a commitment to lend to a domestic bank.

Commercial banks in countries where saving accounts and loans in foreign currency are allowed may face two types of risks:

- Currency mismatch risk: Assets and liabilities on the balance sheets may be in different denominations. This may arise if the bank converts foreign currency deposits into local currency and lends in local currency or vice versa.
- Default risk: Arises if the bank uses the foreign currency deposits to lend in foreign currency.

However, currency substitution eliminates the probability of a currency crisis that negatively affects the banking system through the balance sheet channel. Currency substitution may reduce the possibility of systematic liquidity shortages and the optimal reserves in the banking system. Research has shown that official currency substitution has played a significant role in improving bank liquidity and asset quality in Ecuador and El Salvador.

Determinants of the Currency Substitution Process

The Dynamics of the Flight from Domestic Money

High and unanticipated inflation rates decrease the demand for domestic money and raise the demand for alternative assets, including forcign currency and assets dominated by foreign currency. This phenomenon is called the "flight from domestic money". It results in a rapid and sizable process of currency substitution. In countries with high inflation rates, the domestic currency tends to be gradually displaced by a stable currency. At the beginning of this process, the store-of-value function of the domestic currency is replaced by the foreign currency. Then, the unit-of-account function of the domestic currency is displaced when many prices are quoted in a foreign currency. A prolonged period of high inflation will induce the domestic currency to lose its function as medium of exchange when the public carries out many transactions in foreign currency.

Ize and Levy-Yeyati examine the determinants of deposit and credit currency substitution, concluding that currency substitution is driven by the volatility of inflation and the real exchange rate. Currency substitution increases with inflation volatility and decreases with the volatility of the real exchange rate.

Institutional Factors

The flight from domestic money depends on a country's institutional factors. The first factor is the level of development of the domestic financial market. An economy with a well-developed financial market can offer a set of alternative financial instruments denominated in domestic currency, reducing the role of foreign currency as an inflation hedge. The pattern of the currency substitution process also varies across countries with different foreign exchange and capital controls. In a country with strict foreign exchange regulations, the demand for foreign currency will be satisfied in the holding of foreign currency assets abroad and outside the domestic banking system. This demand often puts pressure on the parallel market of foreign currency and on the country's international reserves. Evidence for this pattern is given in the absence of currency substitution during the pre-reform period in most transition economies, because of constricted controls on foreign exchange and the banking system. In contrast, by increasing foreign currency reserves, a country might mitigate the shift of assets abroad and strengthen its external reserves in exchange for a currency substitution process. However, the effect of this regulation on the pattern of currency substitution depends on the public's expectations of macroeconomic stability and the sustainability of the foreign exchange regime.

ROLLOVER

A rollover may entail a number of actions, most popularly the transfer of the holdings of one retirement plan to another without creating a taxable event. A rollover may also entail reinvesting funds from a mature security into a new issue of the same or a similar security, or moving a FOREX (FX) position to the following delivery date, in which case the rollover incurs a charge.

In the context of retirement assets, the distribution from a retirement plan is reported on IRS Form 1099-R and may be limited to one per annum for each individual retirement account (IRA). The forex rollover fee arising from the difference in interest rates between the two currencies underlying a transaction is paid to the broker.

Rollovers often occur as a way of making money for a specific purpose, such as immediate income from day trading or for saving on taxes, as with retirement plans. A rollover IRA or IRA rollover is a transfer of funds from a retirement account into a traditional IRA or a Roth IRA. As shown by the following examples, the benefits of rollovers vary among different types of investments.

Rollover in Retirement Accounts

With a direct rollover, the retirement plan administrator may pay the plan's proceeds directly to another plan or to an IRA. The distribution may be issued as a check made payable to the new account. When receiving a distribution from an IRA through a trustee-to-trustee transfer, the institution holding the IRA may distribute the funds from the IRA to the other IRA or a retirement plan.

Taxes are typically not paid when performing a direct rollover or trustee-to-trustee transfer. However, distributions from a 60-day rollover and funds not rolled over are typically taxable.

Rollover in Forex Positions

Long-term forex day traders can make money in the market by trading from the positive side of the rollover equation. Traders begin by computing swap points, which is the difference between the forward rate and the spot rate of a specific currency pair as expressed in pips. Traders base their calculations on interest rate parity, which implies that investing in varying currencies should result in hedged returns that are equal, regardless of the currencie's interest rates.

Traders compute the swap points for a certain delivery date by considering the net benefit or cost of lending one currency and borrowing another against it during the time between the spot value date and the forward delivery date. Therefore, the trader makes money when he is on the positive side of the interest rollover payment.

FOREIGN EXCHANGE OPTION

In finance, a foreign exchange option (commonly shortened to just FX option or currency option) is a derivative financial instrument that gives the right but not the obligation to exchange money denominated in one currency into another currency at a pre-agreed exchange rate on a specified date.

The foreign exchange options market is the deepest, largest and most liquid market for options of any kind. Most trading is over the counter (OTC) and is lightly regulated, but a fraction is traded on exchanges like the International Securities Exchange, Philadelphia Stock Exchange, or the Chicago Mercantile Exchange for options on futures contracts. The global market for exchange-traded currency options was notionally valued by the Bank for International Settlements at $158.3 trillion in 2005.

For example, a GBPUSD contract could give the owner the right to sell £1,000,000 and buy $2,000,000 on December 31. In this case the pre-agreed exchange rate, or strike price, is 2.0000 USD per GBP (or GBP/USD 2.00 as it is typically quoted) and the notional amounts (notionals) are £1,000,000 and $2,000,000.

This type of contract is both a call on dollars and a put on sterling, and is typically called a GBPUSD put, as it is a put on the exchange rate; although it could equally be called a USDGBP call.

If the rate is lower than 2.0000 on December 31 (say 1.9000), meaning that the dollar is stronger and the pound is weaker, then the option is exercised, allowing the owner to sell GBP at 2.0000 and immediately buy it back in the spot market at 1.9000, making a profit of (2.0000 GBPUSD – 1.9000 GBPUSD) × 1,000,000 GBP = 100,000 USD in the process. If instead they take the profit in GBP (by selling the USD on the spot market) this amounts to 100,000 / 1.9000 = 52,632 GBP.

Trading

The difference between FX options and traditional options is that in the latter case the trade is to give an amount of money and receive the right to buy or sell a commodity, stock or other non-money asset. In FX options, the asset in question is also money, denominated in another currency. For example, a call option on oil allows the investor to buy oil at a given price and date. The investor on the other side of the trade is in effect selling a put option on the currency.

To eliminate residual risk, traders match the *foreign* currency notionals, not the local currency notionals, else the foreign currencies received and delivered do not offset.

In the case of an FX option on a *rate*, as in the above example, an option on GBPUSD gives a USD value that is linear in GBPUSD using USD as the numéraire (a move from 2.0000 to 1.9000 yields a.10 * $2,000,000 / $2.0000 = $100,000 profit), but has a non-linear GBP value. Conversely, the GBP value is linear in the USDGBP rate, while the USD value is non-linear. This is because inverting a rate has the effect of $x \mapsto 1/x$, which is non-linear.

Hedging

Corporations primarily use FX options to hedge *uncertain* future cash flows in a foreign currency. The general rule is to hedge *certain* foreign currency cash flows with *forwards*, and *uncertain* foreign cash flows with *options*.

Suppose a United Kingdom manufacturing firm expects to be paid US$100,000 for a piece of engineering equipment to be delivered in 90 days. If the GBP strengthens against the US$ over the next 90 days the UK firm loses money, as it will receive less GBP after converting the US$100,000 into GBP. However, if the GBP weakens against the US$, then the UK firm receives more GBP. This uncertainty exposes the firm to FX risk. Assuming that the cash flow is certain, the firm can enter into a forward contract to deliver the US$100,000 in 90 days time, in exchange for GBP at the current forward rate. This forward contract is free, and, presuming the expected cash arrives, exactly matches the firm's exposure, perfectly hedging their FX risk.

If the cash flow is uncertain, a forward FX contract exposes the firm to FX risk in the *opposite* direction, in the case that the expected USD cash is *not* received, typically making an option a better choice.

Using options, the UK firm can purchase a GBP call/USD put option (the right to sell part or all of their expected income for pounds sterling at a predetermined rate), which:

- Protects the GBP value that the firm expects in 90 day's time (presuming the cash is received).

- Costs at most the option premium (unlike a forward, which can have unlimited losses).
- Yields a profit if the expected cash is not received but FX rates move in its favor.

Valuation: The Garman–Kohlhagen model.

As in the Black–Scholes model for stock options and the Black model for certain interest rate options, the value of a European option on an FX rate is typically calculated by assuming that the rate follows a log-normal process.

The earliest currency options pricing model was published by Biger and Hull. The model preceded the Garmam and Kolhagen's Model. In 1983 Garman and Kohlhagen extended the Black–Scholes model to cope with the presence of two interest rates (one for each currency). Suppose that r_d is the risk-free interest rate to expiry of the domestic currency and r_f is the foreign currency risk-free interest rate (where domestic currency is the currency in which we obtain the value of the option; the formula also requires that FX rates both strike and current spot be quoted in terms of "units of domestic currency per unit of foreign currency"). The results are also in the same units and to be meaningful need to be converted into one of the currencies.

Then the domestic currency value of a call option into the foreign currency is,

$$c = S_0 e^{-r_f T} \mathcal{N}(d_1) - K e^{-r_d T} \mathcal{N}(d_2).$$

The value of a put option has value:

$$p = K e^{-r_d T} \mathcal{N}(-d_2) - S_0 e^{-r_f T} \mathcal{N}(-d_1)$$

where,

$$d_1 = \frac{\ln(S_0 / K) + (r_d - r_f + \sigma^2 / 2)T}{\sigma\sqrt{T}}$$

$$d_2 = d_1 - \sigma\sqrt{T}$$

S_0 is the current spot rate,

K is the strike price,

$\mathcal{N}(x)$ is the cumulative normal distribution function,

r_d is domestic risk free simple interest rate,

r_f is foreign risk free simple interest rate,

T is the time to maturity (calculated according to the appropriate day count convention), and σ is the volatility of the FX rate.

Risk Management

An earlier pricing model was published by Biger and Hull, Financial Management, spring 1983. The model preceded Garmam and Kolhagen Model. A wide range of techniques are in use for calculating the options risk exposure, (as for example the Vanna-Volga method). Although the option prices produced by every model agree (with Garman–Kohlhagen), risk numbers can vary significantly depending on the assumptions used for the properties of spot price movements, volatility surface and interest rate curves.

After Garman–Kohlhagen, the most common models are SABR and local volatility, although when agreeing risk numbers with a counterparty (e.g. for exchanging delta, or calculating the strike on a 25 delta option) Garman–Kohlhagen is always used.

FOREIGN EXCHANGE RISK

Foreign exchange risk (also known as FX risk, exchange rate risk or currency risk) is a financial risk that exists when a financial transaction is denominated in a currency other than the domestic currency of the company. The exchange risk arises when there is a risk of an unfavourable change in exchange rate between the domestic currency and the denominated currency before the date when the transaction is completed.

Foreign exchange risk also exists when the foreign subsidiary of a firm maintains financial statements in a currency other than the domestic currency of the consolidated entity.

Investors and businesses exporting or importing goods and services, or making foreign investments, have an exchange-rate risk but can take steps to manage (i.e. reduce) the risk.

Many businesses were unconcerned with, and did not manage, foreign exchange risk under the international Bretton Woods system. It wasn't until the switch to floating exchange rates, following the collapse of the Bretton Woods system, that firms became exposed to an increased risk from exchange rate fluctuations and began trading an increasing volume of financial derivatives in an effort to hedge their exposure. The currency crises of the 1990s and early 2000s, such as the Mexican peso crisis, Asian currency crisis, 1998 Russian financial crisis, and the Argentine peso crisis, led to substantial losses from foreign exchange and led firms to pay closer attention to their foreign exchange risk.

Types of Foreign Exchange Risk

Economic Risk

A firm has *economic risk* (also known as *forecast risk*) to the degree that its market value is influenced by unexpected exchange-rate fluctuations, which can severely affect the firm's market share with regard to its competitors, the firm's future cash flows, and ultimately the firm's value. Economic risk can affect the present value of future cash flows. An example of an economic risk would be a shift in exchange rates that influences the demand for a good sold in a foreign country.

Another example of an economic risk is the possibility that macroeconomic conditions will influence an investment in a foreign country. Macroeconomic conditions include exchange rates, government regulations, and political stability. When financing an investment or a project, a company's operating costs, debt obligations, and the ability to predict economically unsustainable circumstances should be thoroughly calculated in order to produce adequate revenues in covering those economic risks. For instance, when an American company invests money in a manufacturing plant in Spain, the Spanish government might institute changes that negatively impact the American company's ability to operate the plant, such as changing laws or even seizing the plant, or to otherwise make it difficult for the American company to move its profits out of Spain. As a result, all possible risks that outweigh an investment's profits and outcomes need to be closely scrutinized and strategically planned before initiating the investment. Other examples of potential economic risk are steep market downturns, unexpected cost overruns, and low demand for goods.

International investments are associated with significantly higher economic risk levels as compared to domestic investments. In international firms, economic risk heavily affects not only investors but also bondholders and shareholders, especially when dealing with the sale and purchase of foreign government bonds. However, economic risk can also create opportunities and profits for investors globally. When investing in foreign bonds, investors can profit from the fluctuation of the foreign-exchange markets and interest rates in different countries. Investors should always be aware of possible changes by the foreign regulatory authorities. Changing laws and regulations regarding sizes, types, timing, credit quality, and disclosures of bonds will immediately and directly affect investments in foreign countries. For example, if a central bank in a foreign country raises interest rates or the legislature increases taxes, the return on investment will be significantly impacted. As a result, economic risk can be reduced by utilizing various analytical and predictive tools that consider the diversification of time, exchange rates, and economic development in multiple countries, which offer different currencies, instruments, and industries.

When making a comprehensive economic forecast, several risk factors should be noted. One of the most effective strategies is to develop a set of positive and negative risks that associate with the standard economic metrics of an investment. In a macroeconomic model, major risks include changes in GDP, exchange-rate fluctuations, and commodity-price and stock-market fluctuations. It is equally critical to identify the stability of the economic system. Before initiating an investment, a firm should consider the stability of the investing sector that influences the exchange-rate changes. For instance, a service sector is less likely to have inventory swings and exchange-rate changes as compared to a large consumer sector.

Contingent Risk

A firm has *contingent risk* when bidding for foreign projects, negotiating other contracts, or handling direct foreign investments. Such a risk arises from the potential of a firm to suddenly face a transnational or economic foreign-exchange risk contingent on the outcome of some contract or negotiation. For example, a firm could be waiting for a project bid to be accepted by a foreign business or government that, if accepted, would result in an immediate receivable. While waiting, the firm faces a contingent risk from the uncertainty as to whether or not that receivable will accrue.

Transaction Risk

Companies will often participate in a transaction involving more than one currency. In order to meet the legal and accounting standards of processing these transactions, companies have to translate foreign currencies involved into their domestic currency. A firm has *transaction risk* whenever it has contractual cash flows (receivables and payables) whose values are subject to unanticipated changes in exchange rates due to a contract being denominated in a foreign currency. To realize the domestic value of its foreign-denominated cash flows, the firm must exchange, or translate, the foreign currency for domestic.

When firms negotiate contracts with set prices and delivery dates in the face of a volatile foreign exchange market, with rates constantly fluctuating between initiating a transaction and its settlement, or payment, those firms face the risk of significant loss. Businesses have the goal of making all monetary transactions profitable ones, and the currency markets must thus be carefully observed.

Applying public accounting rules causes firms with transnational risks to be impacted by a process known as "re-measurement". The current value of contractual cash flows are remeasured on each balance sheet.

Translation Risk

A firm's *translation risk* is the extent to which its financial reporting is affected by exchange-rate movements. As all firms generally must prepare consolidated financial statements for reporting purposes, the consolidation process for multinationals entails translating foreign assets and liabilities, or the financial statements of foreign subsidiaries, from foreign to domestic currency. While translation risk may not affect a firm's cash flows, it could have a significant impact on a firm's reported earnings and therefore its stock price.

Translation risk deals with the risk to a company's equities, assets, liabilities, or income, any of which can change in value due to fluctuating foreign exchange rates when a portion is denominated in a foreign currency. A company doing business in a foreign country will eventually have to exchange its host country's currency back into their domestic currency. When exchange rates appreciate or depreciate, significant, difficult-to-predict changes in the value of the foreign currency can occur. For example, U.S. companies must translate Euro, Pound, Yen, etc., statements into U.S. dollars. A foreign subsidiary's income statement and balance sheet are the two financial statements that must be translated. A subsidiary doing business in the host country usually follows that country's prescribed translation method, which may vary, depending on the subsidiary's business operations.

Subsidiaries can be characterized as either an integrated or a self-sustaining foreign entity. An integrated foreign entity operates as an extension of the parent company, with cash flows and business operations that are highly interrelated with those of the parent. A self-sustaining foreign entity operates in its local economic environment, independent of the parent company. Both integrated and self-sustaining foreign entities operate use functional currency, which is the currency of the primary economic environment in which the subsidiary operates and in which day-to-day operations are transacted. Management must evaluate the nature of its foreign subsidiaries to determine the appropriate functional currency for each.

There are three translation methods: current-rate method, temporal method, and U.S. translation procedures. Under the current-rate method, all financial statement line items are translated at the "current" exchange rate. Under the temporal method, specific assets and liabilities are translated at exchange rates consistent with the timing of the item's creation. The U.S. translation procedures differentiate foreign subsidiaries by functional currency, not subsidiary characterization. If a firm translates by the temporal method, a zero net exposed position is called fiscal balance. The temporal method cannot be achieved by the current-rate method because total assets will have to be matched by an equal amount of debt, but the equity section of the balance sheet must be translated at historical exchange rates.

Measuring Risk

If foreign-exchange markets are efficient—such that purchasing power parity, interest rate parity, and the international Fisher effect hold true—a firm or investor needn't concern itself with foreign exchange risk. A deviation from one or more of the three international parity conditions generally needs to occur for there to be a significant exposure to foreign-exchange risk. Financial risk is most commonly measured in terms of the variance or standard deviation of a quantity such as percentage returns or rates of change. In foreign exchange, a relevant factor would be the rate of change of the foreign currency spot exchange rate. A variance, or spread, in exchange rates indicates enhanced risk, whereas standard deviation represents exchange-rate risk by the amount exchange rates deviate, on average, from the mean exchange rate in a probabilistic distribution. A higher standard deviation would signal a greater currency risk. Because of its uniform treatment of deviations and for the automatically squaring of deviation values, economists have criticized the accuracy of standard deviation as a risk indicator. Alternatives such as average absolute deviation and semivariance have been advanced for measuring financial risk.

Value at Risk

Practitioners have advanced, and regulators have accepted, a financial risk management technique called value at risk (VaR), which examines the tail end of a distribution of returns for changes in exchange rates, to highlight the outcomes with the worst returns. Banks in Europe have been authorized by the Bank for International Settlements to employ VaR models of their own design in establishing capital requirements for given levels of market risk. Using the VaR model helps risk managers determine the amount that could be lost on an investment portfolio over a certain period of time with a given probability of changes in exchange rates.

Managing Risk

Transaction Hedging

Firms with exposure to foreign-exchange risk may use a number of hedging strategies to reduce that risk. Transaction exposure can be reduced either with the use of money markets, foreign exchange derivatives—such as forward contracts, options, futures contracts, and swaps—or with operational techniques such as currency invoicing, leading and lagging of receipts and payments, and exposure netting. Each hedging strategy comes with its own benefits that may make it more suitable than another, based on the nature of the business and risks it may encounter.

Forward and futures contracts serve similar purposes: they both allow transactions that take place in the future—for a specified price at a specified rate—that offset otherwise adverse exchange fluctuations. Forward contracts are more flexible, to an extent, because they can be customized to specific transactions, whereas futures come in standard amounts and are based on certain commodities or assets, such as other currencies. Because futures are only available for certain currencies and time periods, they cannot entirely mitigate risk, because there is always the chance that exchange rates will move in your favor. However, the standardization of futures can be a part of what makes them attractive to some: they are well-regulated and are traded only on exchanges.

Two popular and inexpensive methods companies can use to minimize potential losses is hedging with options and forward contracts. If a company decides to purchase an option, it is able to set a rate that is "at-worst" for the transaction. If the option expires and it's out-of-the-money, the company is able to execute the transaction in the open market at a favorable rate. If a company decides to take out a forward contract, it will set a specific currency rate for a set date in the future.

Currency invoicing refers to the practice of invoicing transactions in the currency that benefits the firm. It is important to note that this does not necessarily eliminate foreign exchange risk, but rather moves its burden from one party to another. A firm can invoice its imports from another country in its home currency, which would move the risk to the exporter and away from itself. This technique may not be as simple as it sounds; if the exporter's currency is more volatile than that of the importer, the firm would want to avoid invoicing in that currency. If both the importer and exporter want to avoid using their own currencies, it is also fairly common to conduct the exchange using a third, more stable currency.

If a firm looks to leading and lagging as a hedge, it must exercise extreme caution. Leading and lagging refer to the movement of cash inflows or outflows either forward or backward in time. For example, if a firm must pay a large sum in three months but is also set to receive a similar amount from another order, it might move the date of receipt of the sum to coincide with the payment. This delay would be termed lagging. If the receipt date were moved sooner, this would be termed leading the payment.

Another method to reduce exposure transaction risk is natural hedging (or netting foreign-exchange exposures), which is an efficient form of hedging because it will reduce the margin that is taken by banks when businesses exchange currencies; and it is a form of hedging that is easy to understand. To enforce the netting, there will be a systematic-approach requirement, as well as a real-time look at exposure and a platform for initiating the process, which, along with the foreign cash flow uncertainty, can make the procedure seem more difficult. Having a back-up plan, such as foreign-currency accounts, will be helpful in this process. The companies that deal with inflows and outflows in the same currency will experience efficiencies and a reduction in risk by calculating the net of the inflows and outflows, and using foreign-currency account balances that will pay in part for some or all of the exposure.

Translation Hedging

Translation exposure is largely dependent on the translation methods required by accounting standards of the home country. For example, the United States Federal Accounting Standards Board specifies when and where to use certain methods. Firms can manage translation exposure by performing a balance sheet hedge, since translation exposure arises from discrepancies between net assets and net liabilities solely from exchange rate differences. Following this logic, a firm could acquire an appropriate amount of exposed assets or liabilities to balance any outstanding discrepancy. Foreign exchange derivatives may also be used to hedge against translation exposure.

A common technique to hedge translation risk is called balance-sheet hedging, which involves speculating on the forward market in hopes that a cash profit will be realized to offset a non-cash loss from translation. This requires an equal amount of exposed foreign currency assets and liabilities on the firm's consolidated balance sheet. If this is achieved for each foreign currency, the net translation exposure will be zero. A change in the exchange rates will change the value of exposed liabilities to an equal degree but opposite to the change in the value of exposed assets.

Companies can also attempt to hedge translation risk by purchasing currency swaps or futures contracts. Companies can also request clients to pay in the company's domestic currency, whereby the risk is transferred to the client.

Strategies other than Financial Hedging

Firms may adopt strategies other than financial hedging for managing their economic or operating exposure, by carefully selecting production sites with a mind for lowering costs, using a policy of flexible sourcing in its supply chain management, diversifying its export market across a greater number of countries, or by implementing strong research and development activities and differentiating its products in pursuit of less foreign-exchange risk exposure.

By putting more effort into researching alternative methods for production and development, it is possible that a firm may discover more ways to produce their outputs locally rather than relying on export sources that would expose them to the foreign exchange risk. By paying attention to currency fluctuations around the world, firms can advantageously relocate their production to other countries. For this strategy to be effective, the new site must have lower production costs. There are many factors a firm must consider before relocating, such as a foreign nation's political and economic stability.

FOREIGN EXCHANGE DERIVATIVE

A foreign exchange derivative is a financial derivative whose payoff depends on the foreign exchange rates of two (or more) currencies. These instruments are commonly used for currency speculation and arbitrage or for hedging foreign exchange risk.

Foreign exchange transactions can be traced back to the fourteenth Century in the UK, but the coming into being and development of foreign exchange derivatives market was in the 1970s with the historical background and economic environment. Firstly, after the collapse of the Bretton Woods system, in 1976, IMF held a meeting in Jamaica and reached the Jamaica agreement. When the floating exchange-rate system replaced a fixed exchange-rate system, many countries relaxed control of interest rates and the risk of financial market increased. In order to reduce and avoid risks and achieve the purpose of hedging, modern financial derivatives came into being. Secondly, economic globalization promoted the globalization of financial activities and financial markets. After the collapse of the Bretton Woods system, much capital flew across the world.

Countries generally relaxed restrictions on domestic and foreign financial institutions and foreign investors. Changes in macroeconomic factors led to market risk and the demand for foreign exchange derivatives market increasing further, what promoted the development of the derivatives market. Under such circumstances, financial institutions continue to create new financial tools to meet the needs of traders for avoiding the risk. Therefore, many foreign exchange derivatives were widely used, making the foreign exchange market expand from the traditional transactions market to the derivatives market, and develop rapidly.

Specific foreign exchange derivatives, and related concepts include:

Instruments

Basic Features

Margin trading which means you could pay part of margin but make full transaction without the practically transferring of your principal. The end of contract mostly adopt the settlement for differences. At the same time, the buyers need not present full payment only when the physical delivery gets performed on the maturity date. Therefore, the characters of trading financial derivatives include the lever effect. When margin decreases, the risk of trading will increase, as the lever effect will increase.

Basic Function

- Avoiding and managing systemically financial risk: According to statistics, the systemic risk accounts for 50% in the risk of financial market investment in developed countries, so preventing and mitigating systemic financial risks is vital in management of financial institutions. All traditional risk-management tools (insurance, asset-liability management, portfolio etc). cannot prevent systemic risk, while foreign exchange derivatives can efficiently avoid systemic risk, which is brought by the adverse change of the prices in basic goods market, by its specific hedging function.
- Increasing financial system's ability to resist risk: Financial derivatives, which contain functions to avoid and shift risk, can transfer the risk to individuals with more risk tolerance. The process turns financial risk that would be excessive for weak-risk-tolerance companies to withstand to small or intermediate impact for powerful enterprises, while some might be converted to speculator's chances to make profit. It strengthens financial system's overall win-resisting ability and consolidates this system's robustness.
- Improving economic efficiency: It mainly refers to raise the efficiency of business running and financial market. The former is embodied as providing business with tools to prevent the risk of finance, reducing the founding cost and increasing economic benefits. The latter reflected as it enriches and completes

financial market system by countless kinds of products, reduces the occurrence of asymmetric information, realizes the desirable arrangement of risk, increases the efficiency in pricing, etc.

Trading Schemes

- Foreign forward swap transaction trading: The parties of a swap contract agree to periodically swap capital in some time.
- Foreign exchange option trading: The contract can agree the option holder to exchange it at a defined price as his right instead of an obligation.
- Forward exchange futures transaction trading: Future contract's buyers or sellers submit margin at the beginning of trading, as a kind of buffering mechanism. The margin needs to make corresponding adjustment on time according to the price of contract.
- Forward forex exchange trading: Similar to futures, but it is an unstandardized agreement without the margin requirement.

Risk and Return

Foreign exchange derivatives can allow investors to engage in risk avoidance to keep value, but also can earn profit through speculation. This kind of specific duality makes derivatives more uncontrollable. Thus, foreign exchange derivative products can be risky while rewardable in addition speculative transactions in the financial market are considered negatively and potentially damaging to the real economy.

INTERNATIONAL FISHER EFFECT

The International Fisher Effect (IFE) is an economic theory stating that the expected disparity between the exchange rate of two currencies is approximately equal to the difference between their countrie's nominal interest rates.

The IFE is based on the analysis of interest rates associated with present and future risk-free investments, such as Treasuries, and is used to help predict currency movements. This is in contrast to other methods that solely use inflation rates in the prediction of exchange rate shifts, instead functioning as a combined view relating inflation and interest rates to a currency's appreciation or depreciation.

The theory stems from the concept that real interest rates are independent of other monetary variables, such as changes in a nation's monetary policy, and provide a better indication of the health of a particular currency within a global market. The IFE provides for the assumption that countries with lower interest rates will likely also experience lower levels of inflation, which can result in increases in the real value of the associated currency when compared to other nations. By contrast, nations with higher interest rates will experience depreciation in the value of their currency.

Calculating the International Fisher Effect

IFE is calculated as:

$$E = \frac{i_1 + i_2}{1 + i_2} \approx\sim i_1 - i_2$$

where:

E = the percent change in the exchange rate.

i_1 = country A's interest rate.

i_2 =country B's interest rate For example, if country A's interest rate is 10% and country B's interest rate is 5%, country B's currency should appreciate roughly 5% compared to country A's currency. The rationale for the IFE is that a country with a higher interest rate will also tend to have a higher inflation rate. This increased amount of inflation should cause the currency in the country with a higher interest rate to depreciate against a country with lower interest rates.

The Fisher Effect and the International Fisher Effect

The Fisher Effect and the IFE are related models but are not interchangeable. The Fisher Effect claims that the combination of the anticipated rate of inflation and the real rate of return are represented in the nominal interest rates. The IFE expands on the Fisher Effect, suggesting that because nominal interest rates reflect anticipated inflation rates and currency exchange rate changes are driven by inflation rates, then currency changes are proportionate to the difference between the two nation's nominal interest rates.

Application of the International Fisher Effect

Empirical research testing the IFE has shown mixed results, and it is likely that other factors also influence movements in currency exchange rates. Historically, in times when interest rates were adjusted by more significant magnitudes, the IFE held more validity. However, in recent years inflation expectations and nominal interest rates around the world are generally low, and the size of interest rate changes is correspondingly relatively small. Direct indications of inflation rates, such as consumer price indexes (CPI), are more often used to estimate expected changes in currency exchange rates.

References

- O'Sullivan, Arthur; Sheffrin, Steven M. (2003). Economics: Principles in Action. Upper Saddle River, New Jersey 07458: Pearson Prentice Hall. p. 462. ISBN 0-13-063085-3
- Foreign-exchange-market-meaning-functions-and-kinds, balance-of-payment, macro-economics-30428: yourarticlelibrary.com, Retrieved 13 March, 2020
- Dooley, M.; Folkerts-Landau, D.; Garber, P. (2009). "Bretton Woods Ii Still Defines the International Monetary System". Pacific Economic Review. 14 (3): 297–311. doi:10.1111/j.1468-0106.2009.00453.x
- What-is-forward-exchange-market, economics-12046: preservearticles.com, Retrieved 30 June, 2020
- Calvo, G.; Reinhart, C. (2002). "Fear of Floating". Quarterly Journal of Economics. 117 (2): 379–408. doi:10.1162/003355302753650274
- Factors-influence-exchange-rates, trading: investopedia.com, Retrieved 26 July, 2020
- Reinhart, C. M.; Rogoff, K. S. (2004). "The Modern History of Exchange Rate Arrangements: A Reinterpretation" (PDF). The Quarterly Journal of Economics. 119: 1. doi:10.1162/003355304772839515

Financial Globalization

CHAPTER 4

The global linkages through cross-border financial flows fall under the domain of financial globalization. It further includes domestic and global financial system, trade finance, etc. The topics elaborated in this chapter will help in gaining a better perspective of financial globalization.

Financial globalization, by definition, means the integration of financial markets of all countries of the world into one. This is only possible provided uniformity can be brought in the terms and conditions across the globe for raising international loans. The existence of different currencies with their different degrees of convertibility prevents uniformity in the terms and the conditions for loans. Consequently, not only does the existence of different currencies act as a barrier to such integration, but it disproportionately benefits the developed countries.

Financial globalization has offered substantial benefits to the national economies and to both investors and wealth creators. However, it has a wreaking effect on financial markets as well.

Driving Forces of Financial Globalization

When we talk about financial globalization, there are four major factors to be considered:

- Advancement in information and communication technologies: Technological advancements have made market players and governments far more efficient in collecting the information needed to manage financial risks.
- Globalization of national economies: Economic globalization has made production, consumption, and investments dispersed over various geographic locations. As barriers to international trade have been lowered, international flows of goods and services have dramatically increased.
- Liberalization of national financial and capital markets: Liberalization and fast improvements in IT and the globalization of national economies have resulted in highly spread financial innovations. It has increased the growth of international capital movements.
- Competition among intermediary services providers: Competition has increased

manifold due to technological advancements and financial liberalization. A new class of nonbank financial entities, including institutional investors, have also emerged.

Changes in Capital Markets

The driving forces of financial globalization have led to four dramatic changes in the structure of national and international capital markets:

- First, banking systems have been under a process of disintermediation. Financial intermediation is happening more through tradable securities and not through bank loans and deposits.
- Second, cross-border financing has increased. Investors are now trying to enhance their returns by diversifying their portfolios internationally. They are now seeking the best investment opportunities from around the world.
- Third, the non-banking financial institutions are competing with banks in national and international markets, decreasing the prices of financial instruments. They are taking advantage of economies of scale.
- Fourth, banks have accessed a market beyond their traditional businesses. It has enabled the banks to diversify their sources of income and the risks.

Benefits and Risks of Financial Globalization

One of the major benefits of Financial Globalization is that the risk of a "credit crunch" has been reduced to extremely low levels. When banks are under strain, they can now raise funds from international capital markets.

Another benefit is that, with more choices, borrowers and investors get a better pricing on their financing. Corporations can finance the investments more cheaply.

The disadvantage is that the markets are now extremely volatile, and this can be a threat to financial stability. Financial globalization has altered the balance of risks in international capital markets.

With financial globalization, creditworthy banks and businesses in emerging markets can now reduce their borrowing costs. However, emerging markets with weak or poorly managed banks are at risk.

Safeguarding Financial Stability

The crises of the 1990s have shown the importance for a prudent sovereign debt management, effective capital account liberalization, and management of domestic financial systems.

Private financial institutions and market players can now contribute to financial stability by managing their businesses well and avoiding unnecessary risk-taking.

As financial stability is a global public good, governments and regulators also play a key role in it. The scope of this role is increasingly getting international.

The IMF is a key role-player as well. Its global surveillance initiatives to enhance its ability to manage international financial stability must also stay in track.

GLOBAL FINANCIAL SYSTEM

The global financial system is the financial system consisting of institutions and regulators that act on the international level, as opposed to those that act on a national or regional level. The main players are the global institutions, such as International Monetary Fund and Bank for International Settlements, national agencies and government departments, e.g., central banks and finance ministries, private institutions acting on the global scale, e.g., banks and hedge funds, and regional institutions, e.g., the Eurozone.

Main Agents

There are four main agents of financial globalization: governments, borrowers, investors, and financial institutions. Each of them is helping countries become more financially integrated.

Governments are one of the main agents of financial globalization. Governments allow globalization by liberalizing restrictions on the domestic financial sector and the capital account of the balance of payments. In the past, governments used to regulate the domestic financial sector by restricting the allocation of credit through controls on prices and quantities. Governments also imposed several constraints on cross-country capital movements. The list of instruments used to restrict the capital account is rather extensive, including restrictions on foreign exchange transactions, derivative transactions, lending and borrowing activities by banks and corporations, and the participation of foreign investors in the local financial system.

Even though the domestic financial sector and the capital account were heavily regulated for a long time, Kaminsky and Schmukler show how the restrictions have been lifted over time.

Borrowers and investors, including households and firms, have also become main agents of financial globalization. By borrowing abroad, firms and individuals can relax their financial constrains to smooth consumption and investment. Firms can expand their financing alternatives by raising funds directly through bonds and equity issues in international markets and thereby reducing the cost of capital, expanding their investor base, and increasing liquidity. More financing alternatives help foreign investors overcome direct and indirect investment barriers. International investors, as argued in Obstfeld and Tesar and Werner, have taken advantage of financial globalization to achieve cross-country risk diversification.

Financial institutions, through the internationalization of financial services, are also a major driving force of financial globalization. As discussed by the International Monetary Fund, changes at the global level and changes in both developed and developing countries explain the role of financial institutions as a force of globalization. At a global level, the gains in information technology have diminished the importance of geography, allowing international corporations to service several markets from one location. In developed countries, increased competition has led banks and other nonbank financial firms to look for expanding their market shares into new businesses and markets, attracting customers from other countries, what allows them to diversify risk. Decreasing costs due to deregulation and technical improvements were accompanied by more competition. Moreover, the liberalization of the regulatory systems has opened the door for international firms to participate in local markets. Macroeconomic stabilization, better business environment, and stronger fundamentals in emerging markets ensured a more attractive climate for foreign investment.

Financial Globalization and Financial Sector Development

Financial globalization can lead to the development of the financial system. A well functioning financial sector provides funds to borrowers (households, firms, and governments) who have productive investment opportunities.

Financial globalization can help improve the functioning of the financial system through two main channels. First, financial globalization can increase the availability of funds. Second, financial globalization can improve the financial infrastructure, what can reduce the problem of asymmetric information. As a consequence, financial globalization can potentially decrease adverse selection and moral hazard, enhancing the availability of credit.

Regarding the first channel, in a financially integrated world, funds can flow freely from countries with excess funds to countries where the marginal product of capital is high. In this context, both foreign institutions and individuals might provide capital to developing countries if they expect these countries to grow faster than developed economies. As a consequence, countries can smooth consumption and make investments financed by foreign capital. This flow of capital from developed to developing countries is reflected in the large current account deficits typically observed in many developing nations.

The effects of capital flows on financial development take place because new sources of funds and more capital become available. New sources of funds mean that borrowers not only depend on domestic funds, they can also borrow from foreign countries willing to invest in domestic assets. The capital available from new sources means that market discipline is now stronger both at the macroeconomic level and at the financial sector level, as now local and foreign investors enforce market discipline on private and public borrowers. Foreign capital is particularly effective in imposing this kind of discipline given its footloose nature; foreign capital can more easily shift investment across countries. Domestic capital tends to have more restrictions to invest internationally.

Thanks in part to the availability of more capital, developing economies have developed their stock and bond markets as well as some of their local financial service industry. Capital markets have developed, in the sense that more domestic equity and bonds are issued and traded, but this does not imply that all domestic financial institutions have become more important. Borrowers and investors can just use international financial intermediaries, like stock exchanges and banks, to conduct their financial transactions. In fact, domestic financial institutions can actually shrink due to competition with international financial institutions. For example, local banks obtain a lower share of the domestic market. Moreover, as Claessens, Klingebiel, and Schmukler argue, many stock markets are shrinking as trading moves from domestic markets to major global stock exchanges.

The second channel is that financial globalization can improve the financial infrastructure. An improved financial sector infrastructure means that borrowers and lenders operate in a more transparent, competitive, and efficient financial system. In this environment, problems of asymmetric information are minimized and credit is maximized.

In theory, there are different ways through which financial globalization can lead to improvements in the financial sector infrastructure. First, financial globalization can lead to a greater competition in the provision of funds, which can generate efficiency gains. Second, the adoption of international accounting standards can increase transparency. Third, the introduction of international financial intermediaries would push the financial sector towards the international frontier. Fourth, Stulz argues that financial globalization improves corporate governance; new shareholders and potential bidders can lead to a closer monitoring of management. Fifth, Crockett claims that the increase in the technical capabilities for engaging in precision financing results in a growing completeness of local and global markets. Sixth, Stiglitz argues that the stringent market discipline imposed by financial globalization has consequences not only on the macro-economy, but also on the business environment and other institutional factors.

Foreign bank entry is another way through which financial globalization can improve the financial infrastructure of developing countries. Mishkin argues that foreign banks enhance financial development for at least three main reasons. First, foreign banks have more diversified portfolios as they have access to sources of funds from all over the world, what means that they are exposed to less risk and are less affected by negative shocks to the home country economy. Second, foreign entry can lead to the adoption of best practices in the banking industry, particularly in risk management but also in management techniques, what leads to a more efficient banking sector. Third, if foreign banks dominate the banking sector, governments are less likely to bail out banks when they have solvency problems. A lower likelihood of bailouts encourages a more prudent behavior by banking institutions, an increased discipline, and a reduction in moral hazard. The World Bank discusses this topic in greater depth.

Major Flaws of the Global Financial System

Billions of People Globally Remain Unbanked

To participate in the global financial sector, whether it is to make a digital payment or manage one's wealth, one must have access to a bank account. However, 1.7 billion adults worldwide remain unbanked, having zero access to an account with a financial institution or a mobile money provider.

Global Financial Literacy Remains Low

For people to successfully use financial services and markets, they must have some degree of financial literacy. According to a recent global survey, just 1-in-3 people show an understanding of basic financial concepts, with most of these people living in high income economies.

Without an understanding of key concepts in finance, it makes it difficult for the majority of the population to make the right decisions and to build wealth.

High Intermediary Costs and Slow Transactions

Once a person has access to financial services, sending and storing money should be inexpensive and fast.

However, just the opposite is true. Around the globe, the average cost of a remittance is 7.01% in fees per transaction – and when using banks, that rises to 10.53%. Even worse, these transactions can take days at a time, which seems quite unnecessary in today's digital era.

Low Trust in Financial Institutions and Governments

The financial sector is the least trusted business sector globally, with only a 57% level of trust according to Edelman. Meanwhile, trust in governments is even lower, with only 40% trusting the U.S. government, and the global country average sitting at 47%.

Rising Global Inequality

In a centralized system, financial markets tend to be dominated by those who are best connected to them.

These are people who have:

- Access to many financial opportunities and asset classes.
- Capital to deploy.
- Informational advantages.
- Access to financial expertise.

Currency Manipulation and Censorship

In a centralized system, countries have the power to manipulate and devalue fiat currencies, and this can have a devastating effect on markets and the lives of citizens.

In Venezuela, for example, the government has continually devalued its currency, creating runaway hyperinflation as a result. The last major currency manipulation in 2018 increased the price of a cup of coffee by over 772,400% in six months.

Further, centralized power also gives governments and financial institutions the ability to financially censor citizens, by taking actions such as freezing accounts, denying access to payment systems, removing funds from accounts, and denying the retrieval of funds during bank runs.

TRADE FINANCE

Trade finance represents the financial instruments and products that are used by companies to facilitate international trade and commerce. Trade finance makes it possible and easier for importers and exporters to transact business through trade. Trade finance is an umbrella term meaning it covers many financial products that banks and companies utilize to make trade transactions feasible.

Working of Trade Finance

The function of trade finance is to introduce a third-party to transactions to remove the payment risk and the supply risk. Trade finance provides the exporter with receivables or payment according to the agreement while the importer might be extended credit to fulfill the trade order.

The parties involved in trade finance are numerous and can include:

- Banks.
- Trade finance companies.

- Importers and exporters.
- Insurers.
- Export credit agencies and service providers.

Trade financing is different than conventional financing or credit issuance. General financing is used to manage solvency or liquidity, but trade financing may not necessarily indicate a buyer's lack of funds or liquidity. Instead, trade finance may be used to protect against international trade's unique inherent risks, such as currency fluctuations, political instability, issues of non-payment, or the creditworthiness of one of the parties involved.

Below are a few of the financial instruments used in trade finance:

- Lending lines of credit can be issued by banks to help both importers and exporters.
- Letters of credit reduce the risk associated with global trade since the buyer's bank guarantees payment to the seller for the goods shipped. However, the buyer is also protected since payment will not be made unless the terms in the LC are met by the seller. Both parties have to honor the agreement for the transaction to go through.
- Factoring is when companies are paid based on a percentage of their accounts receivables.
- Export credit or working capital can be supplied to exporters.
- Insurance can be used for shipping and the delivery of goods and can also protect the exporter from nonpayment by the buyer.

Although international trade has been in existence for centuries, trade finance facilitates its advancement. The widespread use of trade finance has contributed to international trade growth.

Trade Financing Reducing Risk

Trade finance can help reduce the risk associated with global trade by reconciling the divergent needs of an exporter and importer. Ideally, an exporter would prefer the importer to pay upfront for an export shipment to avoid the risk that the importer takes the shipment but refuses to pay for the goods. However, if the importer pays the exporter upfront, the exporter may accept the payment but refuse to ship the goods.

A common solution to this problem is for the importer's bank to provide a letter of credit to the exporter's bank that provides for payment once the exporter presents documents that prove the shipment occurred, like a bill of lading. The letter of credit guarantees that once the issuing bank receives proof that the exporter shipped the goods and the terms of the agreement have been met, it will issue the payment to the exporter.

With the letter of credit, the buyer's bank assumes the responsibility of paying the seller. The buyer's bank would have to ensure the buyer was financially viable enough to honor the transaction. Trade finance helps both importers and exporters build trust in dealing with each other and thus facilitating trade.

References

- International-financial-globalization.htm, international-finance: tutorialspoint.com, Retrieved 25 May, 2020
- Benefits-and-Risks-of-Financial-Globalization-Challenges-for-Developing-Countries- 239922-690: researchgate.net, Retrieved 17 January, 2020
- 7-major-flaws-global-financial-system: visualcapitalist.com, Retrieved 30 March, 2020
- Tradefinance, terms: investopedia.com, Retrieved 26 May, 2020

International Trade

5 CHAPTER

The exchange of goods, capital and services across international borders and territories is known as international trade. Some of the aspects studied under it are export and import trade, international trade theory, mercantilism, etc. All the aspects related to international trade have been carefully analyzed in this chapter.

International trade allows countries to expand their markets for both goods and services that otherwise may not have been available domestically. As a result of international trade, the market contains greater competition, and therefore more competitive prices, which brings a cheaper product home to the consumer.

Working of International Trade

International trade gives rise to a world economy, in which supply and demand, and therefore prices, both affect and are affected by global events. Political change in Asia, for example, could result in an increase in the cost of labor, thereby increasing the manufacturing costs for an American sneaker company based in Malaysia, which would then result in an increase in the price charged at your local mall. A decrease in the cost of labor, on the other hand, would likely result in you having to pay less for your new shoes.

A product that is sold to the global market is called an export, and a product that is bought from the global market is an import. Imports and exports are accounted for in a country's current account in the balance of payments.

Comparative Advantage: Increased Efficiency of Trading Globally

Global trade allows wealthy countries to use their resources—whether labor, technology or capital—more efficiently. Because countries are endowed with different assets and natural resources (land, labor, capital, and technology), some countries may produce the same good more efficiently and therefore sell it more cheaply than other countries. If a country cannot efficiently produce an item, it can obtain the it by trading with another country that can. This is known as specialization in international trade.

Let's take a simple example. Country A and Country B both produce cotton sweaters and wine. Country A produces ten sweaters and six bottles of wine a year while Country B produces six sweaters and ten bottles of wine a year. Both can produce a total of 16 units. Country A, however, takes three hours to produce the ten sweaters and two hours to produce the six bottles of wine (total of five hours). Country B, on the other hand, takes one hour to produce ten sweaters and three hours to produce six bottles of wine (a total of four hours).

But these two countries realize that they could produce more by focusing on those products with which they have a comparative advantage. Country A then begins to produce only wine, and Country B produces only cotton sweaters. Each country can now create a specialized output of 20 units per year and trade equal proportions of both products. As such, each country now has access to 20 units of both products.

We can see then that for both countries, the opportunity cost of producing both products is greater than the cost of specializing. More specifically, for each country, the opportunity cost of producing 16 units of both sweaters and wine is 20 units of both products (after trading). Specialization reduces their opportunity cost and therefore maximizes their efficiency in acquiring the goods they need. With the greater supply, the price of each product would decrease, thus giving an advantage to the end consumer as well.

Note that, in the example above, Country B could produce both wine and cotton more efficiently than Country A (less time). This is called an absolute advantage, and Country B may have it because of a higher level of technology.

Criticisms of Comparative Advantage

Why doesn't the world have open trading between countries? When there is free trade, why do some countries remain poor at the expense of others? There are many reasons, but the most influential is something that economists call rent-seeking. Rent-seeking occurs when one group organizes and lobbies the government to protect its interests.

Say, for example, the producers of American shoes understand and agree with the free-trade argument—but they also know that their narrow interests would be negatively impacted by cheaper foreign shoes. Even if laborers would be most productive by switching from making shoes to making computers, nobody in the shoe industry wants to lose his or her job or see profits decrease in the short run.

This desire could lead the shoemakers to lobby for special tax breaks for their products and extra duties (or even outright bans) on foreign footwear. Appeals to save American jobs and preserve a time-honored American craft abound—even though, in the long run, American laborers would be made relatively less productive and American consumers relatively poorer by such protectionist tactics.

Other Possible Benefits of Trading Globally

International trade not only results in increased efficiency but also allows countries to participate in a global economy, encouraging the opportunity for foreign direct investment (FDI), which is the amount of money that individuals invest into foreign companies and assets. In theory, economies can therefore grow more efficiently and can more easily become competitive economic participants.

For the receiving government, FDI is a means by which foreign currency and expertise can enter the country. It raises employment levels, and theoretically, leads to a growth in gross domestic product. For the investor, FDI offers company expansion and growth, which means higher revenues.

Free Trade vs. Protectionism

As with all theories, there are opposing views. International trade has two contrasting views regarding the level of control placed on trade: free trade and protectionism. Free trade is the simpler of the two theories: a laissez-faire approach, with no restrictions on trade. The main idea is that supply and demand factors, operating on a global scale, will ensure that production happens efficiently. Therefore, nothing needs to be done to protect or promote trade and growth, because market forces will do so automatically.

In contrast, protectionism holds that regulation of international trade is important to ensure that markets function properly. Advocates of this theory believe that market inefficiencies may hamper the benefits of international trade, and they aim to guide the market accordingly. Protectionism exists in many different forms, but the most common are tariffs, subsidies, and quotas. These strategies attempt to correct any inefficiency in the international market.

As it opens up the opportunity for specialization, and therefore more efficient use of resources, international trade has the potential to maximize a country's capacity to produce and acquire goods. Opponents of global free trade have argued, however, that international trade still allows for inefficiencies that leave developing nations compromised. What is certain is that the global economy is in a state of continual change, and, as it develops, so too must its participants.

TRADE AND DEVELOPMENT

Trade can be a key factor in economic development. The prudent use of trade can boost a country's development and create absolute gains for the trading partners involved. Trade has been touted as an important tool in the path to development by prominent economists. However trade may not be a panacea for development as important questions surrounding how free trade really is and the harm trade can cause domestic infant industries to come into play.

The current consensus is that trade, development, and poverty reduction are intimately linked. Sustained economic growth over longer periods is associated with poverty reduction, while trade and growth are linked. Countries that develop invariably increase their integration with the global economy. while export-led growth has been.

Continents, countries and sectors that have not developed and remain largely poor have comparative advantage in three main areas:

- Natural resource exploitation, i.e. running down of natural capital such as rain forest timber.
- Low-education labor-intensive manufacturing, due to high population densities and little suitable land per person.
- Agriculture, due to low population densities and relatively large areas of suitable land per person.

Crucially for poverty reduction, the latter two at least are labor-intensive, helping to ensure that growth in these sectors will be poverty-reducing. However, low value-added, price instability and sustainability in these commodity sectors means they should be used only temporarily and as stepping stones in the path to economic development.

Agriculture

In many developing countries, agriculture employs a large proportion of the labor force, while food consumption accounts for a large share of household income. The United Nations Conference on Trade and Development (UNCTAD) notes that this means that "even small changes in agricultural employment opportunities, or prices, can have major socio-economic effects in developing countries". Thus whatever the development strategy a particular country adopts, the role of agriculture will often be crucial. In 1994, the agricultural sector employed over 70% of the labor force in low-income countries, 30% in middle-income countries, and only 4% in high-income countries.

In poor countries with low population densities and enough suitable land area, which includes most countries in Africa and Latin America, agriculture is central to the economy. In poor regions and rural areas within middle-income developing countries, the concentration of poverty in rural areas of otherwise better-off developing countries makes the development of agriculture vital there. Finally, in Net Food Importing Developing Countries (NFIDCs), there is a positive link between growing agricultural exports and increases in local food production, which makes agricultural development if anything even more important, as food security and the financial stability of the government are also at stake. In Vietnam in the 1990s, increases in production and export of coffee of 15% a year contributed to a nearly 50% rise in food production in the same period. As agricultural GDP grew 4.6% per year, rural poverty fell from 66% in 1993 to 45% in 1998.

Anderson estimate annual welfare losses of $19.8 billion for developing countries from agricultural tariffs – even after Uruguay Round reforms. This is three times the loss from OECD import restrictions on textiles and clothing. A combination of better market access, and domestic reforms and foreign aid to enhance the ability of developing countries to take advantage of it, could have a significant impact on poverty reduction, and help to meet the Millennium Development Goals.

The largest beneficiaries of agricultural liberalization would be OECD countries themselves: welfare losses of $62.9bn a year are estimated as resulting from the distortionary policies. Nor is the traditional objective of OECD agricultural subsidy (supporting small farmers) achieved by this system in a manner that could be characterised as efficient: most of the producer support incomes goes to better-off farmers, with the poorest 40% receiving just 8% of the support spent.

Market Access

Market Access to Developed Countries

The issue of market access to high-income countries is a thorny but crucial one. The issues fall into three main groups: first, those relating to deliberately imposed barriers to trade, such as tariffs, quotas, and tariff escalation. Second, barriers to trade resulting from domestic and external producer support, primarily in the form of subsidies, but also including, for example, export credits. Third, those relating to indirect barriers to trade resulting from developing countrie's lack of institutional capacity to engage in the global economy and in multilateral institutions (e.g., the World Trade Organization) on equal terms.

Barriers to Trade

- High tariffs are imposed on agriculture in high-income countries, the average tariff rate on agriculture is almost double the tariff for manufactures. And more than one third of the European Union's agricultural tariff lines, for instance, carry duties above 15%. Tariff peaks within agriculture occur most frequently on processed products and temperate commodities, rather than the major export crops of least developed countries (unprocessed fruits and vegetables and tropical commodities). However, many developing countries in temperate zones have the potential of competing as lower-cost producers in temperate commodities. Thus liberalization could open up new development-through-trade possibilities.

- Strong tariff escalation is typically imposed on agricultural and food products by high-income countries. This strongly discourages the development of high value added exports, and hinders diversification in particular as well as development in general. In high-income countries, tariffs on agricultural products escalate steeply, especially in the EU and Japan. ('Tariff escalation' is the imposition of higher import tariffs on processed products than the tariffs applied to unprocessed ingredients).

- Complex tariffs make it more difficult for developing country exporters to access industrialised-country markets because of the disadvantages developing countries face in accessing, and in their capacity to process, information. Not only are price signals distorted, they are often unclear, subject to change (for example seasonally) and difficult to interpret.

- Tariff-rate quotas (TRQs), introduced by the Uruguay Round with the aim of securing a minimum level of market access, have performed poorly. Average fill rates have been low and declining, from 67% in 1995 to 63% in 1998, with about a quarter of TRQs filled to less than 20%. The low fill rate may reflect high in-quota rates. Overall, the UR tariffication process which produced them has not resulted in the increased market access developing countries hoped for.

Producer Support

- Support to agricultural producers remains sizable, at about five times the level of international development assistance - $245 billion in 2000. Total support to agriculture, as defined by the OECD, reaches $327 billion - 1.3% of OECD countrie's GDP. To some extent these can be justified by "multifunctionality" arguments, but it remains a priority to find means of support which effectively meet the primary objectives without the negative developmental and environmental consequences that have been seen in the past.

- The dumping of unwanted production surpluses onto the world market through export subsidies has depressed prices for many temperate agricultural commodities, with EU surpluses of exportable wheat a prime example. (Despite several Common Agricultural Policy reforms, domestic support for wheat - as measured by OECD producer support estimates - declined only marginally from an average 52% of gross farm receipts in 1986-88, to around 48% in 1998-2000.) The URAA has been relatively unsuccessful in disciplining export subsidies, with the proportion of subsidised exports in total exports increasing in many products of export interest for developing countries: for example for wheat, from 7% in 1995 to 25% in 1998. The cost to developing country production and exports is considerable, and only partially offset by the lower food prices available to NFIDC consumers. This form of transfer from high-income country taxpayers to low-income consumers is in any case rather inefficient, and the lower prices may harm production for local consumption even in NFIDCs. Agricultural reform as a whole, including the removal of export subsidies, would only result in quite small price rises for developing-country consumers.

- The counter-cyclical nature of producer support is also harmful to developing-country producers. High-income farmers are insulated from changes in world prices, making production less responsive to swings in demand. As a result, world commodity prices are more volatile, and the burden of adjustment falls disproportionately on developing-country producers.

Lack of Capacity

This includes non-tariff barriers such as food regulations and standards, which developing countries are often not (or not effectively) involved in setting, and which may be deliberately used to reduce competition from developing countries. In any case, the lack of capacity to meet implement regulations and ensure compliance with standards constitutes a barrier to trade, and must be met by increasing that capacity.

Researchers at the Overseas Development Institute have identified many capacity related issues that developing economies face aside from tariff barriers:

- Traders and potential traders must know about an agreement and its details, however, the interests and skills of good producers lie in production and not in legal rules, only the largest firms can afford policy advisers.
- Markets and suppliers must share information - producer associations, industrial organisations, and chambers of commerce exchange information among their members and this information exchange must then take place across borders.
- A successful agreement must be flexible and governments need to accept that it will need to evolve.
- Trade agreements must generate relevant reforms in areas such as customs documentation, but also more fundamentally in relaxing rules for cross-border transportation.
- Selling to new markets requires adequate finance.
- Poor or wrong infrastructure can restrict trade.
- Governments can support producers or traders in other ways.

The benefits of trade agreements for developing countries are not automatic, especially for SMEs whether or not they are already exporting as the costs of entering a new market are greater for them than for large companies when compared to their potential revenue.

Market Access to Developing Countries

- Average applied tariffs in agriculture are higher in developing countries (although most of the very high rates, over 100%, are found in developed countries). With an increasing share of agricultural exports directed toward other developing countries, high levels of tariff protection in the South may impede prospects for export-led growth. This may be particularly true for the export opportunities of low-income countries, which have increased export market share in agriculture.

- "Open regionalism" holds the potential to stimulate global trade and improve the efficiency of regional producers. But regional arrangements can also become a vehicle for protection, trade diversion, and unintended inefficiency. Agreements in particular between richer and poorer developing countries risk generating trade losses for the poorer ones when their imports are diverted toward the richer members whose firms are not internationally competitive. However, where regional arrangements lead to the reduction of non-tariff barriers, trade creation is likely, and the dynamic benefits of effective regional integration in terms of improved governance and regional stability are likely to outweigh diversion concerns. The World Bank suggests that key conditions to benefit from expanded trade and investment include lowering common external trade barriers, stimulating competition, reducing transaction costs, and reinforcing nondiscriminatory investment and services policies. The greater structural differences between North and South economies mean that North-South arrangements hold the greatest promise for economic convergence and trade creation, including in agricultural products, underlining the importance of links between South-South arrangements and northern economies.
- Trade liberalization. According to the World Bank, "most analyses suggest that unilateral reduction in barriers can produce the greatest and the quickest gains". Some countries, such as Chile, China and Costa Rica, have undertaken domestic policy reforms. Caution must however be employed: as the case of Haiti shows, liberalization when institutions and the economy are not strong enough to face risks and opportunities can be harmful. And while reforms may be beneficial in the long run, for example by reducing possibilities for customs corruption, in the short run they create both winners and losers. Low-income consumers, unskilled workers in sheltered industries, and previously shielded producers may suffer in the transition period as the economy adapts to changed incentive structures. Temporary safety nets can help cushion the blow and ensure trade-led growth is pro-poor. Specific assistance to meet costs of adaptation – for example of switching to a different crop – may be appropriate.

Market Access is Vital, but not Enough

It is important to recognise that the issues facing LDCs and middle-income developing countries differ significantly. For the middle-income countries, the primary issue is market access. Many of the world's poor live in these countries, and so market access alone can have significant poverty-reducing effects in these countries. However, for the least developed countries, the principal problem is not market access, but lack of production capacity to achieve new trading opportunities. This is recognised by paragraph 42 of the Doha Development Agenda:

We recognize that the integration of the LDCs into the multilateral trading system requires meaningful market access, support for the diversification of their production and export base, and trade-related technical assistance and capacity building.

So while the further development of middle-income countries, and in particular the tackling of rural poverty in these countries, can be achieved most importantly through increased market access in agriculture, lower-income countries need additional help, not only to take advantage of new opportunities, but to be able to adapt to changing conditions due to the loss of preferences. This additional help must take three main forms: support for developing-country agricultural production; support for participation in trade; and support for good policies and good governance.

Support for Agricultural Production

- Support for agricultural modernization and development investment in productive capacity in agriculture and food processing.
- Support for agricultural-related development institutions which are not trade-distorting, e.g. research; e.g. risk-management of agricultural product price fluctuations; e.g. diversification.

Support for Participation in Trade and the Global Economy

Cases such as Haiti's post-1986 liberalization show that the opportunities thereby created will not be taken advantage of if macroeconomic policies, institutions, and the investment climate are not favorable. This includes:

- Trade-related infrastructure: the cost of exporting must be low enough to ensure competitiveness in rapidly expanding high-value agricultural markets where competition is stiff – such as fruits and vegetables.
- It also includes related issues that are part of the general investment climate but can be particularly important for exports, such as a weak financial sector. Here, export finance "is often a major constraint inhibiting exports in many low-income countries".
- Other issues are more specific to exports: developing countries and their exporters may have difficulty with both the implementation of, and showing compliance with, international product standards and other multilateral agreements. Low-income developing countries need both technical and financial assistance in this area.
- Technical Assistance for negotiations is also needed to further developing-country interests in multilateral and bilateral arenas and ensure the success of future negotiations and agreements.
- Marketing of exports is also a challenge for low-income countries: product and country brands need to be built, and quality concerns met.

Given the importance of agriculture for poverty reduction, additional policies and institutional capacity are needed to ensure an effective supply response to market incentives provide by better market access. Rural infrastructure is particularly important in enabling agricultural exports in developing countries. Sufficient credit at competitive conditions is important for private sector investment in storage, transportation and marketing of agricultural products. Investment in skills and education in rural areas is needed to bolster agricultural productivity. Trade policy reforms must address any remaining anti-export bias. Efficient land policies and land tenure institutions are needed to ensure the functioning of land markets, property rights, and efficient farm structures.

World Trade Organization Negotiations

The most recent round of World Trade Organization negotiations (the Doha "Development" Round) was promoted as being directed at the interests of developing countries, addressing issues of developed country protectionism. The introduction of the (investment-related) Singapore issues together with a lack of sufficient concessions to developing countrie's interests has put the success of the negotiations in doubt.

TYPES OF INTERNATIONAL TRADE

Here are the types of international trades:

Export Trade

An export in international trade is a good or service produced in one country that is bought by someone in another country. The seller of such goods and services is an *exporter*; the foreign buyer is an *importer*.

Export of goods often requires involvement of customs authorities. An export's reverse counterpart is an import.

Exporting

Many manufacturing firms began their global expansion as exporters and only later switched to another mode for serving a foreign market. Exporting refers to sending of goods and services from a home country to a foreign country.

Process

Methods of exporting a product or good or information include mail, hand delivery, air shipping, shipping by vessel, uploading to an internet site, or downloading from an internet site. Exports also include distribution of information sent as email, an email attachment, fax or in a telephone conversation.

Barriers

Trade barriers are government laws, regulations, policy, or practices that either protect domestic products from foreign competition or artificially stimulate exports of particular domestic products. While restrictive business practices sometimes have a similar effect, they are not usually regarded as trade barriers. The most common foreign trade barriers are government-imposed measures and policies that restrict, prevent, or impede the international exchange of goods and services.

Strategic

International agreements limit trade in and the transfer of, certain types of goods and information e.g. goods associated with weapons of mass destruction, advanced telecommunications, arms and torture, and also some art and archaeological artefacts. For example:

- Nuclear Suppliers Group limits trade in nuclear weapons and associated goods (45 countries participate).
- The Australia Group limits trade in chemical & biological weapons and associated goods (39 countries).
- Missile Technology Control Regime limits trade in the means of delivering weapons of mass destruction (35 countries).
- The Wassenaar Arrangement limits trade in conventional arms and technological developments (40 countries).

Tariffs

A tariff is a tax placed on a specific good or set of goods exported from or imported to a countryside, creating an economic barrier to trade. Usually the tactic is used when a country's domestic output of the good is falling and imports from foreign competitors are rising, particularly if the country has strategic reasons to retain a domestic production capability. Some failing industries receive a protection with an effect similar to subsidies; tariffs reduce the industry's incentives to produce goods quicker, cheaper, and more efficiently. The third reason for a tariff involves addressing the issue of dumping. Dumping involves a country producing highly excessive amounts of goods and *dumping* the goods on another country at prices that are "too low", for example, pricing the good lower in the export market than in the domestic market of the country of origin. In dumping the producer sells the product at a price that returns no profit, or even amounts to a loss. The purpose and expected outcome of a tariff is to encourage spending on domestic goods and services rather than imports.

Tariffs can create tension between countries. Examples include the United States steel tariff of 2002 and when China placed a 14% tariff on imported auto parts. Such tariffs usually lead to a complaint with the World Trade Organization (WTO). If that fails, the country may put a tariff of its own against the other nation in retaliation, and to increase pressure to remove the tariff.

Vessel at altenwerder container terminal.

Advantages of Exporting

- Exporting has two distinct advantages. First, it avoids the often substantial cost of establishing manufacturing operations in the host country.
- Second, exporting may help a company achieve experience curve effects and location economies.

Ownership advantages are the firm's specific assets, international experience, and the ability to develop either low-cost or differentiated products within the contacts of its value chain. The locational advantages of a particular market are a combination of market potential and investment risk. Internationalization advantages are the benefits of retaining a core competence within the company and threading it though the value chain rather than to license, outsource, or sell it.

In relation to the eclectic paradigm, companies that have low levels of ownership advantages do not enter foreign markets. If the company and its products are equipped with *ownership advantage* and *internalization advantage*, they enter through low-risk modes such as exporting. Exporting requires significantly lower level of investment than other modes of international expansion, such as FDI. The lower risk of export typically results in a lower rate of return on sales than possible though other modes of international business. In other words, the usual return on export sales may not be tremendous, but neither is the risk. Exporting allows managers to exercise operation control but does not provide them the option to exercise as much marketing control. An exporter usually resides far from the end consumer and often enlists various intermediaries to manage marketing activities. After two straight months of contraction, exports from India rose by 11.64% at $25.83 billion in July 2013 against $23.14 billion in the same month of the previous year.

Disadvantages of Exporting

Exporting has a Number of Drawbacks

- Exporting from the firm's home base may not be appropriate if lower-cost locations for manufacturing the product can be found abroad. It may be preferable to manufacture where conditions are most favorable to value creation, and to export to the rest of the world from that location.
- A second drawback to exporting, is that high transport cost can make exporting uneconomical, particularly for bulk products. One way to fix this, is to manufacture bulk products regionally.
- Another drawback, is that high tariff barriers can make exporting uneconomical and very risky.

For small and medium enterprises (SMEs) with fewer than 250 employees, selling goods and services to foreign markets can be more difficult than serving the domestic market. The lack of knowledge of trade regulations, cultural differences, different languages and foreign-exchange situations, as well as the strain of resources and staff, interact like a block for exporting. Indeed, there are some SMEs which are exporting, but nearly two-thirds of them sell to only one foreign market.

Export Motivations and Perceptions

Motivational factors are "all those factors triggering the decision of the firm to initiate and develop export activities". In the literature, export barriers are divided into four large categories: motivational, informational, operational/resource-based, and knowledge.Export motivators can be separated into specific dimensions leading to potential selection bias. In addition, the importance of size, knowledge of foreign markets, and unsolicited orders show an association with the perceptions of motivator stimuli toward specific dimensions (research, external, reactive).

In Macroeconomics

In macroeconomics, exports demanded by a country's foreign customers are one of the components of the demand for the country's gross domestic product, the other components being domestic consumption, physical investment, and government spending. Foreign demand for a country's exports depends positively on income in foreign countries and negatively on the strength of the producing country's currency (i.e., on how expensive it is for foreign customers to buy the producing country's currency in the foreign exchange market).

Entrepot Trade

Re-exportation, also called entrepot trade, may occur when one member of a free trade agreement charges lower tariffs to external nations to win trade, and then re-exports the same product to another partner in the trade agreement, but tariff-free. Re-exportation can be used to avoid sanctions by other nations.

Re-exports consist of foreign goods exported in the same state as previously imported, from the free circulation area, premises for inward processing or industrial free zones, directly to the rest of the world and from premises for customs warehousing or commercial free zones, to the rest of the world.

When dealing with trade data, it is essential to subtract re-exports from normal exports to arrive at the final value of exports. This is necessary because re-exports do not undergo any value-added processes, so cannot be counted towards a nation's exports.

Examples:

For example, the United Arab Emirates may have engaged in re-exportation of goods to Iran as a way for Iran to avoid U.S. trade sanctions against it. Thus re-exportation involves export without further processing or transformation of a good that has been imported. In contrast, Finland imported crude oil from the Soviet Union as part of bilateral trade between these two countries and refined the oil for export to other Western European countries, while the Soviet Union did not intend to sell oil to these capitalist countries, but this was not re-exportation because thc crude oil was refined before selling. Dubai has emerged as the major re-export center for the entire Middle East region.

Import Trade

The import trade is referred to goods and services purchased into one nation from another. The word "import"originates from the word "port" considering the fact that the products are frequently transported via ship to foreign countries. Similar to exports, imports are also the backbone of international trade. Here, if the expense of a country's imports is more than the value of its exports than the country has a negative balance of trade (BOT), which is also known as a trade deficit.

Every country import goods and services that the domestic country cannot manufacture, maybe because the country cannot produce effectively or cheaply like another exporting country. Few countries sometimes also import commodities and raw materials which are not available on their premises. For instance, many nations import oil they cannot manufacture it locally or cannot provide sufficient to meet the demand.

Objectives of Import Trade

To Speed up Industrialisation

- Developing countries import scarce raw materials, capital goods and advanced technology required for rapid industrial development.

To Meet Domestic Demand

- The goods which are in demand but are not available in the country are imported.

To Overcome Natural Disasters

- During drought, flood, earthquake and other natural calamities country import food grains and other essential commodities to prevent starvation.

To Improve Standard of Living

- Imports enable consumers in the home country to enjoy a wide variety of products of high quality.
- It helps in improving the standard of living of masses.

To Ensure National Defence

- The importer must get the receipt of credit from his concerned bank and send it to the foreign supplier.

Important Steps Involved in a Typical Import Transaction:

Trade Enquiry and Sending Quotations

- The domestic buyer who wishes to buy the goods from the other country sends an inquiry relating to price, desired quality, terms, and conditions for the export of goods.
- The exporter sends a reply to the inquiry in the form of 'Quotation'.
- The quotation is also known as 'Proforma Invoice' which contains information about the selling price, quantity, quality, mode of delivery, etc.

Procurement of Import License

- Goods can be imported only upon the license, the importer requires to obtain an import license.

Obtaining Foreign Exchange

- The overseas supplier asks payment in a foreign currency.
- Payment requires the exchange of Indian currency into foreign currency.
- In India, transaction related to foreign exchange are governed by Reserve Bank of India (RBI) under the Exchange Control Department.

Placing Order or Indent

- After the receipt of the 'Quotation', if the prospective buyer finds the information suitable to him, he places the 'Order/Indent' for the import of goods.

Obtaining Letter of Credit

- The importer must get the receipt of credit from his concerned bank and send it to the foreign supplier.

Arrangement of Finance

- The importer makes the finance settlements in advance to remunerate to the exporter when the shipment arrives at the destination.

Receipt of Shipment Advice

- After storing the consignment on the ship, the foreign supplier sends the shipment advice to the importer.
- The shipment advice includes data about the shipment of products such as:
  - Invoicc number.
  - The landing or airways bill date and number.
  - Name of the ship with date.
  - Port or Destination of export.
  - Classification of goods and quantity.
  - Date of the sailing of the vessel.

Arrival of Goods

- The overseas supplier dispatches the Goods as per the contract.

Customs Clearance and Release of Goods

- In India, all the imported goods have to have a clearance from customs after they pass the Indian borders.
- When the ship arrives at the port, the importer has to obtain a delivery order/endorsement for delivery on the back of the bill of lading from the concerned shipping company.

TRADE AGREEMENTS

A trade agreement (also known as trade pact) is a wide-ranging taxes, tariff and trade treaty that often includes investment guarantees. It exists when two or more countries agree on terms that helps them trade with each other. The most common trade agreements are of the preferential and free trade types are concluded in order to reduce (or eliminate) tariffs, quotas and other trade restrictions on items traded between the signatories.

The logic of formal trade agreements is that they outline what is agreed upon and the punishments for deviation from the rules set in the agreement. Trade agreements therefore make misunderstandings less likely, and create confidence on both sides that cheating will be punished; this increases the likelihood of long-term cooperation. An international organization, such as the IMF, can further incentivize cooperation by monitoring compliance with agreements and reporting third countries of the violations. Monitoring by international agencies may be needed to detect non-tariff barriers, which are disguised attempts at creating trade barriers.

Trade pacts are frequently politically contentious since they may change economic customs and deepen interdependence with trade partners. Increasing efficiency through "free trade" is a common goal. For the most part, governments are supportive of further trade agreements.

There have been however some concerns expressed by the WTO. According to Pascal Lamy, Director-General of the WTO, the proliferation of regional trade agreements (RTAs) "is breeding concern – concern about incoherence, confusion, exponential increase of costs for business, unpredictability and even unfairness in trade relations". The position of the WTO is that while the typical trade agreements (called *preferential* or *regional* by the WTO) are useful to a degree, it is much more beneficial to focus on global agreements in the WTO framework such as the negotiations of the current Doha round.

The anti-globalization movement opposes such agreements almost by definition, but some groups normally allied within that movement, e.g. green parties, seek fair trade or safe trade provisions that moderate real and perceived ill effects of globalization.

Classification of Trade Pacts

By Number and Type of Signatories

There are three different types of trade agreements. The first is *unilateral* trade agreement, this is what happens when a country wants certain restrictions to be enforced but no other countries want them to be imposed. This also allows countries to decrease the amount of trade restrictions. That is also something that does not happen often and could impair a country.

The second is classified as *bilateral* (BTA) when signed between two sides, where each side could be a country (or other customs territory), a trade bloc or an informal group of countries (or other customs territories). When both countries loosen their trade restrictions to help out businesses so that they can prosper better between the different countries this definitely helps lower taxes and it helps them converse about their trade statu's. Usually this revolves around subsided domestic industries. Mainly the industries fall under automotive, oil, or food industries.

A trade agreement signed between more than two sides (typically neighboring or in the same region) is classified as *multilateral*. These face the most obstacles- when negotiating substance, and for implementation. The more countries that are involved, the harder it is to reach mutual satisfaction. Once this type of trade agreement is settled on, it becomes a very powerful agreement. The larger the GDP of the signatories, the greater the impact on other global trade relationships. The largest multilateral trade agreement is the North American Free Trade Agreement between the United States, Canada, and Mexico.

By Level of Integration

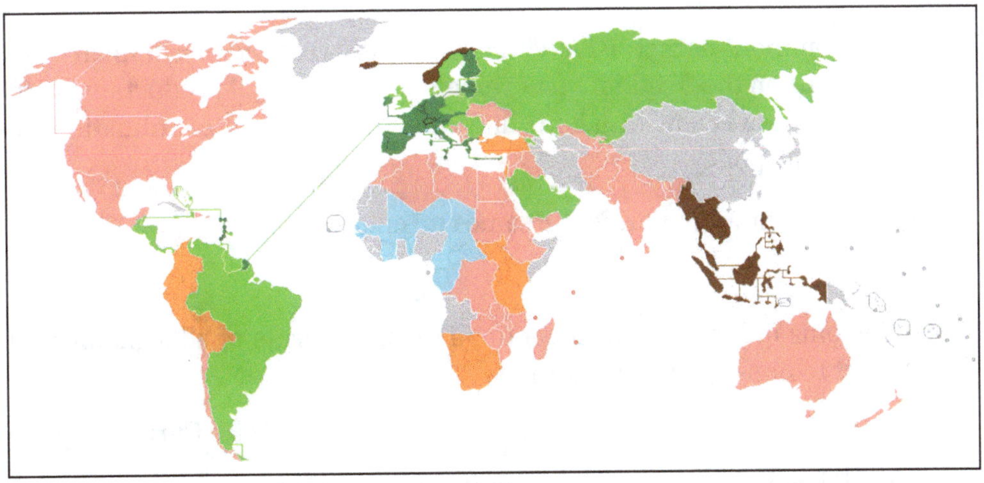

Stages of economic integration around the World (each country colored according to the most integrated form that it participates with):

- Economic and monetary union (CSME/EC$, EU/€, Switzerland–Liechtenstein/CHF)
- Economic union (CSME, EU, EAEU, MERCOSUR, GCC, SICA)
- Customs and monetary union (CEMAC/XAF, UEMOA/XOF)
- Common market (EEA–Switzerland, ASEAN
- Customs union (CAN, EAC, EUCU, SACU)
- Multilateral Free Trade Area (CEFTA, CISFTA, COMESA, CPTPP, DCFTA, EFTA, GAFTA, NAFTA, SAFTA, AANZFTA, PAFTA, SADCFTA)

There are a variety of trade agreements; with some being quite complex (European Union), while others are less intensive (North American Free Trade Agreement). The resulting level of economic integration depends on the specific type of trade pacts and policies adopted by the trade bloc:

- Separate.
    - Trade and Investment Framework Agreement (TIFA).
    - Bilateral Investment Treaty (BIT).
    - Preferential Trade Arrangement (PTA): Limited scope and depth of tariffs reduction between the customs territories.
        - Free Trade Agreement establishing a Free Trade Area (FTA): Extensive reduction or elimination of tariffs on substantially all trade allowing for the free movement of goods and in more advanced agreements also reduction of restrictions on investment and establishment allowing for the free movement of capital and free movement of services.
        - Common market: FTA with significantly reduced or eliminated restrictions on the freedom of movement of all factors of production, including free movement of labour and of enterprise; and coordination in economic policy.
    - Currency union: Sharing the same currency.
- Composite.
    - Customs union: FTA with common external tariffs of all signatories in respect to non-signatory countries.
        - Customs and monetary union: Customs union with Currency union.
        - Economic union: Customs union with Common market.
        - Economic and monetary union (EMU): Economic union with Currency Union.
        - Fiscal Union: Common coordination of substantial parts of the fiscal policies *(proposed step between EMU and Complete economic integration)*

Special Agreements

- World Trade Organization treaty.
    - Agreements in the WTO framework (Textile Agreement and others).
- The now defunct Multilateral Agreement on Investment (in the OECD framework).

U.S. Regional Trade Agreements

These are between countries in a certain area. The most powerful ones include a few countries that are near each other in a geographical area. These countries usually have similar histories, demographics and even economic goals.

North American Free Trade Agreement (NAFTA) January 1, 1989 was when it was put into effect, this is between United States, Canada, and Mexico this agreement was designed to get rid of tariff barriers between the separate countries.

Regional trade agreements are very hard to establish and commit to when the countries are more diverse.

Association of Southeast Asian Nations(ASEAN) this was formed in 1967 between the countries of Indonesia, Malaysia, the Philippines, Singapore, and Thailand the reasoning was so that they could engage political and economic encouragement and it helps them all keep regional stability.

By the World Trade Organization

Typically the benefits and obligations of the trade agreements apply only to their signatories.

In the framework of the World Trade Organization, different agreement types are concluded (mostly during new member accessions), whose terms apply to all WTO members on the so-called most-favored basis (MFN), which means that beneficial terms agreed bilaterally with one trading partner will apply also to the rest of the WTO members.

All agreements concluded outside of the WTO framework (and granting additional benefits beyond the WTO MFN level, but applicable only between the signatories and not to the rest of the WTO members) are called *preferential* by the WTO. According to WTO rules these agreements are subject to certain requirements such as notification to the WTO and general reciprocity (the preferences should apply equally to each of the signatories of the agreement) where unilateral preferences (some of the signatories gain preferential access to the market of the other signatories, without lowering their own tariffs) are allowed only under exceptional circumstances and as temporary measure.

The trade agreements called *preferential* by the WTO are also known as *regional* (RTA), despite not necessarily concluded by countries within a certain region. There are currently 205 agreements in force as of July 2007. Over 300 have been reported to the WTO. The number of FTA has increased significantly over the last decade. Between 1948 and 1994, the General Agreement on Tariffs and Trade (GATT), the predecessor to the WTO, received 124 notifications. Since 1995 over 300 trade agreements have been enacted.

The WTO is further classifying these agreements in the following types:

- Goods covering:
    - Basic preferential trade agreement (a.k.a. partial scope agreement).
    - Free trade agreement.
    - Customs union.
- Services covering:
    - Economic Integration Agreement–any agreement, including a basic PTA, that covers also services.

INTERNATIONAL TRADE THEORY

International trade theories are simply different theories to explain international trade. Trade is the concept of exchanging goods and services between two people or entities. *International trade* is then the concept of this exchange between people or entities in two different countries.

People or entities trade because they believe that they benefit from the exchange. They may need or want the goods or services. While at the surface, this many sound very simple, there is a great deal of theory, policy, and business strategy that constitutes international trade.

MERCANTILISM

Seaport at sunrise, a French seaport painted by Claude Lorrain in 1639, at the height of mercantilism.

Mercantilism is a national economic policy that is designed to maximize the exports, and minimize the imports, of a nation. These policies aim to reduce a possible current account deficit or reach a current account surplus. Mercantilism includes a national economic policy aimed at accumulating monetary reserves through a positive balance of trade, especially of finished goods. Historically, such policies frequently led to war and also motivated colonial expansion. Mercantilist theory varies in sophistication from one writer to another and has evolved over time.

Mercantilism was dominant in modernized parts of Europe from the 16th to the 18th centuries, a period of proto-industrialization, before falling into decline, although some commentators argue that it is still practiced in the economies of industrializing countries, in the form of economic interventionism. It promotes government regulation of a nation's economy for the purpose of augmenting state power at the expense of rival national powers. High tariffs, especially on manufactured goods, were an almost universal feature of mercantilist policy.

With the efforts of supranational organizations such as the World Trade Organization to reduce tariffs globally, non-tariff barriers to trade have assumed a greater importance in neomercantilism.

Merchants in Venice.

Theory

Most of the European economists who wrote between 1500 and 1750 are today generally considered mercantilists; this term was initially used solely by critics, such as Mirabeau and Smith, but was quickly adopted by historians. Originally the standard English term was "mercantile system". The word "mercantilism" was introduced into English from German in the early 19th century.

The bulk of what is commonly called "mercantilist literature" appeared in the 1620s in Great Britain. Smith saw the English merchant Thomas Mun as a major creator of the mercantile system, especially in his posthumously published *Treasure by Foreign Trade*, which Smith considered the archetype or manifesto of the movement. Perhaps the last major mercantilist work was James Steuart's *Principles of Political Economy*, published in 1767.

Mercantilist literature also extended beyond England. Italy and France produced noted writers of mercantilist themes, including Italy's Giovanni Botero and Antonio Serra and, in France, Jean Bodin and Colbert. Themes also existed in writers from the German historical school from List, as well as followers of the American system and British free-trade imperialism, thus stretching the system into the 19th century. However, many British writers, including Mun and Misselden, were merchants, while many of the writers from other countries were public officials. Beyond mercantilism as a way of understanding the wealth and power of nations, Mun and Misselden are noted for their viewpoints on a wide range of economic matters.

The Austrian lawyer and scholar Philipp Wilhelm von Hornick, one of the pioneers of Cameralism, detailed a nine-point program of what he deemed effective national economy in his *Austria Over All, If She Only Will* of 1684, which comprehensively sums up the tenets of mercantilism:

- That every little bit of a country's soil be utilized for agriculture, mining or manufacturing.
- That all raw materials found in a country be used in domestic manufacture, since finished goods have a higher value than raw materials.
- That a large, working population be encouraged.
- That all exports of gold and silver be prohibited and all domestic money be kept in circulation.
- That all imports of foreign goods be discouraged as much as possible.
- That where certain imports are indispensable they be obtained at first hand, in exchange for other domestic goods instead of gold and silver.
- That as much as possible, imports be confined to raw materials that can be finished in the home country.
- That opportunities be constantly sought for selling a country's surplus manufactures to foreigners, so far as necessary, for gold and silver.
- That no importation be allowed if such goods are sufficiently and suitably supplied at home.

Other than Von Hornick, there were no mercantilist writers presenting an overarching scheme for the ideal economy, as Adam Smith would later do for classical economics. Rather, each mercantilist writer tended to focus on a single area of the economy. Only later did non-mercantilist scholars integrate these "diverse" ideas into what they called mercantilism. Some scholars thus reject the idea of mercantilism completely, arguing that it gives "a false unity to disparate events". Smith saw the mercantile system as an enormous conspiracy by manufacturers and merchants against consumers, a view that has led some authors, especially Robert E. Ekelund and Robert D. Tollison, to call mercantilism "a rent-seeking society". To a certain extent, mercantilist doctrine itself made a general theory of economics impossible. Mercantilists viewed the economic system as a zero-sum game, in which any gain by one party required a loss by another. Thus, any system of policies that benefited one group would by definition harm the other, and there was no possibility of economics being used to maximize the commonwealth, or common good. Mercantilist's writings were also generally created to rationalize particular practices rather than as investigations into the best policies.

Mercantilist domestic policy was more fragmented than its trade policy. While Adam Smith portrayed mercantilism as supportive of strict controls over the economy, many mercantilists disagreed. The early modern era was one of letters patent and government-imposed monopolies; some mercantilists supported these, but others acknowledged the corruption and inefficiency of such systems. Many mercantilists also realized that the inevitable results of quotas and price ceilings were black markets. One notion that mercantilists widely agreed upon was the need for economic oppression of the working population; laborers and farmers were to live at the "margins of subsistence". The goal was to maximize production, with no concern for consumption. Extra money, free time, and education for the lower classes were seen to inevitably lead to vice and laziness, and would result in harm to the economy.

The mercantilists saw a large population as a form of wealth that made possible the development of bigger markets and armies. Opposite to mercantilism was the doctrine of physiocracy, which predicted that mankind would outgrow its resources. The idea of mercantilism was to protect the markets as well as maintain agriculture and those who were dependent upon it.

Policies

Mercantilist ideas were the dominant economic ideology of all of Europe in the early modern period, and most states embraced it to a certain degree. Mercantilism was centred on England and France, and it was in these states that mercantilist policies were most often enacted.

The policies have included:

- High tariffs, especially on manufactured goods.
- Forbidding colonies to trade with other nations.
- Monopolizing markets with staple ports.
- Banning the export of gold and silver, even for payments.
- Forbidding trade to be carried in foreign ships, as per, for example, the Navigation Acts.

- Subsidies on exports.
- Promoting manufacturing and industry through research or direct subsidies.
- Limiting wages.
- Maximizing the use of domestic resources.
- Restricting domestic consumption through non-tariff barriers to trade.

France

Mercantilism arose in France in the early 16th century soon after the monarchy had become the dominant force in French politics. In 1539, an important decree banned the import of woolen goods from Spain and some parts of Flanders. The next year, a number of restrictions were imposed on the export of bullion.

Over the rest of the 16th century, further protectionist measures were introduced. The height of French mercantilism is closely associated with Jean-Baptiste Colbert, finance minister for 22 years in the 17th century, to the extent that French mercantilism is sometimes called Colbertism. Under Colbert, the French government became deeply involved in the economy in order to increase exports. Protectionist policies were enacted that limited imports and favored exports. Industries were organized into guilds and monopolies, and production was regulated by the state through a series of more than one thousand directives outlining how different products should be produced.

To encourage industry, foreign artisans and craftsmen were imported. Colbert also worked to decrease internal barriers to trade, reducing internal tariffs and building an extensive network of roads and canals. Colbert's policies were quite successful, and France's industrial output and the economy grew considerably during this period, as France became the dominant European power. He was less successful in turning France into a major trading power, and Britain and the Netherlands remained supreme in this field.

New France

France imposed its mercantilist philosophy on its colonies in North America, especially New France. It sought to derive the maximum material benefit from the colony, for the homeland, with a minimum of imperial investment in the colony itself. The ideology was embodied in New France through the establishment under Royal Charter of a number of corporate trading monopolies including La Compagnie des Marchands, which operated from 1613 to 1621, and the Compagnie de Montmorency, from that date until 1627. It was in turn replaced by La Compagnie des Cent-Associés, created in 1627 by King Louis XIII, and the Communauté des habitants in 1643. These were the first corporations to operate in what is now Canada.

Great Britain

In England, mercantilism reached its peak during the Long Parliament government. Mercantilist policies were also embraced throughout much of the Tudor and Stuart periods, with Robert Walpole being another major proponent. In Britain, government control over the domestic economy was far less extensive than on the Continent, limited by common law and the steadily increasing power of Parliament. Government-controlled monopolies were common, especially before the English Civil War, but were often controversial.

The Anglo-Dutch Wars were fought between the English and the Dutch for control over the seas and trade routes.

With respect to its colonies, British mercantilism meant that the government and the merchants became partners with the goal of increasing political power and private wealth, to the exclusion of other empires. The government protected its merchants—and kept others out—through trade barriers, regulations, and subsidies to domestic industries in order to maximize exports from and minimize imports to the realm. The government had to fight smuggling, which became a favorite American technique in the 18th century to circumvent the restrictions on trading with the French, Spanish, or Dutch. The goal of mercantilism was to run trade surpluses so that gold and silver would pour into London. The government took its share through duties and taxes, with the remainder going to merchants in Britain. The government spent much of its revenue on a superb Royal Navy, which not only protected the British colonies but threatened the colonies of the other empires, and sometimes seized them. Thus the British Navy captured New Amsterdam (New York) in 1664. The colonies were captive markets for British industry, and the goal was to enrich the mother country.

British mercantilist writers were themselves divided on whether domestic controls were necessary. British mercantilism thus mainly took the form of efforts to control trade. A wide array of regulations were put in place to encourage exports and discourage imports. Tariffs were placed on imports and bounties given for exports, and the export of some raw materials was banned completely. The Navigation Acts expelled foreign merchants from England's domestic trade. The nation aggressively sought colonies and once under British control, regulations were imposed that allowed the colony to only produce raw materials and to only trade with Britain. This led to friction with the inhabitants of these colonies, and mercantilist policies (such as forbidding trade with other empires and controls over smuggling) were a major irritant leading to the American Revolution.

Mercantilism taught that trade was a zero-sum game, with one country's gain equivalent to a loss sustained by the trading partner. Overall, however, mercantilist policies had a positive impact on Britain helping turn it into the world's dominant trader and the global hegemon. One domestic policy that had a lasting impact was the conversion of "wastelands" to agricultural use. Mercantilists believed that to maximize a nation's power, all land and resources had to be used to their highest and best use, and this era thus saw projects like the draining of The Fens.

Other Countries

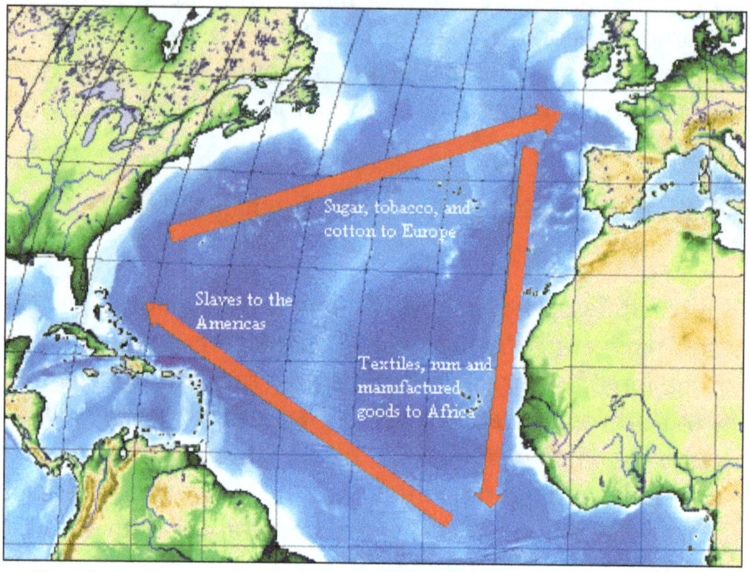

Mercantilism helped create trade patterns such as the triangular trade in the North Atlantic, in which raw materials were imported to the metropolis and then processed and redistributed to other colonies.

The other nations of Europe also embraced mercantilism to varying degrees. The Netherlands, which had become the financial centre of Europe by being its most efficient trader, had little interest in seeing trade restricted and adopted few mercantilist policies. Mercantilism became prominent in Central Europe and Scandinavia after the Thirty Year's War, with Christina of Sweden, Jacob Kettler of Courland, and Christian IV of Denmark being notable proponents.

The Habsburg Holy Roman Emperors had long been interested in mercantilist policies, but the vast and decentralized nature of their empire made implementing such notions difficult. Some constituent states of the empire did embrace Mercantilism, most notably Prussia, which under Frederick the Great had perhaps the most rigidly controlled economy in Europe.

Spain benefited from mercantilism early on as it brought a large amount of precious metals such as gold and silver into their treasury by way of the new world. In the long run, Spain's economy collapsed as it was unable to adjust to the inflation that came with the large influx of bullion. Heavy intervention from the crown put crippling laws for the protection of Spanish goods and services. Mercantilist protectionist policy in Spain caused the long-run failure of the Castilian textile industry as the efficiency severely dropped off with each passing year due to the production being held at a specific level. Spain's heavily protected industries led to famines as much of its agricultural land was required to be used for sheep instead of grain. Much of their grain was imported from the Baltic region of Europe which caused a shortage of food in the inner regions of Spain. Spain limiting the trade of their colonies is one of the causes that lead to the separation of the Dutch from the Spanish Empire. The culmination of all of these policies lead to Spain defaulting in 1557, 1575, and 1596.

During the economic collapse of the 17th century, Spain had little coherent economic policy, but French mercantilist policies were imported by Philip V with some success. Russia under Peter I (Peter the Great) attempted to pursue mercantilism, but had little success because of Russia's lack of a large merchant class or an industrial base.

HECKSCHER–OHLIN MODEL

Basic situation: Two identical countries (A and B) have different initial factor endowments. Autarky equilibrium (A^A, A^B): no trade, individual production equals consumption. Trade equilibrium: both countries consume the same ($C^A = C^B$), especially beyond their own Production–possibility frontier; production and consumption points are divergent.

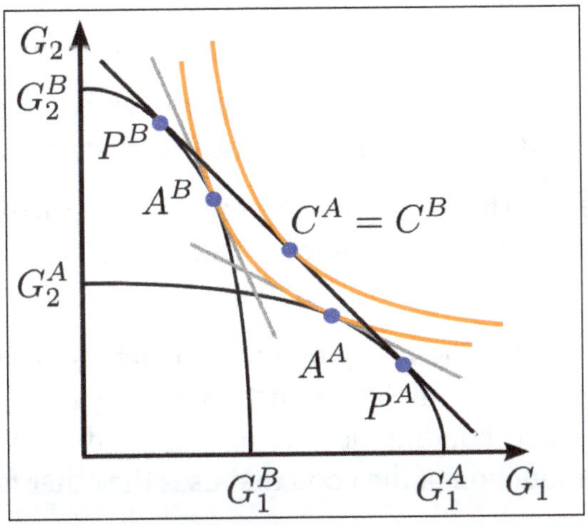

The Heckscher–Ohlin theorem is one of the four critical theorems of the Heckscher–Ohlin model, developed by Swedish economist Eli Heckscher and Bertil Ohlin. In the two-factor case, it states: "A capital-abundant country will export the capital-intensive good, while the labor-abundant country will export the labor-intensive good".

The critical assumption of the Heckscher–Ohlin model is that the two countries are identical, except for the difference in resource endowments. This also implies that the aggregate preferences are the same. The relative abundance in capital will cause the capital-abundant country to produce the capital-intensive good cheaper than the labor-abundant country and vice versa.

Initially, when the countries are not trading:

- The price of the capital-intensive good in the capital-abundant country will be bid down relative to the price of the good in the other country,
- The price of the labor-intensive good in the labor-abundant country will be bid down relative to the price of the good in the other country.

Once trade is allowed, profit-seeking firms will move their products to the markets that have (temporary) higher price. As a result:

- The capital-abundant country will export the capital-intensive good,
- The labor-abundant country will export the labor-intensive good.

The Leontief paradox, presented by Wassily Leontief in 1951, found that the U.S. (the most capital-abundant country in the world by any criterion) exported labor-intensive commodities and imported capital-intensive commodities, in apparent contradiction with the Heckscher–Ohlin theorem. However, if labor is separated into two distinct factors, skilled labor and unskilled labor, the Heckscher–Ohlin theorem is more accurate. The U.S. tends to export skilled-labor-intensive goods, and tends to import unskilled-labor-intensive goods.

Related Theorems

- Factor price equalization: The relative prices for two identical factors of production will eventually be equalized across countries because of international trade.
- Stolper–Samuelson theorem: A rise in the relative price of a good will lead to a rise in the return to that factor which is used most intensively in the production of the good, and conversely, to a fall in the return to the other factor.
- Rybczynski theorem: When only one of two factors of production is increased there is a relative increase in the production of the good using more of that factor. This leads to a corresponding decline in that good›s relative price as well as a decline in the production of the good that uses the other factor more intensively.

INTERNATIONAL TRADE AND STATE SECURITY

International economic structures range from complete autarky to complete market openness. This structure has undergone numerous changes since the beginning of the nineteenth century. The state-power theory as put into perspective by Stephen Krasner explains that the structure of international trade is determined by the interests and power of states acting to maximize their aggregate national income, social stability, political power and economic growth. Such state interests can be achieved under free trade.

The relationship between these interests and the level of openness depends upon the economic power of states. Power is dependent upon a states size and level of economic development. Krasner contends that distributions of potential power may vary from multipolar to hegemonic; and different international trading structures are made of either of these. The key to this argument is that a hegemonic distribution of potential economic power is likely to result in an open trading system. Since states act to maximize their aggregate economic utility, maximum global welfare is achieved under free trade.

Neoclassical trade theory posits that the greater the degree of openness in the international trading system, the greater the level of aggregate economic income.

Theoretical Perspectives

Realism

Robert Gilpin and Stephen Krasner are advocates of the realist tradition, which emphasises the hegemonic system. The hegemonic system contends that there are states that are much larger and more developed than their trading partners and therefore, the costs and benefits of openness are not symmetrical for all members of the system. Krasner contends that the hegemonic state will have a preference for an open structure because it will increase its aggregate national income and power.

Realism emphasizes state's demands for power and security. Military force is therefore, the most important power resource. States must rely ultimately on their own resources and must strive to maintain their power positions in the system, even at high economic costs. For realism, the most important variables are the economic and military strength of hegemonic states; and international hostilities are mainly because of variations in the distribution of political-military capabilities between states.

Hegemonic Stability

The theory of hegemonic stability by the realist school argues that dominance of one country is necessary for the existence of an open and stable international economy. The relationship between hegemony and an open, stable economy has been challenged by some scholars "As US behaviour during the interwar period illustrates, the possession of superior resources by a nation does not translate automatically into great influence or beneficial outcomes for the world".

Development Policy

Realist trade encourages Import substitution industrialization (ISI) replacing imports with domestic production. Realism recognises that trade regulations can be used to correct domestic distortions and to promote new industries.

Under realism, states possess a high degree of discretionary power to influence many variables and prices in the economy. The government influences the distribution of investment, thus protecting national industries.

International Institutions

Realists with their focus on power and the struggle for survival in an anarchical world, criticize the role of international institutions that govern the world economy, such as the World Bank, World Trade Organization (WTO), EU, and the International Monetary Fund (IMF). Scholars argue that the influence exerted by international institutions is dependent upon the states that form part of them, and therefore international institutions have little independent impact. Accordingly, the realist school emphasises the impact of state power over the strength of the institution per se.

Liberalism

The liberal tradition consists of two schools of thought on the causes of peace, one emphasises representative government and international institutions and the other advocates global markets and economic development.

Liberalism traces back to Immanuel Kant. Kantian Liberalism posits that democracy, economic interdependence and international organisations are optimal solutions for reducing the incidence of conflict. It is not individual factors, which lead to a more peaceful world, but rather all three elements working in conjunction, which eliminates conflict.

Oneal and Russett's research design has become a standard choice of replications in studies assessing the Kantian peace triangle where democracies tend to be interdependent and members of the same International Government Organisations (IGOs). Their research is consistent with the argument that democratic peace advocates economic interdependence and a joint need to attain membership in IGOs in order to prevent the incidence of conflict. However, the empirical findings on the Kantian peace triangle as a joint force to eliminate conflict presents some limitations, as one study found that the three Kantian peace variables are less robust in explaining leader's conflict behaviour. Keohane and Nye go further to include the lack of additional components in this theory including environmental and military measurements.

Trade

Liberals emphasise two main aspects of the benefits of trade. First, trade promotes states to work together and cooperatively, reinforcing peaceful relations among trading partners. The second benefit is based on the expected utility model of trade and conflict which emphasises the potential economic consequences of a disruption in trade. Countries are therefore deterred from initiating conflict against a trading partner for fear of losing the welfare gains associated with trade.

Interdependence

Liberals argue that economic interdependence between states reduces conflict because conflict discourages commerce. Recent cost-benefit calculations of trade take into account information as an important component in the explanation of the pacifying aspect of economic interdependence. Through open trade, states reveal their intentions and capabilities and thus "relations become more transparent and reduce uncertainty".

Furthermore, economic interdependence makes costly signals possible. If military action did not entail loss, national leaders would not be able to communicate their capabilities and resolve. This acts as a deterrent and promotes peace between states. "Mechanisms that facilitate the transmission of credible information across international boundaries limit bargaining failure, enhancing interstate peace".

There is some disagreement about the interdependence liberal thesis among some scholars. Kenneth Waltz, for example, argues that since "close interdependence means closeness of contact and raises the prospect of at least occasional conflict. the liberal myth of interdependence. asserts a false belief about the conditions that may promote peace". Despite the scrutiny, there is a long-held position that economic interdependence has a pacifying effect on interstate relations.

According to the liberal view, the costly nature of conflict is central to contemporary bargaining theory. Keohane & Nye put forth four conditions that make the use of force by large states costly:

- Risks of nuclear escalation.
- Resistance by people in poor or weak countries.
- Uncertain and possibly negative effects on the achievement of economic goals.
- Domestic opinion opposed to the human costs of the use of force.

Development Policy

Liberal trade encourages export led growth (ELG), leaving traders and consumers dependent on foreign markets. Liberals argue that these actors have an incentive to avoid hostilities with their trading partners, since any disruption in commercial relations would be costly.

International institutions are a key feature of the liberal peace, because they represent credible signals of resolve to defend member states in times of crisis, regulate state behaviour, facilitate communication and create common security interests between member states.

The Argument about Trade and Conflict

The relationship between international trade and conflict has been a source of controversy among international relations scholars. Some scholars argue that trade does not reduce conflict even though conflict reduces trade; while others report that international trade fosters a peaceful disposition among states, which are less likely to resort to armed conflict in times of crisis.

The argument that open trade inhibits conflict dates back to the classical liberal movement of free trade and world peace. This view argues that increasing interaction among traders and consumers (interdependence) promotes peace; free trade fosters a sense of international community that reduce interstate conflict and tensions. Liberals posit that free markets and economic development contribute to a reduction in interstate conflict. The contrasting contemporary view is that open trade dampens political conflict by promoting economic dependence.

Economic dependence has negative consequences for interstate conflict. Albert O. Hirschman for example, has pointed out that the "gains from trade do not accrue to states proportionately and the distribution of these gains can affect interstate power relations. Moreover, shifts in power relations are widely regarded as a potent source of military conflict".

Economic Interdependence

Economic interdependence and greater openness exposes domestic economies to the exigencies of the world market. Social instability is therefore increased by exposure to international competition. This negative force undermines the Kantian peace and remains a cause for concern in international conflict. Although this concern seems legitimate given the economic disparities between developed and developing countries, studies fail to provide comprehensive empirical evidence.

Another view at odds with liberalism is that technological innovation and industrialization increase the ability of some countries to exercise power. As trade flows and the level of interdependence increases, so do the incentives for states to take military actions to reduce their economic vulnerability.

The adverse effect of trade on state security is difficult to determine, however the more competition, the more aggressive the environment. Openness and competition increases social instability because domestic prices need to adjust to changes in international prices. Consistent with the realists view that states are essentially always in conflict, social instability and resource competition are motives for conflict and states will rely on the use of force to attain their own political goals and interests.

The Role of Military Power

A number of international relations scholars, notably Xiang, recognise the role of military power in initiating conflict, as well as the role militarily powerful countries play in international trade. One argument suggests that militarily capable countries are more likely to have the motivation to initiate armed conflict due to their awareness of their capabilities and to their confidence in achieving favourable outcomes.

A second argument suggests that power facilitates trade. Third, there are positive benefits from economic interdependence on military power. Finally, the economic stature of a country determines both the military power and level of trade of that country, hinting that economic powerful states trade more. Because powerful countries are better positioned to take advantage of the benefits resulting from international trade and to transform welfare gains into military power, they also are more likely to use force when their positions are threatened.

Similarly, Gartzke & Hewitt argue that the "extension of economic and other interests beyond national borders increases incentives to police relevant regions and exercise influence, sometimes through force".

Unequal Peace

The motives for conflict, which historically were concentrated among the powerful and their ambitious challengers, are today clustered among the poor, and between the poor and the rich. Theory has prompted to inequality as a potential source of internal conflict. "Inequalities within the same countries has increased, not through impoverishment of the masses, but because while wealth is created many people remain left behind in poverty. Thus, we have an unequal peace". Around 60 countries suffer not only from low GDP per capita but also low or negative growth. These countries tend to be caught in armed conflict among other development traps. Some argue that the evidence surrounding inequality and conflict remains inconclusive, calling for further empirical studies.

Studies show that states with the most dissimilar interests possess a motive for conflict but whether they experience conflict (or not) depends on external determinants of bargaining success or failure. These determinants include uncertainty about the balance of power, opponent's resolve as well as policy dissimilarities between competing states. Interests are important determinants of whether conflict occurs. According to Gartzke & Hewitt, promoting democratic interests, or even imposing them for peace, is not likely to reduce conflict "it may even lead to a weakening of the actual determinants of liberal peace", thereby increasing interstate tensions. Contemporary research demonstrates that promoting free markets and economic development helps mitigate conflict and promote peace.

Capitalist Peace

The capitalist peace thesis suggests that free markets and economic development contribute to a reduction in interstate conflict.

Research on the capitalist peace has chosen to pursue the liberal political economy school, with a particular focus on Kant's Perpetual Peace. The same set of theoretical frameworks that evolved in democratic peace research now asserts itself in the capitalist peace.

The capitalist peace sees capitalism as creating conditions to make war more costly and therefore undesirable by trading states. Traditional interpretations of the capital peace contend that development and global markets will eventually eliminate resource competition as a motive for war. This view was eventually deemed outdated, as "it became clear that needed raw materials would continue to make their way to industrial centers through free markets, rather than through mercantilist autarkies. The capitalist theory contends that as economies become stronger, prosperous capitalist states no longer need to threaten one another over access to inputs to production. Consequently, the security dilemma loses its relevance.

Scholars like Michael Mousseau argue that democracies are only peaceful in pairs. Other research has demonstrated that the democratic peace is even more exclusive than previously imagined, limiting the finding to developed democracies. Gartzke and Hewitt challenged this by demonstrating that it is economic development and market freedoms, rather than political liberty that result in interstate peace.

Deterrent Effect of Institutional Ties

International Government Organisations (IGOs) are designed to promote cooperation and inhibit political disputes. Institutional ties promote the exchange of information about the economic gains and losses of participating member states, thereby reducing uncertainty about the distribution of benefits.

Regional institutions also present great influence in addressing issues beyond trade. Regional economic institutions help develop trade expectations for the future. "High economic stakes that states have in the continuation and growth of economic activity in the context of economic regionalism lead to a security community in which states develop a genuine interest in not only keeping peace with each other, but also defending their relationship against outside aggressors". In addition to their role in dispute settlement, regional arrangements can deter aggressors from targeting institutionally connected states.

Aydin makes an important contribution to the extended deterrence literature and economic peace research through his empirical study on the deterrent effect of economic integration. This study shows that trade has a general deterrent effect on attackers when the target is economically integrated with potential defenders through regional trade institutions. When trade is conducted in an institutionalised setting it can have political implications beyond bilateral interdependence.

Research shows that economic integration decreases the opportunities to fight and enhances the opportunities to intervene in crisis. Mansfield & Pevehouse present strong evidence that "the combination of PTA membership (preferential trading arrangements) and a high level of trade is quite likely to discourage belligerence".

Many PTAs have become venues for addressing political disputes between participants and fostering cooperation. Observers have widely acknowledged, for example, that ASEAN has helped to manage tensions in Southeast Asia. Mercado Comun del Sur (MERCOSUR) has done likewise, improving political-military relations throughout the southern cone. The reciprocal nature of this system helps guarantee that economic concessions made by one state will be repaid, rather than exploited by its counterpart.

International Investment Flows

Another area to add to the existing literature on economic integration is the impact of militarized conflict on foreign investment.

Bussman's contribution to the liberal notion that conflict inhibits foreign investment, complements the liberal peace arguments in conflict studies. Bussman's research shows that international conflict reduces international investment flows considerably. Bussman contends that "as with trade, foreign investment could be an important factor in promoting peace. States might avoid violent conflict in order not to deter foreign investors". By ensuring political stability, states can thus create an environment that is desirable to foreign investors. It is therefore, in the best interest of states to keep away from belligerent behaviour as they could potentially miss out on the welfare gains associated with foreign investment. As a result, states that benefit from foreign direct investment flows are less likely to experience the onset of militarized conflict.

INTRA-INDUSTRY TRADE

Intra-industry trade refers to the exchange of similar products belonging to the same industry. The term is usually applied to international trade, where the same types of goods or services are both imported and exported.

Examples of this kind of trade include automobiles, foodstuffs and beverages, computers and minerals. Europe exported 2.6 million motor vehicles in 2002, and imported 2.2 million of them. Japan exported 4.7 million vehicles in 2002 (1 million of which went to Europe, and 2 million to North America), and imported 0.3 million.

Why do countries at the same time import and export the products of the same industry, or import and export the same kinds of goods? According to Nigel Grimwade, "An explanation cannot be found within the framework of classical or neo-classical trade theory. The latter predicts only inter-industry specialisation and trade". However, this is far from the case.

The traditional model of trade were set out by the model of David Ricardo and the Heckscher–Ohlin model, which tried to explain the occurrence of international trade.

Both models used the idea of comparative advantage and an explanation of why countries trade. However, many economists have made the point of claiming that these models provide no explanation towards intra-industry trade as under their assumptions countries with identical factor endowments would not trade and produce goods domestically. Hence, as intra-industry trade has developed many economists have looked at other explanations.

One attempt to explain IIT was made by Finger, who thought that occurrence of intra-industry trade was "unremarkable" as existing classifications place goods of heterogeneous factor endowments in a single industry. However, evidence shows that even when industries are disaggregated to extremely fine levels IIT still occurs, so this argument can be ignored.

Another potential explanation is provided by Flavey & Kierzkowski. They produced a model that tried to get rid of the idea that all products are produced under identical technical conditions. Their model showed that on the demand side goods are distinguished by the perceived quality of that good and high quality goods are produced under conditions of high capital intensity. However, this explanation has also been dismissed. It is questioned whether the model applies to IIT at all, as it does not address directly trade between goods of similar factor endowments.

The most comprehensive and widely accepted explanation, at least within economic theory, is that of Paul Krugman's New Trade Theory. Krugman argues that economies specialise to take advantage of increasing returns, not following differences in regional endowments (as contended by neoclassical theory). In particular, trade allows countries to specialize in a limited variety of production and thus reap the advantages of increasing returns (i.e., economies of scale), but without reducing the variety of goods available for consumption.

Yet, Donald Davis believed that both the Heckscher–Ohlin and Ricardian models were still relevant in explaining intra-industry trade. He developed the Heckscher-Ohlin-Ricardo model, which showed that even with constant returns to scale that intra-industry trade could still occur under the traditional setting. The Heckscher-Ohlin-Ricardo model explained that countries of identical factor endowments would still trade due to differences in technology, as this would encourage specialisation and therefore trade, in exactly the same matter that was set out in the Ricardian model.

Types

There are three types of intra-industry trade:

- Trade in Homogeneous Goods.
- Trade in Horizontally Differentiated Goods.
- Trade in Vertically Differentiated Goods.

Although the theory and measurement of intra-industry trade initially focused on trade in goods, especially industrial products, it has also been observed that there is substantial intra-industry trade in the international trade of services.

Measurement

Intra-industry trade is difficult to measure statistically because regarding products or industries as "the same" is partly a matter of definition and classification. For a very simple example, it could be argued that although a BMW and a Ford are both motor cars, and although a Budweiser and a Heineken are both beers, they are really all different products.

Various indexes of IIT have been created, including the Grubel–Lloyd index, the Balassa index, the Aquino index, the Bergstrand index and the Glesjer index. Research suggests that:

- IIT is not simply a fiction or artifact produced by statistical classifications and definitions, but very much a reality.
- the share of IIT in total international trade is growing all the time, at about 4–5% a year. Thus, more and more, countries are importing the same kinds of products they are also exporting.

"Intra-industry trade has been considered in international trade literature as the explanation of the unexpectedly large expansion of industrial trade among OECD countries, for which it represented more than two-thirds of their total international trade by the beginning of the seventies".

COMPARATIVE ADVANTAGE

The law of comparative advantage describes how, under free trade, an agent will produce more of and consume less of a good for which they have a comparative advantage.

In an economic model, agents have a comparative advantage over others in producing a particular good if they can produce that good at a lower relative opportunity cost or autarky price, i.e. at a lower relative marginal cost prior to trade. Comparative advantage describes the economic reality of the work gains from trade for individuals, firms, or nations, which arise from differences in their factor endowments or technological progress. (One should not compare the monetary costs of production or even the resource costs (labor needed per unit of output) of production. Instead, one must compare the opportunity costs of producing goods across countries).

David Ricardo developed the classical theory of comparative advantage in 1817 to explain why countries engage in international trade even when one country's workers are more efficient at producing *every* single good than workers in other countries. He demonstrated that if two countries capable of producing two commodities engage in the free market, then each country will increase its overall consumption by exporting the good for which it has a comparative advantage while importing the other good, provided that there exist differences in labor productivity between both countries. Widely regarded as one of the most powerful yet counter-intuitive insights in economics, Ricardo's theory implies that comparative advantage rather than absolute advantage is responsible for much of international trade.

Classical Theory and David Ricardo's Formulation

Adam Smith first alluded to the concept of *absolute advantage* as the basis for international trade in 1776, in *The Wealth of Nations*:

> If a foreign country can supply us with a commodity cheaper than we ourselves can make it, better buy it off them with some part of the produce of our own industry employed in a way in which we have some advantage. The general industry of the country, being always in proportion to the capital which employs it, will not thereby be diminished but only left to find out the way in which it can be employed with the greatest advantage.

Writing several decades after Smith in 1808, Robert Torrens articulated a preliminary definition of comparative advantage as the loss from the closing of trade:

> If I wish to know the extent of the advantage, which arises to England, from her giving France a hundred pounds of broadcloth, in exchange for a hundred pounds of lace, I take the quantity of lace which she has acquired by this transaction, and compare it with the quantity which she might, at the same expense of labour and capital, have acquired by manufacturing it at home. The lace that remains, beyond what the labour and capital employed on the cloth, might have fabricated at home, is the amount of the advantage which England derives from the exchange.

Ricardo's Example

Graph illustrating Ricardo's example:

In case I (diamonds), each country spends 3600 hours to produce a mixture of cloth and wine. In case II (squares), each country specializes in its comparative advantage, resulting in greater total output.

In a famous example, Ricardo considers a world economy consisting of two countries, Portugal and England, each producing two goods of identical quality. In Portugal, the *a priori* more efficient country, it is possible to produce wine and cloth with less labor than it would take to produce the same quantities in England. However, the relative costs of producing those two goods differ between the countries.

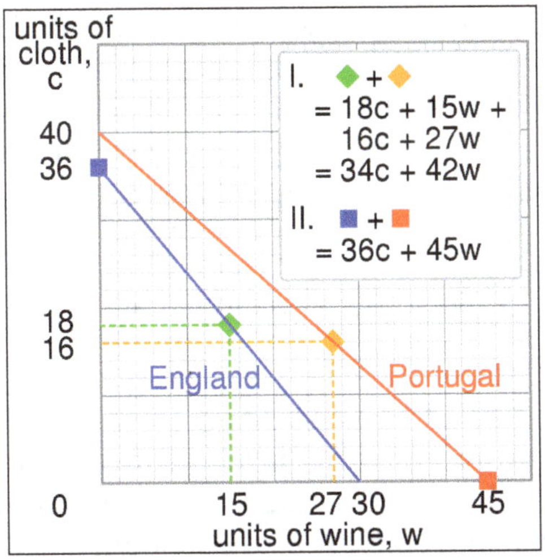

Hours of work necessary to produce one unit		
Produce Country	Cloth	Wine
England	100	120
Portugal	90	80

In this illustration, England could commit 100 hours of labor to produce one unit of cloth, or produce 5/6 units of wine. Meanwhile, in comparison, Portugal could commit 90 hours of labor to produce one unit of cloth, or produce 9/8 units of wine. So, Portugal possesses an *absolute advantage* in producing cloth due to fewer labor hours, but England has a *comparative advantage* in producing cloth due to lower opportunity cost.

In the absence of trade, England requires 220 hours of work to both produce and consume one unit each of cloth and wine while Portugal requires 170 hours of work to produce and consume the same quantities. England is more efficient at producing cloth than wine, and Portugal is more efficient at producing wine than cloth. So, if each country specializes in the good for which it has a comparative advantage, then the global production of both goods increases, for England can spend 220 labor hours to produce 2.2 units of cloth while Portugal can spend 170 hours to produce 2.125 units of wine. Moreover, if both countries specialize in the above manner and England trades a unit of its cloth for 5/6 to 9/8 units of Portugal's wine, then both countries can consume at least a unit each of cloth and wine, with 0 to 0.2 units of cloth and 0 to 0.125 units of wine remaining in each respective country to be consumed or exported. Consequently, both England and Portugal can consume more wine and cloth under free trade than in autarky.

Ricardian Model

The Ricardian model is a general equilibrium mathematical model of international trade. Although the idea of the Ricardian model was first presented in the *Essay on*

Profits (a single-commodity version) and then in the *Principles* (a multi-commodity version) by David Ricardo, the first mathematical Ricardian model was published by William Whewell in 1833. The earliest test of the Ricardian model was performed by G.D.A MacDougall, which was published in *Economic Journal* of 1951 and 1952. In the Ricardian model, trade patterns depend on productivity differences.

The following is a typical modern interpretation of the classical Ricardian model. In the interest of simplicity, it uses notation and definitions, such as opportunity cost, unavailable to Ricardo.

The world economy consists of two countries, Home and Foreign, which produce wine and cloth. Labor, the only factor of production, is mobile domestically but not internationally; there may be migration between sectors but not between countries. We denote the labor force in Home by L, the amount of labor required to produce one unit of wine in Home by a_{LW}, and the amount of labor required to produce one unit of cloth in Home by a_{LC}. The total amount of wine and cloth produced in Home are Q_W and Q_C respectively. We denote the same variables for Foreign by appending a prime. For instance, a'_{LW} is the amount of labor needed to produce a unit of wine in Foreign.

We don't know if Home is more productive than Foreign in making cloth. That is, we don't know that $a_{LC} < a'_{LC}$. Similarly, we don't know if Home has an absolute advantage in wine. However, we will assume that Home is more *relatively* productive in cloth than Foreign:

$$a_{LC} / a'_{LC} < a_{LW} / a'_{LW}.$$

Equivalently, we may assume that Home has a comparative advantage in cloth in the sense that it has a lower opportunity cost for cloth in terms of wine than Foreign:

$$a_{LC} / a_{LW} < a'_{LC} / a'_{LW}.$$

In the absence of trade, the relative price of cloth and wine in each country is determined solely by the relative labor cost of the goods. Hence the relative autarky price of cloth is a_{LC} / a_{LW} in Home and a'_{LC} / a'_{LW} in Foreign. With free trade, the price of cloth or wine in either country is the world price P_C or P_W.

nstead of considering the world demand (or supply) for cloth and wine, we are interested in the world *relative demand* (or *relative supply*) for cloth and wine, which we define as the ratio of the world demand (or supply) for cloth to the world demand (or supply) for wine. In general equilibrium, the world relative price P_C / P_W will be determined uniquely by the intersection of world relative demand *RD* and world relative supply *RS* curves.

We assume that the relative demand curve reflects substitution effects and is decreasing with respect to relative price. The behavior of the relative supply curve, however, warrants closer study. Recalling our original assumption that Home has a comparative advantage in cloth, we consider five possibilities for the relative quantity supplied at a given price.

- If $P_C / P_W = a_{LC} / a_{LW} < a'_{LC} / a'_{LW}$,, then Foreign specializes in wine, for the wage P'_W / a'_{LW} in the wine sector is greater than the wage P'_C / a'_{LC} in the cloth sector. However, Home workers are indifferent between working in either sector. As a result, the quantity supplied can take any value.

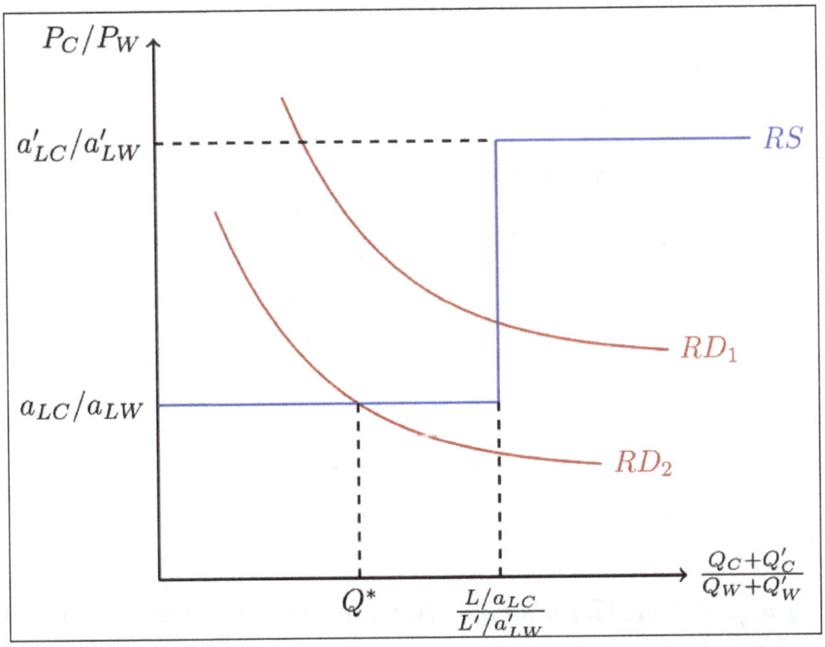

The demand for cloth relative to wine decreases with the relative price of cloth in terms of wine; the supply *RS* of cloth relative to wine increases with relative price. Two relative demand curves RD_1 and RD_2 are drawn for illustrative purposes.

- If $P_C / P_W < a_{LC} / a_{LW} < a'_{LC} / a'_{LW}$,, then both Home and Foreign specialize in wine, for similar reasons as above, and so the quantity supplied is zero.
- If $a_{LC} / a_{LW} < P_C / P_W < a'_{LC} / a'_{LW}$,, then Home specializes in cloth whereas Foreign specializes in wine. The quantity supplied is given by the ratio $\frac{L / a_{LC}}{L' / a'_{LW}}$ of the world production of cloth to the world production of wine.
- If $a_{LC} / a_{LW} < a'_{LC} / a'_{LW} < P_C / P_W$,, then both Home and Foreign specialize in cloth. The quantity supplied tends to infinity as the quantity of wine supplied approaches zero.
- If $a_{LC} / a_{LW} < a'_{LC} / a'_{LW} = P_C / P_W$,, then Home specializes in cloth while Foreign workers are indifferent between sectors. Again, the relative quantity supplied can take any value.

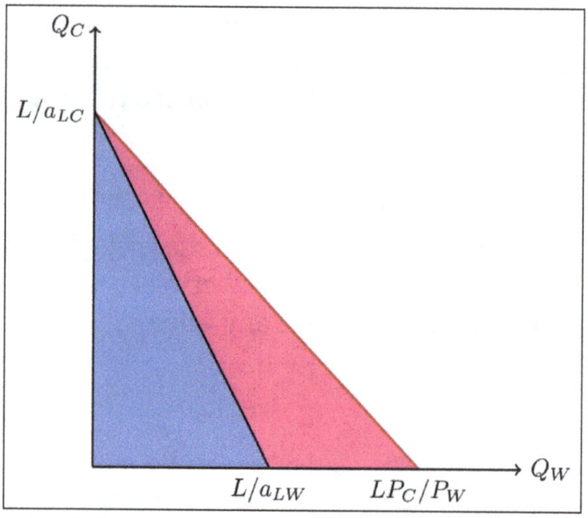

The blue triangle depicts Home's original production (and consumption) possibilities. By trading, Home can also consume bundles in the pink triangle despite facing the same productions possibility frontier.

As long as the relative demand is finite, the relative price is always bounded by the inequality,

$$a_{LC} / a_{LW} \leq P_C / P_W \leq a'_{LC} / a'_{LW}.$$

In autarky, Home faces a production constraint of the form,

$$a_{LC}Q_C + a_{LW}Q_W \leq L,$$

from which it follows that Home's cloth consumption at the production possibilities frontier is,

$$Q_C = L / a_{LC} - (a_{LW} / a_{LC})Q_W.$$

With free trade, Home produces cloth exclusively, an amount of which it exports in exchange for wine at the prevailing rate. Thus Home's overall consumption is now subject to the constraint,

$$a_{LC}Q_C + a_{LC}(P_W / P_C)Q_W \leq L$$

while its cloth consumption at the *consumption possibilities* frontier is given by,

$$Q_C = L / a_{LC} - (P_W / P_C)Q_W \geq L / a_{LC} - (a_{LW} / a_{LC})Q_W.$$

A symmetric argument holds for Foreign. Therefore, by trading and specializing in a good for which it has a comparative advantage, each country can expand its consumption possibilities. Consumers can choose from bundles of wine and cloth that they could not have produced themselves in closed economies.

Terms of Trade

Terms of trade is the rate at which one good could be traded for another. If both countries specialize in the good for which they have a comparative advantage then trade, the terms of trade for a good (that benefit both entities) will fall between each entities opportunity costs. In the example above one unit of cloth would trade for between $\frac{5}{6}$ units of wine and $\frac{9}{8}$ units of wine.

Haberler's Opportunity Costs Formulation

In 1930 Gottfried Haberler detached the doctrine of comparative advantage from Ricardo's labor theory of value and provided a modern opportunity-cost formulation. Haberler's reformulation of comparative advantage revolutionized the theory of international trade and laid the conceptual groundwork of modern trade theories.

Haberler's innovation was to reformulate the theory of comparative advantage such that the value of good X is measured in terms of the forgone units of production of good Y rather than the labor units necessary to produce good X, as in the Ricardian formulation. Haberler implemented this opportunity-cost formulation of comparative advantage by introducing the concept of a production possibility curve into international trade theory.

Modern Theories

Since 1817, economists have attempted to generalize the Ricardian model and derive the principle of comparative advantage in broader settings, most notably in the neoclassical *specific factors* Ricardo-Viner and *factor proportions* Heckscher–Ohlin models. Subsequent developments in the new trade theory, motivated in part by the empirical shortcomings of the H–O model and its inability to explain intra-industry trade, have provided an explanation for aspects of trade that are not accounted for by comparative advantage. Nonetheless, economists like Alan Deardorff, Avinash Dixit, Gottfried Haberler, and Victor D. Norman have responded with weaker generalizations of the principle of comparative advantage, in which countries will only *tend* to export goods for which they have a comparative advantage.

Dornbusch 's Continuum of Goods Formulation

In both the Ricardian and H–O models, the comparative advantage theory is formulated for a 2 countries/2 commodities case. It can be extended to a 2 countries/many commodities case, or a many countries/2 commodities case. Adding commodities in order to have a smooth continuum of goods is the major insight of the seminal paper by Dornbusch, Fisher, and Samuelson. In fact, inserting an increasing number of goods into the chain of comparative advantage makes the gaps between the ratios of the labor requirements negligible, in which case the three types of equilibria around any good in the original model collapse to the same outcome. It notably allows for transportation costs to be incorporated, although the framework remains restricted to two countries. But in the case with many countries (more than 3 countries) and many commodities (more than 3 commodities), the notion of comparative advantage requires a substantially more complex formulation.

Deardorff's General Law of Comparative Advantage

Skeptics of comparative advantage have underlined that its theoretical implications hardly hold when applied to individual commodities or pairs of commodities in a world of multiple commodities. Deardorff argues that the insights of comparative advantage remain valid if the theory is restated in terms of averages across all commodities. His models provide multiple insights on the correlations between vectors of trade and vectors with relative-autarky-price measures of comparative advantage. What has become to be known as the "Deardorff's general law of comparative advantage" is a model incorporating multiple goods, and which takes into account tariffs, transportation costs, and other obstacles to trade.

Alternative Approaches

Recently, Y. Shiozawa succeeded in constructing a theory of international value in the tradition of Ricardo's cost-of-production theory of value. This was based on a wide range of assumptions: Many countries; Many commodities; Several production techniques for a product in a country; Input trade (intermediate goods are freely traded); Durable capital goods with constant efficiency during a predetermined lifetime; No transportation cost (extendable to positive cost cases).

In a famous comment McKenzie pointed that "A moment's consideration will convince one that Lancashire would be unlikely to produce cotton cloth if the cotton had to be grown in England". However, McKenzie and later researchers could not produce a general theory which includes traded input goods because of the mathematical difficulty. As John Chipman points it, McKenzie found that "introduction of trade in intermediate product necessitates a fundamental alteration in classical analysis". Durable capital goods such as machines and installations are inputs to the productions in the same title as part and ingredients.

In view of the new theory, no physical criterion exists. The competitive patterns are determined by the traders trials to find cheapest products in a world. The search of cheapest product is achieved by world optimal procurement. Thus the new theory explains how the global supply chains are formed.

Empirical Approach to Comparative Advantage

Comparative advantage is a theory about the benefits that specialization and trade would bring, rather than a strict prediction about actual behavior. (In practice, governments restrict international trade for a variety of reasons; under Ulysses S. Grant, the US postponed opening up to free trade until its industries were up to strength, following the example set earlier by Britain). Nonetheless there is a large amount of empirical work testing the predictions of comparative advantage. The empirical works usually involve testing predictions of a particular model. For example, the Ricardian model predicts that technological differences in countries result in differences in labor productivity. The differences in labor productivity in turn determine the comparative advantages across different countries. Testing the Ricardian model for instance involves looking at the relationship between relative labor productivity and international trade patterns. A country that is relatively efficient in producing shoes tends to export shoes.

Direct Test: Natural Experiment of Japan

Assessing the validity of comparative advantage on a global scale with the examples of contemporary economies is analytically challenging because of the multiple factors driving globalization: indeed, investment, migration, and technological change play a role in addition to trade. Even if we could isolate the workings of open trade from other processes, establishing its causal impact also remains complicated: it would require a comparison with a counterfactual world without open trade. Considering the durability of different aspects of globalization, it is hard to assess the sole impact of open trade on a particular economy.

Daniel Bernhofen and John Brown have attempted to address this issue, by using a natural experiment of a sudden transition to open trade in a market economy. They focus on the case of Japan. The Japanese economy indeed developed over several centuries under autarky and a quasi-isolation from international trade but was, by the mid-19th century, a sophisticated market economy with a population of 30 million. Under Western military pressure, Japan opened its economy to foreign trade through a series of unequal treaties.

In 1859, the treaties limited tariffs to 5% and opened trade to Westerners. Considering that the transition from autarky, or self-sufficiency, to open trade was brutal, few changes to the fundamentals of the economy occurred in the first 20 years of trade. The general law of comparative advantage theorizes that an economy should, on average, export goods with low self-sufficiency prices and import goods with high self-sufficiency prices. Bernhofen and Brown found that by 1869, the price of Japan's main export, silk and derivatives, saw a 100% increase in real terms, while the prices of numerous imported goods declined of 30-75%. In the next decade, the ratio of imports to gross domestic product reached 4%.

Structural Estimation

Another important way of demonstrating the validity of comparative advantage has consisted in 'structural estimation' approaches. These approaches have built on the Ricardian formulation of two goods for two countries and subsequent models with many goods or many countries. The aim has been to reach a formulation accounting for both multiple goods and multiple countries, in order to reflect real-world conditions more accurately. Jonathan Eaton and Samuel Kortum underlined that a convincing model needed to incorporate the idea of a 'continuum of good's developed by Dornbusch for both goods and countries. They were able to do so by allowing for an arbitrary (integer) number i of countries, and dealing exclusively with unit labor requirements for each good (one for each point on the unit interval) in each country (of which there are i).

Earlier Empirical Work

Two of the first tests of comparative advantage were by MacDougall. A prediction of a two-country Ricardian comparative advantage model is that countries will export goods where output per worker (i.e. productivity) is higher. That is, we expect a positive relationship between output per worker and number of exports. MacDougall tested this relationship with data from the US and UK, and did indeed find a positive relationship. The statistical test of this positive relationship was replicated with new data by Stern and Balassa.

Dosi conduct a book-length empirical examination that suggests that international trade in manufactured goods is largely driven by differences in national technological competencies.

One critique of the textbook model of comparative advantage is that there are only two goods. The results of the model are robust to this assumption. Dornbusch generalized the theory to allow for such a large number of goods as to form a smooth continuum. Based in part on these generalizations of the model, Davis provides a more recent view of the Ricardian approach to explain trade between countries with similar resources.

More recently, Golub and Hsieh presents modern statistical analysis of the relationship between relative productivity and trade patterns, which finds reasonably strong correlations, and Nunn finds that countries that have greater enforcement of contracts specialize in goods that require relationship-specific investments.

Taking a broader perspective, there has been work about the benefits of international trade. Zimring & Etkes finds that the Blockade of the Gaza Strip, which substantially restricted the availability of imports to Gaza, saw labor productivity fall by 20% in three years. Markusen reports the effects of moving away from autarky to free trade during the Meiji Restoration, with the result that national income increased by up to 65% in 15 years.

Considerations

Development Economics

The theory of comparative advantage, and the corollary that nations should specialize, is criticized on pragmatic grounds within the import substitution industrialization theory of development economics, on empirical grounds by the Singer–Prebisch thesis which states that terms of trade between primary producers and manufactured goods deteriorate over time, and on theoretical grounds of infant industry and Keynesian economics. In older economic terms, comparative advantage has been opposed by mercantilism and economic nationalism. These argue instead that while a country may initially be comparatively disadvantaged in a given industry (such as Japanese cars in the 1950s), countries should shelter and invest in industries until they become globally competitive. Further, they argue that comparative advantage, as stated, is a static theory – it does not account for the possibility of advantage changing through investment or economic development, and thus does not provide guidance for long-term economic development.

Much has been written since Ricardo as commerce has evolved and cross-border trade has become more complicated. Today trade policy tends to focus more on "competitive advantage" as opposed to "comparative advantage". One of the most in-depth research undertakings on "competitive advantage" was conducted in the 1980s as part of the Reagan administration's Project Socrates to establish the foundation for a technology-based competitive strategy development system that could be used for guiding international trade policy.

Criticism

Several arguments have been advanced against using comparative advantage as a justification for advocating free trade, and they have gained an audience among economists. For example, James Brander and Barbara Spencer demonstrated how, in a strategic setting where a few firms compete for the world market, export subsidies and import restrictions can keep foreign firms from competing with national firms, increasing welfare in the country implementing these so-called strategic trade policies.

However, the overwhelming consensus of the economics profession remains that while these arguments against comparative advantage are theoretically valid under certain conditions or assumptions, these assumptions do not usually hold. Thus, these arguments should not be used to guide trade policy. Gregory Mankiw, chairman of the Harvard Economics Department, has stated: "Few propositions command as much consensus among professional economists as that open world trade increases economic growth and raises living standards."

There are some economists who dispute the claims of the benefit of comparative advantage. James K. Galbraith has stated that "free trade has attained the status of a god" and that " none of the world's most successful trading regions, including Japan, Korea, Taiwan, and now mainland China, reached their current status by adopting neoliberal trading rules". He argues that " comparative advantage is based upon the concept of constant returns: the idea that you can double or triple the output of any good simply by doubling or tripling the inputs. But this is not generally the case. For manufactured products, increasing returns, learning, and technical change are the rule, not the exception; the cost of production falls with experience. With increasing returns, the lowest cost will be incurred by the country that starts earliest and moves fastest on any particular line. Potential competitors have to protect their own industries if they wish them to survive long enough to achieve competitive scale". According to Galbraith, nations trapped into specializing in agriculture are condemned to perpetual poverty, as agriculture is dependent on land, a finite non-increasing natural resource. Galbraith summarizes: "Comparative advantage has very little practical use for trade strategy. Diversification, not specialization, is the main path out of underdevelopment, and effective diversification requires a strategic approach to trade policy. It cannot mean walling off the outside world, but it is also a goal not easily pursued under a dogmatic commitment to free trade".

According to historian Cecil Woodham-Smith, Ireland in the 1800s is an example of the dangers of over-specialization. When the union with Great Britain was formed in 1800, Irish textile industries protected by tariffs were exposed to world markets where England had a comparative advantage in technology, experience and scale of operation which devastated the Irish industry. Ireland was forced to specialize in the export of grain while the displaced Irish labor was forced into subsistence farming and relying on the potato for survival. When the potato blight occurred the resulting famine killed at least one million Irish in one of the worst famines in European history. As Woodham-Smith would later comment, "the Irish peasant was told to replace the potato by eating his grain, but Trevelyan once again refused to take any steps to curb the export of food from Ireland. 'Do not encourage the idea of prohibiting exports,' he wrote, on September 3, 'perfect free trade is the right course'".

The classical and neoclassical formulations of comparative advantage theory differ in the tools they use but share the same basis and logic. Comparative advantage theory says that market forces lead all factors of production to their best use in the economy. It indicates that international free trade would be beneficial for all participating countries as well as for the world as a whole because they could increase their overall production and consume more by specializing according to their comparative advantages. Goods would become cheaper and available in larger quantities. Moreover, this specialization would not be the result of chance or political intent, but would be automatic. However, at least some theories of free trade and comparative advantage require certain assumptions to achieve an ideal, or optimal, scenario. While these assumptions are not necessary for comparative advantage to produce positive results, situations where these assumptions are not true will produce less effective results. These assumptions include:

Assumption 1 - Capital and Labour are not Internationally Mobile

The international immobility of labour and capital is essential to the theory of comparative advantage. Without this, there would be no reason for international free trade to be regulated by comparative advantages. Classical and neoclassical economists all assume that labour and capital do not circulate between nations. At the international level, only the goods produced can move freely, with capital and labour trapped in countries. David Ricardo was aware that the international immobility of labour and capital is an indispensable hypothesis. He devoted half of his explanation of the theory to it in his book. He even explained that if labour and capital could move internationally, then comparative advantages could not determine international trade. Ricardo assumed that the reasons for the immobility of the capital would be:

The fancied or real insecurity of capital, when not under the immediate control of its owner, together with the natural disinclination which every man has to quit the country of his birth and connexions, and intrust himself with all his habits fixed, to a strange government and new laws.

However, this criticism does not apply to modern theories. Neoclassical economists, for their part, argue that the scale of these movements of workers and capital is irrelevant. They developed the theory of price compensation by factor that makes these movements superfluous:

While ricardo assumes that capital and labour cannot move internationally, modern theories assume that international mobility is unnecessary because international commodity trade will lead to the same result through an equalisation of factor prices.

Assumption 2 - There are no Externalities

An externality is the term used when the price of a product does not reflect its cost or real economic value. The classic negative externality is environmental degradation, which reduces the value of natural resources without increasing the price of the product that has caused them harm. The classic positive externality is technological encroachment, where one company's invention of a product allows others to copy or build on it, generating wealth that the original company cannot capture. If prices are wrong due to positive or negative externalities, free trade will produce sub-optimal results.

For example, goods from a country with lax pollution standards will be too cheap. As a result, its trading partners will import too much. And the exporting country will export too much, concentrating its economy too much in industries that are not as profitable as they seem, ignoring the damage caused by pollution.

On the positive externalities, if an industry generates technological spinoffs for the rest of the economy, then free trade can let that industry be destroyed by foreign competition because the economy ignores its hidden value. Some industries generate new technologies, allow improvements in other industries and stimulate technological advances throughout the economy; losing these industries means losing all industries that would have resulted in the future.

Assumption 3 - Productive Resources move Easily from one Industry to Another

Comparative advantage theory deals with the best use of resources and how to put the economy to its best use. But this implies that the resources used to manufacture one product can be used to produce another object. If they cannot, imports will not push the economy into industries better suited to its comparative advantage and will only destroy existing industries.

For example, when workers cannot move from one industry to another - perhaps because they do not have the right skills and cannot be trained, or do not live in the right place and cannot move - changes in the economy's comparative advantage will not shift them to a more appropriate industry, but rather to unemployment or precarious and unproductive jobs.

Assumption 4 - The Gains Resulting from International Trade are only Static Gains

Comparative advantage theory allows for a "static" and not a "dynamic" analysis of the economy. That is, it examines the facts at a single point in time and determines the best response to those facts at that point in time, given our productivity in various industries. But when it comes to long-term growth, it says nothing about how the facts can change tomorrow and how they can be changed in someone's favour. It does not indicate how best to transform factors of production into more productive factors in the future.

According to theory, the only advantage of international trade is that goods become cheaper and available in larger quantities. Improving the static efficiency of existing resources would therefore be the only advantage of international trade. And the neoclassical formulation assumes that the factors of production are given only exogenously. Exogenous changes can come from population growth, industrial policies, the rate of capital accumulation (propensity for security) and technological inventions, among others. Dynamic developments endogenous to trade such as economic growth are not integrated into Ricardo's theory. And this is not affected by what is called "dynamic comparative advantage". In these models, comparative advantages develop and change over time, but this change is not the result of trade itself, but of a change in exogenous factors.

However, the world, and in particular the industrialized countries, are characterized by dynamic gains endogenous to trade, such as technological growth that has led to an increase in the standard of living and wealth of the industrialized world. In addition, dynamic gains are more important than static gains.

Assumption 5 - Trade will Always be Balanced and there is an Adjustment Mechanism

A crucial assumption for ideal results in both the classical and neoclassical formulation of comparative advantage theory is that trade is balanced, which means that the value of imports is equal to the value of each country's exports. The volume of trade may change, but international trade will always be balanced at least after a certain adjustment period. The balance of trade is essential for theory because the resulting adjustment mechanism is responsible for transforming the comparative advantages of production costs into absolute price advantages. And this is necessary because it is the absolute price differences that determine the international flow of goods. Since consumers buy a good from the one who sells it cheapest, comparative advantages in terms of production costs must be transformed into absolute price advantages. In the case of floating exchange rates, it is the exchange rate adjustment mechanism that is responsible for this transformation of comparative advantages into absolute price advantages. In the case of fixed exchange rates, neoclassical theory suggests that trade is balanced by changes in wage rates.

So if trade were not balanced in itself and if there were no adjustment mechanism, there would be no reason to achieve a comparative advantage. In the short term, trade imbalances are the norm and balanced trade is in practice only an exception. However, this criticism becomes irrelevant in the long term.

Assumption 6 - International Trade is Understood as Bartering

The assumption that trade will always be balanced is a corollary of the fact that trade is understood as barter. The definition of international trade as barter trade is the basis for the assumption of balanced trade. Ricardo insists that international trade takes place as if it were purely a barter trade, a presumption that is maintained by subsequent classical and neoclassical economists. The quantity of money theory, which Ricardo uses, assumes that money is neutral and neglects the velocity of a currency. Money has only one function in international trade, namely as a means of exchange to facilitate trade.

In practice, however, the velocity of circulation is not constant and the quantity of money is not neutral for the real economy. A capitalist world is not characterized by a barter economy but by a market economy. The main difference in the context of international trade is that sales and purchases no longer necessarily have to coincide. The seller is not necessarily obliged to buy immediately. Thus, money is not only a means of exchange. It is above all a means of payment and is also used to store value, settle debts and transfer wealth. Thus, unlike the barter hypothesis of the comparative advantage theory, money is not a commodity like any other. Rather, it is of practical importance to specifically own money rather than any commodity. And money as a store of value in a world of uncertainty has a significant influence on the motives and decisions of wealth holders and producers.

Asumption 7 - Labour or Capital is used to its Full Potential

Older theories of comparative advantage, including Ricardo and later classical economists assume that labour tends towards full employment and that capital is always fully used in a liberalized economy, because no capital owner will leave its capital unused but will always seek to make a profit from it. That there is no limit to the use of capital is a consequence of Jean-Baptiste Say's law, which presumes that production is limited only by resources and is also adopted by neoclassical economists.

From a theoretical point of view, comparative advantage theory must assume that for optimal results, labour or capital is used to its full potential and that only resources limit production. There are two reasons for this: the realization of gains through international trade and the adjustment mechanism. If significant unemployment (or underutilized resources) exists, there is less chance of opportunity costs, because the production of one good could be increased without reducing the production of another good. Since comparative advantages are determined by opportunity costs, a reduction in opportunity costs reduces the comparative advantage.

If a country's resources were not fully utilized, production and consumption could be increased more at the national level, and less as a result of international trade. In this case, a country could earn more by focusing on domestic policy and stimulating domestic production, as this would allow it to employ more labour and capital and increase national income.

References

- Washington, Charles W. L. Hill, University of (2015). International business : competing in the global marketplace (Tenth edition. ed.). p. 454. ISBN 978-0-07-811277-5
- What-is-international-trade, insights: investopedia.com, Retrieved 11 March, 2020
- Lamy, Pascal (2007-09-10). "Proliferation of regional trade agreements 'breeding concern'". Geneva: World Trade Organization. Retrieved 2008-07-20
- What-is-import-trade, commerce: byjus.com, Retrieved 16 June, 2020
- Aydin, Aysegul (2010). "The deterrent effects of economic integration". Journal of Peace Research. 47: 523–533. doi:10.1177/0022343310370290
- Giorgio Riello, Tirthankar Roy (2009). How India Clothed the World: The World of South Asian Textiles, 1500-1850. Brill Publishers. p. 174. ISBN 9789047429975

PERMISSIONS

All chapters in this book are published with permission under the Creative Commons Attribution Share Alike License or equivalent. Every chapter published in this book has been scrutinized by our experts. Their significance has been extensively debated. The topics covered herein carry significant information for a comprehensive understanding. They may even be implemented as practical applications or may be referred to as a beginning point for further studies.

We would like to thank the editorial team for lending their expertise to make the book truly unique. They have played a crucial role in the development of this book. Without their invaluable contributions this book wouldn't have been possible. They have made vital efforts to compile up to date information on the varied aspects of this subject to make this book a valuable addition to the collection of many professionals and students.

This book was conceptualized with the vision of imparting up-to-date and integrated information in this field. To ensure the same, a matchless editorial board was set up. Every individual on the board went through rigorous rounds of assessment to prove their worth. After which they invested a large part of their time researching and compiling the most relevant data for our readers.

The editorial board has been involved in producing this book since its inception. They have spent rigorous hours researching and exploring the diverse topics which have resulted in the successful publishing of this book. They have passed on their knowledge of decades through this book. To expedite this challenging task, the publisher supported the team at every step. A small team of assistant editors was also appointed to further simplify the editing procedure and attain best results for the readers.

Apart from the editorial board, the designing team has also invested a significant amount of their time in understanding the subject and creating the most relevant covers. They scrutinized every image to scout for the most suitable representation of the subject and create an appropriate cover for the book.

The publishing team has been an ardent support to the editorial, designing and production team. Their endless efforts to recruit the best for this project, has resulted in the accomplishment of this book. They are a veteran in the field of academics and their pool of knowledge is as vast as their experience in printing. Their expertise and guidance has proved useful at every step. Their uncompromising quality standards have made this book an exceptional effort. Their encouragement from time to time has been an inspiration for everyone.

The publisher and the editorial board hope that this book will prove to be a valuable piece of knowledge for students, practitioners and scholars across the globe.

INDEX

www.ingramcontent.com/pod-product-compliance
Lightning Source LLC
LaVergne TN
LVHW080617210926
848485LV00003B/173